Vocabulary Development

Vocabulary Development

Special Issue Editors

Timothy Rasinski
William H. Rupley

MDPI • Basel • Beijing • Wuhan • Barcelona • Belgrade

Special Issue Editors
Timothy Rasinski
Kent State University
USA

William H. Rupley
Texas A&M University
USA

Editorial Office
MDPI
St. Alban-Anlage 66
4052 Basel, Switzerland

This is a reprint of articles from the Special Issue published online in the open access journal *Education Sciences* (ISSN 2227-7102) from 2018 to 2019 (available at: https://www.mdpi.com/journal/education/special_issues/Vocabulary_Development)

For citation purposes, cite each article independently as indicated on the article page online and as indicated below:

LastName, A.A.; LastName, B.B.; LastName, C.C. Article Title. *Journal Name* **Year**, *Article Number*, Page Range.

ISBN 978-3-03897-734-6 (Pbk)
ISBN 978-3-03897-735-3 (PDF)

Contents

About the Special Issue Editors

Timothy Rasinski is a professor of literacy education at Kent State University and director of its award winning reading clinic. He also holds the Rebecca Tolle and Burton W. Gorman Endowed Chair in Educational Leadership. Tim has written over 200 articles and has authored, co-authored or edited over 50 books or curriculum programs on reading education. He is author of the best selling books on reading fluency *The Fluent Reader* and *The Megabook of Fluency*. Tim's scholarly interests include reading fluency and word study, reading in the elementary and middle grades, and readers who struggle. His research on reading has been cited by the National Reading Panel and has been published in journals such as *Reading Research Quarterly*, *The Reading Teacher*, *Reading Psychology*, and *the Journal of Educational Research*. Tim is the first author of the fluency chapter for the *Handbook of Reading Research, Volume IV*.

Tim served a three year term on the Board of Directors of the International Reading Association and was co-editor of *The Reading Teacher*, the world's most widely read journal of literacy education. He has also served as co-editor of the *Journal of Literacy Research*. Rasinski is past-president of the College Reading Association and he has won the A. B. Herr and Laureate Awards from the College Reading Association for his scholarly contributions to literacy education. In 2010 Tim was elected to the International Reading Hall of Fame.

Prior to coming to Kent State Tim taught literacy education at the University of Georgia. He taught for several years as an elementary and middle school classroom and Title I teacher in Omaha, Nebraska.

Professional Development Areas of Expertise

- Working with Struggling Readers

- Developing Foundational Reading Skills in Young Readers

- Effective Teaching of Phonics and Word Study

- Teaching Fluency: The Neglected but Critical Goal of the Reading Curriculum

- Parental Involvement in Reading

William H. Rupley, Professor, Distinguish Research Fellow, and a Regents Scholar in the department of Teaching, Learning, and Culture, College of Education and Human Development at Texas A&M University. Professor Rupley is the Editor-in-Chief of *Reading Psychology: An International Journal*. Much of his research has used randomized designs to explore the effects of teachers' instructional strategies on students' reading achievement and structural equation modeling and canonical analyses to explore cognitive and conceptual components of reading acquisition in elementary students. He has been either the principal or co-principal investigator for over five million dollars in federal and state professional development and teacher training grants since 2000. He has published more than 150 articles and columns in both application and research journals and is coauthor of four books on reading instruction and reading assessment. Professor Rupley teaches both undergraduate and graduate classes in literacy and literacy language in STEM.

Preface to "Vocabulary Development"

Vocabulary knowledge has long been recognized as an essential component of reading comprehension and is a contributing factor for using reading as means of learning. Vocabulary can and does impact meaningful comprehension of text for struggling through accomplished readers. Simply put, readers who know the meaning to the words they encounter when reading a text are more likely to comprehend that text; readers with large vocabularies tend to be more proficient readers. Therefore, vocabulary emphasis should be a major feature of every reading instruction program. Vocabulary can be thought of as hooks for background knowledge, concepts about the world, understanding discipline content, integration of new learning with what is known and representation of abstract understandings. Simply stated, the breadth and depth of our vocabulary enables the interaction with and the comprehension of text.

As you read the following chapters of this book, you probably will encounter words that are either new to you or different in meaning from those with which you are familiar. You may figure out the meaning of the word by using the context, because it is the context in which words appear that determine their meaning. For example, the word set has 464 definitions in the Oxford English Dictionary. Each definition is dependent upon context: I will set the glass on the table. I am all set to go. I can only play one set of tennis. Thus, the relationship between getting meaning from text and vocabulary is a shared one. Vocabulary growth is a partial outcome of comprehending what is read and comprehension capabilities are inextricably bound with knowledge of word meaning in context.

Words for which readers know the meaning in context represent the concepts and informational knowledge available to them to make sense of what they read. Enhancement and growth of vocabulary knowledge facilitates the reader's processing of text and engagement with the author's writing. Through such engagement, readers can formulate and validate concepts, meaning, and new learnings. This fabric of comprehension is a result of weaving together the shared vocabulary that forms the experiences of author and reader.

Growth in word knowledge is a continuum from no knowledge; to a gist level of knowing; such as knowing that bruhaha refers to some sort of unrest; to a narrow contextual grasp of meaning; to a rich, decontextualized level of word meaning. Definitional knowledge is a narrow form of word knowledge that at the outset of comprehending its meaning is limited by how it is defined within a resource such as a dictionary. However, although such resources are of minimal help in understanding the word and all its derivations, definitional knowledge of words has potential to ripen into knowing such words learned through definitional examples contribute to text cohesiveness in multiple text encounters.

Competent readers construct meaning as they read and use context to grasp the meaning of unknown words as they are encountered by using their knowledge of language structure integrated with their experiences and background knowledge. Experiences with language and concepts facilitates the growth, refinement, and concrete construction of new vocabulary knowledge. The direct implication for reading instruction is that to increase learners' vocabularies they must encounter new words in both spoken and written language, facilitating their abilities to construct meaning for new words representative of their background knowledge.

In the classroom, it is our view that vocabulary learning should include both direct/explicit instruction and opportunities for incidental learning. Both types of learning need to provide practice and application of the new words in reading, speaking and writing. We are not referring to Instructional practices that require rote memorization and meaningless construction of written sentences using the word. Such practices limit a learners' developing any cognitive connection with the value of learning the words' meanings. Learning words' meaning within the context of reading text, writing text, and understanding oral language makes such learning functionally important to the learners and will promote new word learning in both narrative and disciplinary texts.

Expanding students' experiential and conceptual backgrounds leads to furthering developing and increasing their knowledge of words. Meaning vocabulary is a salient factor in practice and application of word recognition strategies, fluency and prosody, comprehension and ultimately learning. Readers who know a word in its fullest sense can associate experiences and concepts with it and continue the life-long process of word learning.

This chapters in this volume offer new insights into vocabulary knowledge and vocabulary teaching. Topics range from a presentation of theories of vocabulary that guide instruction, to features of words that affect vocabulary difficulty, to innovative methods and approaches for teaching vocabulary. Particular emphasis is placed on teaching academic and discipline-related words that are critical to success in content area learning. Our hope for this volume is that it may spark a renewed interest in research into vocabulary and vocabulary instruction and move toward making vocabulary instruction an even more integral part of all literacy and disciplinary instruction.

Timothy Rasinski, William H. Rupley
Special Issue Editors

Article

Vocabulary Instruction: A Critical Analysis of Theories, Research, and Practice

Stephanie Moody *, Xueyan Hu , Li-Jen Kuo , Mohammed Jouhar , Zhihong Xu and Sungyoon Lee

Department of Teaching, Learning, and Culture, Texas A&M University, 4232 TAMU, College Station, TX 77843, USA; brittanyhxy@tamu.edu (X.H.); lijenkuo@tamu.edu (L.-J.K.); mjq8@tamu.edu (M.J.); xuzhihong@tamu.edu (Z.X.); tsy2i@tamu.edu (S.L.)
* Correspondence: smmoody@tamu.edu; Tel.: +1-979-845-8384

Received: 31 July 2018; Accepted: 17 October 2018; Published: 23 October 2018

Abstract: Much is known about the impact of vocabulary instruction on reading skills, word knowledge, and reading comprehension. However, knowledge of the underlying theories that guide vocabulary instruction and their potential impact on teachers' performance and/or students' achievement has not been investigated. In this content analysis, articles published in *The Reading Teacher* and *Journal of Adolescent and Adult Literacy* between 2007 and 2017 were dissected to identify and code embedded word-learning strategies, grade levels addressed, target student populations, and desired outcomes (receptive or productive vocabulary). Our primary goal was to examine the embedded word-learning strategies within the articles, and to identify the theories on which they were built. Findings showed that a combination of theories guided most strategy recommendations: Social constructivism and sociocultural theories, schema and psycholinguistic theories, motivation theory, and dual coding theory. We also parallel-coded our findings with a recent review of literature on vocabulary instruction by Wright and Cervetti (2017), and found that they corresponded with the original coding. Follow-up quantitative studies can use the salient theories detected in this content analysis to investigate whether knowledge of underlying theories has an impact on teachers' performance and student vocabulary and reading comprehension achievement.

Keywords: vocabulary; content analysis; practitioners; teachers; elementary; middle school; high school; reading theories

1. Introduction

A well-developed vocabulary has long been recognized as essential for success in reading [1], and literature has repeatedly affirmed that vocabulary size is one of the strongest predictors of reading development [2–5]. Vocabulary can contribute to reading comprehension through multiple avenues. First, larger vocabularies enable readers to access richer semantic resources to activate relevant background knowledge and integrate new information with existing knowledge, which leads to better comprehension [6]. Second, vocabulary has been found to predict the acquisition of critical aspects of metalinguistic awareness. For example, young children with large vocabularies tend to outperform their peers on measures of phonological awareness [7], which facilitates the development of decoding skills through the ability to isolate and manipulate smaller sound units, and to map sub-syllabic sounds to graphemes in written text. Vocabulary size is also predictive of morphological awareness (i.e., understanding of principles that guide the way morphemes are combined to form words) [8,9], which in turn will contribute to expansion of vocabulary [10,11]. Finally, just as the relationship between vocabulary and morphological awareness is reciprocal [12], so is the relationship between vocabulary and reading: Learners with large vocabulary repertoires tend to read more often, which contributes to the expansion of their vocabulary [6,13]. Therefore, initial gaps in word knowledge may grow exponentially if no intervention is provided.

For young children, early vocabulary development is critical. Most children acquire oral vocabulary through parent–children conversations, interactions with peers and siblings, and shared storybook readings [14]. Research has shown that vocabulary knowledge assists with critical literacy skills, such as letter–sound knowledge [9], decoding [8], and morphological awareness [15], when formal reading instruction begins. In the case of early second language (L2) acquisition, lack of L2 vocabulary may hinder the development of basic reading skills and text comprehension in the target language. In the US, for example, English language learners (ELLs) begin school trailing significantly behind their peers in word knowledge [16]. Research has highlighted the necessity of repeated exposure to vocabulary words, explicit instruction on learning strategies, and sufficient time to engage with new words to close vocabulary gaps between students, particularly L2 learners and those in beginning reading programs [17]. Thus, vocabulary instruction must constitute an integral component of every reading and language arts program.

Still, a large corpus of vocabulary remains crucial in the middle and high school grades, as learners are increasingly required to define and use challenging academic words [18]. Many older students struggle with vocabulary; in the US, results from the 2014 National Assessment of Educational Progress (NAEP) found that only 36% of eighth graders read at a basic level, with vocabulary cited as one of the primary barriers to reading comprehension [19]. To counteract this, research suggests that middle- and high-school students be provided with multifaceted instruction on the use of context clues and morphology, as well as opportunities for active use of new words [6].

While much research has investigated strategies for word learning [6], none have critically examined the theories underlying these strategies. The present study seeks to uncover the theories behind the vocabulary instructional practices recommended for practitioners, and to cross-reference our findings with those of a literature review of empirical vocabulary studies [5]. In the following sections, the effects of vocabulary instruction on word acquisition and the impact of vocabulary instruction on reading comprehension will be reviewed, as well as teacher attitudes towards theories.

1.1. Effects of Vocabulary Instruction on Vocabulary

A variety of studies and syntheses have been conducted about the effects of vocabulary instruction on word learning [6,20–22]. Below, we will focus on the findings from several review papers to present an overview of recent studies on vocabulary instruction.

Hairrell, Rupley, and Simmons engaged in a systematic review of vocabulary research and determined that targeted vocabulary instruction leads to increased word knowledge for elementary students [21]. The authors described three of the most common strategies to build vocabulary reported in empirical research: (1) Contextual analysis, (2) semantic strategies, and (3) repeated exposure [21]. While all were found to impact general word knowledge, semantic strategies, including the use of dictionaries, graphic organizers, discussions, etc., were seldom used in isolation [21], making it difficult to determine the extent of their influence. Additionally, the moderating factors underlying each reviewed study were not reported, so we are unsure if these strategies were found to be effective with learners from different cultural or linguistic backgrounds.

By contrast, Ford-Connors and Paratore reported that wide reading contributes to vocabulary development [6]. However, moderating variables such as text complexity, frequency of engaging in wide reading, and language proficiency were found to influence the relationship between wide reading and vocabulary development. Readers with high English proficiency who regularly engaged in reading complex texts were determined to be the most likely to benefit from word reading [6], suggesting that student background plays a key role in word learning.

In one meta-analysis, Marulis and Neuman reported that explicit vocabulary instruction embedded within meaningful texts and combined with multiple opportunities to practice results in significant vocabulary gains for at-risk children [22]. Interventions such as teaching sight words with picture books, implementing storybook reading to develop oral vocabulary, and adopting a multidimensional vocabulary instruction approach were found to be effective for at-risk children. Word knowledge was shown to increase the most in small-group and one-on-one instructional settings. Finally, the type of intervenor was shown to affect the vocabulary gains. Negligible vocabulary gains were associated with uncertified and ill-equipped teachers. Such findings underscore the importance of knowledgeable teachers who not only provide meaningful word-learning experiences, but are also aware of how to customize instruction according to students' needs.

Finally, Chiu examined the impact of computer-mediated instruction on second-language (L2) vocabulary acquisition, and determined that it had a moderate effect [20]. Electronic flashcards with annotations, visuals, and digital word games were shown to be the most influential for increasing L2 vocabulary [20]. These findings indicate that computer-mediated instruction leads to vocabulary gains through multiple exposures and the meaningful contextualization of unknown words. With the ever-increasing presence of technology in 21st century classrooms, this review provides a critical look into the promises and pitfalls of technology for vocabulary instruction.

1.2. Effects of Vocabulary Instruction on Comprehension

Given the direct relationship between vocabulary and reading [5], it stands to reason that vocabulary instruction would have an impact on reading comprehension; such relationships, however, have not been well established in the literature. Nagy and Townsend reviewed studies on academic vocabulary interventions and found that, while most were successful in helping students learn to use academic words, there is a lack of evidence that vocabulary interventions lead to generalized improvements in academic language or enhanced reading comprehension [23]. The conditions in which instruction on academic words can be generalized beyond the specific words taught needs to be further researched [23].

Similarly, Wright and Cervetti reviewed vocabulary interventions with comprehension outcomes, analyzing the measure used, type of intervention, and characteristics of the instructional recommendations [5]. Like Nagy and Townsend, they found inadequate evidence to suggest that direct teaching of word meanings can advance generalized comprehension [23]. They also argued against the notion that instruction on one or two strategies will lead to generalized comprehension, instead advocating for teaching flexible word-learning strategies and techniques for self-monitoring to improve comprehension [5].

Both reviews indicate the lack of evidence linking vocabulary instruction to improvements in general reading comprehension, particularly when only a handful of strategies are employed. We can postulate that vocabulary instruction may be more effective if strategies based on a variety of theoretical frameworks are utilized and if recommendations focus less on learning individual words and more on tools that can be used to facilitate word knowledge across a variety of contexts.

1.3. Attitudes towards Theories

While vocabulary instruction based on a range of theoretical frameworks may be recommended, the massive boom of empirical reading research has not been associated with matching access to theories [24]. Practitioner-oriented articles, for example, focus on describing the characteristics of strategies and providing tips for their implementation. Rarely do these articles state the underlying theories on which the recommended learning strategies are grounded [25]. Cain and Parilla attribute this to the fact that no single theory has been able to capture the reading process in its entirety, due its complexity and dependence on several components [24]. Likewise, there are currently very few learning or reading theories that specifically address vocabulary development and instruction.

Perhaps because of this, many teachers fail to see the relevance of theories to their classrooms [26]. Most teachers are equipped with a plethora of prior knowledge about teaching and learning, and are less likely to accept theories that do not match their prior knowledge [27,28]. Furthermore, teachers are mostly interested in learning explicit teaching strategies that can be directly put into practice [27,29,30], and they tend to value and appreciate the testimonies and suggestions of their fellow teachers more than recommendations from theorists, researchers, or even teacher educators [27–29,31]. This is compounded by the fact that the many demands placed on teachers limit their free time, making it less likely that it will be spent identifying the theoretical basis of instructional practices. Similarly, some educators believe that those who are distanced from the daily reality of teaching, such as researchers, are not in a position to offer educational insights, and thus receive research with skepticism [27–29,31]. In this content analysis study, we seek to determine the salient theories that underlie vocabulary instructional practices and strategies recommended in two practitioner-oriented journals. Through this, we will ensure that whatever time spent by teachers studying and understanding theories is directly related to their classroom practices.

1.4. Justification for Present Study

Students bring their own background knowledge and experiences (i.e., world knowledge) into the classroom. This knowledge is organized in students' minds in abstract forms called schemas, which emerge through social interactions. Social interactions activate stored schemas and facilitate the building of new ones [32], all of which is mediated by vocabulary. If students lack sufficient vocabulary knowledge, their capacity to make self-to-world connections and inferences is hindered [33,34]. It is also important to recognize that word knowledge is not an all-or-nothing phenomenon [35], but instead falls along a continuum. Word knowledge incrementally increases from no knowledge to context-bound knowledge, context-free knowledge, and finally metaphorical knowledge [36]. Teachers who understand the development of word knowledge are more readily able to select vocabulary instructional practices based on theories that support the acquisition of vocabulary.

Teachers who are knowledgeable about vocabulary development make sure that word-learning strategies associated with teacher–student and student–student interactions are incorporated in their vocabulary lessons. Examples of such strategies include semantic maps and other forms of graphic organizers, read-aloud discussions, student-generated definitions, word walls, word games, and shared journal/class books. The social dialogue generated through these strategies allows students to make semantic connections, use newly-learned words in their appropriate contexts, and predict unfamiliar meanings [37]. As this social dialogue becomes habitual in classrooms, we can then expect students to move forward in the word knowledge continuum [36] and take ownership of word meanings. Additionally, many teachers include the use of visuals within vocabulary instruction, which is based on the premise of Dual Coding Theory (DCT). A common misconception amongst teachers is that students will naturally realize the connections between visuals and words [38]. When teachers understand DCT, they recognize that instruction must include a purposeful focus on contextual referents [39] so that all students will understand and internalize new words.

It is also important to realize that "one size" of vocabulary instruction does not necessarily fit all. Students display individual differences in terms of their needs, interests, and prior word knowledge. Motivation theory provides a framework for teachers to customize their instruction to match the needs of all students. Teachers can choose to motivate students and enhance self-efficacy through consistent modeling and the application of self-regulation strategies [40]. Another strategy teachers can use to motivate students involves the incorporation of technology, which has been reported to have a positive influence on students' attitudes towards word learning [41–44]. Knowledge of motivation theory leads teachers to understand how to differentiate instruction to satisfy students' needs, interests, and style of learning.

Thus far, we have built the case that theories have natural implications for vocabulary instruction. Theories help teachers understand how vocabulary knowledge develops, and signals to teachers why some practices are fruitless. Practitioner-oriented articles provide teachers with a plethora of instructional practices and strategies. Teachers may be aware of these strategies and how they are used; however, awareness of the underlying theoretical bases of *why* these were created increases the likelihood that teachers will recognize their utility. Understanding these theories also allows teachers to reflect upon their performance, evaluate their effectiveness, and justify their choice of strategies. Theories enable teachers to choose, manipulate, and modify their vocabulary instructional practices according to students' need and characteristics of words. Despite this, most teachers are not consciously aware of the theoretical basis of their instructional practices [26].

In this content analysis, articles published between 2007 and 2017 in *The Reading Teacher* and *Journal of Adolescent and Adult Literacy* were dissected to identify and code: (1) The embedded word-learning strategies, (2) grade levels addressed, (3) target student population, and (4) desired outcome (i.e., receptive or productive word knowledge). The primary focus was to examine the embedded word-learning strategies, and to identify the underlying theories on which these strategies rest. Identification of these theories will enable teachers to understand under which circumstances a certain strategy works and provide them with the tools to reflect upon and modify their instructional practices. Through this article, we hope to encourage the explicit disclosure of the theoretical underpinnings of instructional practices reported within practitioner journals and to guide future researchers to investigate how teacher knowledge of theories increases the effectiveness of teachers' performance and enhances students' achievement.

1.5. Description of Theories

The following theories guided our analysis: (1) Social constructivism/sociocultural theories; (2) schema/psycholinguistic theories; (3) dual-coding theory; and (4) motivation theory. We selected these because they were identified by the International Literacy Association as having exerted substantial influence over reading research [45] and had been utilized by previous content analyses [25]. Below, information about each theory will be provided.

1.5.1. Social Constructivism and Sociocultural Theories

A core assumption of both social constructivism and sociocultural theory is that knowledge is constructed via interaction with others during social activities [45]. More knowledgeable others are believed to facilitate the understanding and internalization of the social context and its contextual elements (e.g., culture and language), through which the construction of reality develops. Sociocultural theory is well-known for its Vygotskian perspectives, particularly the Zone of Proximal Development (ZPD), scaffolding, psychological tools, and inner speech [46,47]. ZPD refers to the zone that mediates what learners can and cannot do, in which learning must be scaffolded by more advanced adults and/or peers. Scaffolding enables learners to accelerate their mastery of psychological tools (e.g., language) and psychological tools allow learners to control and utilize their higher order mental processes. Bruner and his colleagues postulate that structured and scaffolded interactions between students and knowledgeable adults leads to growth in students' thinking, language, skills, and knowledge [48]. Students start these interactions dependent upon adults, which later fades when skills are mastered and self-regulation is achieved.

These theories imply that all individuals are active participants in the meaning-making process [49], so vocabulary instruction should be perceived as a social dialogue through which meanings are constructed via scaffolding and collaboration. Therefore, tasks where students work cooperatively to construct definitions of words and participate in collaborative discussions about new vocabulary [50] are rooted in social constructivism and sociocultural theory [51,52].

1.5.2. Schema and Psycholinguistic Theories

Schema theory refers to the cognitive and conceptual structure and representation of knowledge [45]. Schemas can be thought of as mental filing cabinets that allow individuals to process, encode, organize, and retrieve information [53]. Comprehension results from the activation of schemas, which provide a framework for explaining objects and events within a text [53]. Similarly, psycholinguistic theory proposes that readers do not rely exclusively on textual clues to make meaning, but instead make predictions as they read [45]. A readers' background knowledge interacts with conceptual abilities and processing strategies to produce comprehension [54]. Both schema and psycholinguistic theories demonstrate the active role of learners when constructing meaning and play a role in vocabulary instruction when students are asked to connect new words to synonyms and antonyms, analyze the morphological features of words [10,11], create concept maps, graphic organizers, and semantic maps [55], and when using prior knowledge to determine word meanings [56].

1.5.3. Dual Coding Theory

The basic premise of dual coding theory (DCT) is that the human mind processes environmental stimuli via two mental systems (or codes), verbal and nonverbal. The two codes, though independent, are connected. The verbal code is responsible for processing and representing language, while the nonverbal code does so for nonlinguistic objects and events. In DCT, cognition occurs when representations from both codes become connected. Verbal-only associations result from a failure to concretize the abstract, producing only shallow understandings [57]. In vocabulary instruction, practices emphasizing the concreteness and imageability of words, such as the use of multiple modalities [58] or the elicitation of mental images [59], are rooted in DCT.

1.5.4. Motivation Theory

Motivation theory, as it pertains to literacy, posits that readers become engaged with a text when it aligns with their goals, desires, and objectives within a particular social milieu [45]. Students become intrinsically driven to read when they are curious about the topic of the book or the author, believe in their reading abilities (self-efficacy), are given autonomy in choice of reading material, or are provided with texts of interest [60]. Motivation also can increase through extrinsic means, such as achieving learning goals based on competition [61] or the desire for external rewards or praise [62]. Vocabulary practices based on motivation theory include the development of word consciousness to enhance student interest [40], the use of word-learning games [63], and technology-based activities [58].

1.6. Research Questions

When teachers have a solid understanding of the theories that drive instruction, they can then recognize why certain strategies are effective, how to properly modify them, and for what purposes each should be used [25] Therefore, the present study seeks to identify the underlying theories behind recommendations made for vocabulary instruction within two practitioner journals, *The Reading Teacher* (RT) and *Journal of Adolescent and Adult Literacy* (JAAL). We selected RT and JAAL for several reasons: (1) We wanted to examine the theories behind practices that are guiding classroom instruction, so practitioner journals were more suitable than empirical research journals, and (2) both RT and JAAL are considered to be high-impact, flagship journals that reach a large audience of classroom teachers and are widely cited in pre-service teacher education textbooks.

Additionally, we chose to do a parallel coding of our study with a recent review published in *Reading Research Quarterly* (RRQ) by Wright and Cervetti [5]. *RRQ* is a leading empirical research journal in the field of literacy and the study by Wright and Cervetti provides a systematic review of vocabulary intervention studies with comprehension outcomes. Through this parallel coding, we sought to determine whether the underlying theories that guide the word-learning strategies recommended in practitioner journals are the same as those recommended in empirical research journals. Additionally, we wanted to determine if there are any word-learning strategies that are exclusively suggested within practitioner-or empirical research, and point out the need for further investigations on these.

Our study is guided by the following research questions:

1. What theories underlie the recommendations for vocabulary instruction made by articles published in practitioner journals?
2. How do the theories underlying recommendations for vocabulary instruction in practitioner journals vary across grade levels, special populations, and desired outcomes (i.e., receptive or productive)?
3. What are the differences and similarities between theories underlying vocabulary instruction made by empirical research articles and practitioner-oriented articles?

2. Methods

2.1. Search Criteria

The current review includes articles that were published in *RT* and *JAAL* between 2007 and 2017. To be selected, the primary focus of each article (over 50%) had to be on vocabulary instructional strategies. Words synonymous with vocabulary, including *word meaning* and *word knowledge*, were used to search the *RT* and *JAAL* databases, yielding an initial 200 articles: 156 from *RT* and 44 from *JAAL*.

2.2. Inclusion and Exclusion Criteria

Following the review by Yang, Kuo, Ji, and McTigue, we included articles that focused on any aspect of word learning or instruction [64]. Articles were excluded if over half of the word count of the entire article was not related to vocabulary instruction or if they were book reviews, commentaries, literature reviews, or editorial columns. This culminated in the identification of 76 articles for analysis, 61 from *RT*, and 15 from *JAAL*.

2.3. Coding Procedures

Five out of the six authors collaborated to code the articles. Each article was read in its entirety and coded for the factors most relevant to the research questions, including: (1) Student characteristics, including grade level and explicit reference to ELLs or struggling learners; (2) the desired outcome, such as *productive* or *receptive*; (3) the reading theories underlying the recommended practices; and (4) explicit or implicit statement of theories [64].

Following Unrau and Alvermann, recommendations for vocabulary instruction were coded as being guided by social constructivism/sociocultural theories, schema/psycholinguistic theories, DCT, or reading motivation theory [45]. Decisions on how to code each practice was based on *why* and *how* it was used within the classroom. For example, using vocabulary journals was coded within social constructivism and sociocultural theories because students were encouraged to work collaboratively to create their own definitions and to share explanatory resources and illustrations. A theory was coded as *explicit* if it was named within the article, and *implicit* if the theory was not stated, but enough evidence was present to suggest that it provided a framework for the practice [61]. Finally, articles could be coded as being guided by more than one theory if sufficient evidence was present [64].

After the initial coding was completed, 20% of the articles ($n = 40$) were stratified and randomly selected for re-coding to establish interrater reliability. Initial results yielded 73% agreement, which was determined to be unsatisfactory. Coders met and discussed all discrepancies, after which a second round of coding was conducted following the revised coding scheme, and an interrater reliability of 85% was reached. Coders met one final time to resolve all remaining differences.

3. Results and Discussion

3.1. Research Question One

Research question one asked, what theories underlie the recommendations for vocabulary instruction made by articles published in practitioner journals? We found that recommendations guided by social constructivism/sociocultural theories were the most prevalent, followed by schema/psycholinguistic theories, motivation theory, and finally DCT (see Table 1). These findings will be discussed in greater detail below.

Eighty-eight percent ($n = 67$) of the recommendations were guided by social constructivism and sociocultural theories, with only 6% ($n = 4$) explicitly naming the theory. This finding is anticipated, as teaching pedagogy has increasingly emphasized learning through social, collaborative discovery [65]. In *RT* and *JAAL*, suggestions based on these theories included the use of cooperative groups to create student-friendly definitions [66], and partner "think–pair–share" work to build meaningful sentences with new words [67].

Table 1. Summary of articles included, presented chronically.

Citation	Grade Level [1]	Explicit References to ELLs	Explicit References to Struggling Readers	Vocabulary Type [2]	Technology	Social Constructivism/ Sociocultural Theories	Schema/ Psycholinguistic	Dual Coding Theory	Motivation Theory
Abrams and Walsh (2014) [41]	HS			R	X[5]		Implicit		Implicit
Adams and Pegg (2012) [68]	HS			P			Implicit		Implicit
Baumann, Ware, and Edwards (2007) [69]	UE			P			Implicit	Implicit	Implicit
Beauchat, Blamey, and Walpole (2009) [70]	PS			R			Implicit	Implicit	
Blamey and Beauchat (2011) [71]	PS			R			Implicit	Implicit	
Boulwar-Gooden (2010) [72]	UE			R			Implicit		
Boyd, Sullivan, Popp, and Hughes (2012) [73]	HS			R			Implicit	Implicit	
Brabham et al. (2012) [42]	EE and UE	X[3]		R	X	Implicit	Implicit		
Briceño (2016) [74]	EE	X		R		Implicit	Implicit		
Bromley (2007) [75]	MS and HS	X		P		Implicit	Implicit		Implicit
Ciechanowski (2009) [76]	UE	X		P		Implicit	Implicit		Implicit
Crosson and Lesaux (2013) [77]	UE	X		P		Implicit	Implicit		
Dalton and Grisham (2011) [58]	UE	X	X[4]	R	X	Implicit	Implicit	Implicit	Implicit
Dashiell and DeBruin-Parecki (2014) [78]	PS		X	R	X	Implicit	Implicit	Implicit	Explicit
Donnelly and Roe (2010) [79]	UE	X		P		Implicit	Implicit		Implicit
Ellery (2010) [66]	*			P		Implicit	Implicit		Implicit
Feezell (2012) [67]	UE	X		P		Implicit	Implicit		
Fisher and Frey (2014) [80]	*			P	X	Implicit	Implicit		Implicit
Flanigan and Greenwood (2007) [81]	MS			R		Implicit	Implicit		Implicit
Flanigan and Greenwood (2007) [81]	MS			R		Implicit	Implicit		Implicit
Flanigan, Templeton, and Hayes (2012) [82]	HS			R		Implicit	Implicit		
Flynt and Brozo (2008) [83]	*	X		P	X	Implicit	Implicit		
Gallagher and Anderson (2016) [84]	UE			R		Implicit	Implicit	Implicit	
Ganske (2016) [85]	EE			R		Implicit	Implicit	Implicit	
Gill (2007) [86]	*			R		Implicit	Implicit	Implicit	
Gillanders, Castro, and Franco (2014) [87]	PS	X		R		Implicit	Implicit	Implicit	Implicit
Gillis (2014) [88]	*			R		Implicit	Implicit		
Giroir, Grimaldo, Vaughn, and Roberts (2015) [37]	EE and UE	X		R		Explicit	Explicit	Implicit	
Goodwin and Perkins (2015) [89]	EE, UE and MS		X	R		Implicit	Implicit		
Goodwin, Cho, and Nichols (2016) [90]	MS		X	R		Implicit	Implicit		
Goodwin, Lipsky, and Ahn (2012) [91]	EE, UE and MS			R		Implicit	Implicit		
Grant et al. (2012) [92]	MS			R		Explicit	Explicit		Explicit
Graves and Watts-Taffe (2008) [93]	*			R		Implicit	Implicit		
Green (2015) [94]	UE			R		Implicit	Implicit		
Greenwood and Flanigan (2007) [95]	UE			P		Implicit	Implicit		
Griffith and Ruan (2007) [96]	EE	X	X	P		Implicit			
Hall (2016) [97]	EE			R		Implicit			
Harmon et al. (2009) [98]	MS			R		Explicit	Implicit	Implicit	
Helman and Burns (2008) [99]	EE	X		R		Implicit	Implicit	Implicit	Implicit
Hendrix and Griffin (2017) [100]	MS			R	X	Implicit	Implicit		Implicit
Hernández (2016) [101]	EE UE	X		P	X	Implicit	Implicit	Implicit	
Kieffer and Lesaux (2007) [102]	MS			R		Implicit	Implicit		Implicit
Kesler (2010) [103]	EE UE			P		Implicit	Implicit	Implicit	Implicit
Kieffer and Lesaux (2010) [102]	UE			R		Implicit	Implicit		
Kieffer and Lesaux (2010) [102]	MS	X		P		Implicit	Implicit		

8

Table 1. *Cont.*

Citation	Grade Level [1]	Explicit References to ELLs	Explicit References to Struggling Readers	Vocabulary Type [2]	Technology	Social Constructivism/ Sociocultural Theories	Schema/ Psycholinguistic	Dual Coding Theory	Motivation Theory
Kindle (2009) [104]	EE			R		Implicit			
Kozdras, Joseph, and Schneider (2015) [43]	UE	X		P	X	Implicit			Implicit
Kucan (2012) [105]	*			R		Implicit	Implicit		
Labbo, Love, and Ryan (2007) [44]	EE			P	X	Implicit	Implicit	Implicit	Implicit
LaBrocca and Morrow (2016) [106]	UE			P		Implicit	Implicit	Implicit	Implicit
Lane and Allen (2010) [40]	EE			P		Implicit			Implicit
Larson (2014) [107]	EE			P		Implicit	Implicit		Implicit
Manyak (2007) [108]	EE UE MS			R		Implicit	Implicit		
Manyak (2010) [109]	UE			R		Implicit	Implicit		Implicit
Manyak and Bauer (2009) [110]	*	X		R		Implicit	Implicit	Implicit	Implicit
Manyak et al. (2014) [111]	UE	X		R		Implicit	Implicit	Implicit	Implicit
McGee and Schickedanz (2007) [112]	PS EE			R	X	Implicit	Implicit	Implicit	Implicit
McKeown et al. (2013) [113]	MS			R		Implicit	Implicit		Implicit
Mountain, L. (2007) [114]	HS			P		Implicit	Implicit		Implicit
Neuman and Roskos (2012) [115]	*			P		Implicit	Implicit	Implicit	Implicit
Picot (2017) [116]	EE UE	X		R		Implicit		Implicit	Implicit
Pierce and Fontaine (2009) [117]	UE			R		Implicit	Implicit		
Pollard-Durodola et al. (2011) [118]	PS			P		Implicit	Implicit	Implicit	Implicit
Putman and Kingsley (2009) [119]	UE			R	X	Implicit	Implicit		Implicit
Rasinski, Padak, Newton, and Newton (2011) [120]	EE UE			R		Implicit	Implicit		
Rodgers (2017) [121]	EE		X	R	X	Implicit	Implicit		
Savino (2011) [122]	MS			P		Implicit	Implicit		Implicit
Snell, Hindman, and Wasik (2015) [123]	PS EE			R		Implicit	Implicit		Implicit
Toth (2013) [124]	EE			R		Implicit	Implicit		
Townsend (2009) [125]	MS	X		R		Implicit	Implicit		Implicit
Wessels (2011) [126]	*	X		R		Explicit			
Williams et al. (2009) [127]	EE			P	X	Implicit	Implicit		Explicit
Winters (2009) [128]	*			R	X	Implicit			
Wolsey, Smetana, and Grisham (2015) [129]	UE			R		Implicit			Implicit
Wright (2014) [130]	EE			R		Implicit	Implicit	Implicit	Implicit
Yopp and Yopp (2007) [131]	*			R		Implicit	Implicit		
Zoski and Erickson (2017) [132]	EE		X	R		Implicit	Implicit		

Note: [1] PS: Preschool; EE: Early elementary (Grades K–2); UE: Upper elementary (Grades 3–5); MS: Middle school (Grades 6–8); HS: High school (Grades 9–12); U: University students; A: Adult; *: Grade level is not indicated in the article; [2] P: Productive vocabulary; R: Receptive vocabulary; [3] X: ELLs are explicitly referred in the article; [4] X: Struggling readers are explicitly referred in the article; [5] X: Technology is applied into vocabulary instruction.

Social constructivism and sociocultural theories may be critical for word learning, as collaborative practices enable teachers to conquer the old-fashioned, deep-rooted notion that vocabulary instruction is solely about providing definitional information while students remain passive listeners. Instead, students engage in the word-learning process interactively, which was evidenced in the suggestion provided by Giroir, Grimaldo, Vaughn, and Roberts; the authors recommended the use of read-aloud discussions to challenge students to "use and predict new language by making meaningful text-to-self and text-to-world connections" [36] (p. 640). Collaborative scaffolding, such as within discussions, fosters multidimensional, world knowledge that goes beyond ability to recall meanings. This knowledge entails fluent access to the precise metaphorical use of words, awareness of oral and written word formats, and the ability to manipulate words across various contexts [35].

Schema and psycholinguistic theories also commonly influenced recommendations for vocabulary instruction, coded in 76% (*n* = 58) of reviewed articles, with 3% (*n* = 2) explicitly naming the theory. This aligns with findings by Wright et al., who determined that practitioner articles about science disciplinary literacy instruction were largely guided by schema theory [25]. In the current review, authors such as Flanigan and Greenwood recommended teaching words through semantic groupings and by comparing and contrasting features of words [81]. Also recommended to support students' development and reorganization of conceptual knowledge was the use of the Frayer Model, a graphic organizer that requires students to define target vocabulary, generate examples and non-examples, provide characteristics, and/or illustrate the word meanings [36]. Briceño asked dual language teachers to create cognate word walls and incorporate students' home language into class discussions to foster understanding about shared semantic meanings and the phonological and orthographic features of each word [74]. Through this, students were able to build rich representations of cognates that went beyond semantics. Afterwards, students were encouraged to use words from the cognate walls within their writing.

The prevalence of Schema/Psycholinguistic strategies indicates that a large chunk of classroom vocabulary instruction centers around the activation of prior knowledge, mental organization of words, and the connection of words to each other. While such strategies play a critical role in word processing, instructional practices that focus only on association (such as categorizing synonyms and antonyms) are not enough for students to gain a deep understanding of words [133]. Strategies such as the Frayer Model must be accompanied by opportunities for students to actively use words in meaningful and authentic ways [14]. Students should be given opportunities to talk about the connections between words, including analyzing word relationships and articulating incidents when one synonym would be preferable over another [14].

Motivation was the third most coded theory, underlying 47% (*n* = 36) of the articles, and explicitly referred to within 9% (*n* = 3). Tenets of motivation theory include the use of rewards, competition, and the generation of student interest, all of which were evidenced in the reviewed articles. The majority of recommendations focused on building intrinsic motivation through word consciousness activities [39,64,69,107,109,133,134] designed to increase student interest in words. To illustrate, Baumann et al. encouraged teachers to promote engagement through an activity where students investigate common slang words used in their homes [69].

Also popular within *RT* and *JAAL* was the use of games for increasing both intrinsic and extrinsic motivation [41,43,58,78,80,106,114,122,125]. Townsend described a variety of games that can be used to build the English vocabulary of ELLs, including picture and music puzzlers, matching and dice games, taboo, jeopardy, and pictionades [125]. She found that the games were "by far, the most engaging part of the intervention, and they were an essential draw to the program for students who would not have been easily convinced of the immediate value of learning words" [125] (p. 250). Technology-based games and programs were also recommended in several articles as a strategy for creating student interest in word learning [41,43,129].

Abrams and Walsh were the only researchers to note the potential of technology for increasing autonomy, as the immediate feedback provided by the computer program in their study facilitated independent learning [41]. This article was unique in that it explores an aspect of motivation theory that has been underused in vocabulary instruction. Aspects such as the development of autonomy, self-efficacy, and personal goal setting were largely overlooked within the other articles in *RT* and *JAAL*. Recommendations for vocabulary instruction that address these, such as the suggestion by Grant, Lapp, Fisher, Johnson, and Frey to use inquiry-based learning to shift the responsibility of learning from teachers to students, should be further examined for their impact on word learning [92]. Additionally, studies involving individualized technology should consider its potential to facilitate multiple aspects of motivation theory, such as the development of goals and self-efficacy [135].

Uncommon within the literature were vocabulary instruction practices based on DCT, found in only 32% (*n* = 24) of the articles, and all implicitly coded. These findings contrast with those of Wright et al., in which DCT was the second most commonly identified theory [25]. In *RT* and *JAAL*, strategies based on DCT revolved around the use of digital books [58] and the incorporation of drama, real objects, and visual images [109]. The use of *mnemonics keywords*, in which students are asked to generate mental images to make words more memorable and concrete, was never mentioned over the past decade in *RT* and *JAAL* [39]. Future studies published in *RT* and *JAAL* could highlight this instructional practice and its role in developing students' vocabulary.

The shortage of recommendations guided by DCT might indicate a failure by teachers and researchers to recognize the association between the different processes in vocabulary learning, or a general misunderstanding about the tenets of DCT. Sadoski and Paivio argue that DCT is frequently misunderstood or mischaracterized, with many believing that it solely encompasses the connection of verbal representations to nonverbal representations [57]. While word learning should include opportunities to activate verbal and nonverbal aspects of vocabulary, word concreteness (e.g., ring) and word context (e.g., wedding ring, boxing ring, telephone ring) must also be acknowledged [39] (p. 223). DCT discourages teachers from using visuals in isolation, as students are then forced to infer appropriate contextual referents and meanings. Thus, it is imperative that educators are provided with explicit theoretical rationales of DCT to overcome misconceptions and unsupported practices.

3.2. Research Question Two

Research question two sought to uncover how the theories underlying vocabulary instructional practices differed across grade levels, special populations, and desired outcomes of vocabulary learning. Findings will be discussed below.

Twenty-eight percent (*n* = 21) of the reviewed articles explicitly focused on vocabulary instruction for ELLs. Of these, 81% (*n* = 17) were driven by theories of social constructivism/socioculturalism, 71% (*n* = 15) by schema/psycholinguistic theories, 52% (*n* = 11) guided by motivation theory, and 33% (*n* = 7) by DCT. Much like the strategies recommended for the general student population, the social nature of word learning and scaffolding was highly valued within ELL instruction. For example, Ciechanowski suggested engaging ELLs in critical discussions using new vocabulary words, so that students could utilize their sociocultural resources to build meaning [76]. In-depth word analysis [136] was also supported within the reviewed articles; most commonly, authors recommended that teachers use morphemic word analysis when working with ELLs [137–139]. Articles that recommended this strategy posited that structured exposure to, and teaching of, meaningful word parts through scaffolding and class discussions is essential for the vocabulary development of ELLs [86].

Aside from the prominence of social constructivism/sociocultural theories, schema theory also played a large role in ELL instruction. This may be due to the widely-held belief that schema theory involves the activation of background knowledge, which has been long recognized as a successful strategy for ELL reading instruction [54]. Future recommendations for ELLs should consider how other aspects of schema theory, such as strategies for "structuring" information in a way that is efficient for encoding, storing, and retrieving words, impacts second-language word learning.

Very few articles that made specific reference to struggling readers (8%, *n* = 6), which is surprising given the fact that, in 2015, only 36% of fourth graders were performing at or above the basic level in reading [19]. Similar to the findings for ELLs, social constructivism/sociocultural theories drove most suggestions (100%, $n = 6$) for struggling readers. Sixty-seven percent ($n = 4$) were based on schema/psycholinguistic theories, whereas 33% ($n = 2$) were rooted in motivation, and 33% ($n = 2$) in DCT.

It is intriguing that more recommendations were not based on motivation theory, given that struggling readers would likely benefit from the development of self-efficacy and personal goal setting. Research has shown that high self-efficacy is correlated with higher achievement [140] and that values, goals, and expectancy mediate the relationship between self-efficacy and achievement [141]. In the present review, one study extolled the use of word-learning technology for igniting the struggling readers' interest in words and for developing self-efficacy [58]; however, the latter was more of an afterthought and not emphasized within the article. Research has consistently shown that technology increases the engagement and interest of struggling readers [142]; however, other aspects of motivation theory need to be considered when planning for instruction. Educators of struggling learners should be careful to include a variety of motivational techniques within their vocabulary instruction.

Similarly, very few articles targeting struggling students were influenced by DCT. This lack may be attributed to the nature of instructional recommendations usually provided for this population, which highlights the use of independent word-learning strategies, such as morphological analysis. While Sadoski argues that DCT encompasses morphological analysis when students analyze words into meaningful parts, then "recombine those parts into meaningful wholes" [39] (p. 233), this argument fails to provide a sufficient explanation for how this connects to the nonverbal code. Because of this concern, we coded the morphological analysis strategy as underlain by the schema, social constructivism, and sociocultural theories.

Eighty percent ($n = 61$) of the identified articles were drawn from *RT*, a journal geared primarily towards teachers of elementary-aged students. Conversely, only 20% percent ($n = 15$) of articles were from *JAAL*, a journal for middle- and high-school practitioners. This paucity is alarming, as it suggests that the focus on vocabulary instruction within research dwindles as students get older. McKeown et al. echoed this concern, noting the lack of intervention studies focusing on word learning that have been conducted with middle- and high-school students [18].

Social constructivism and sociocultural theories were found to significantly underlie most vocabulary instructional recommendations, particularly for the elementary grade levels. Seventy-three percent ($n = 11$) of the articles in *JAAL* were based on these theories, indicating the possibility that middle- and high-school students are using social constructivist/socioculturally-rooted activities to develop academic word knowledge.

Teachers of elementary students were also frequently directed to use strategies based on schema/psycholinguistic theories for building word knowledge. This aligns with findings by Chilton and Ehri, who determined that third graders learned the meaning of vocabulary words better when using cohesive sentences (schema theory) than unconnected sentences [143]. Thus, elementary teachers would benefit from a solid understanding of these theories in order to effectively design and modify vocabulary instruction for their students.

Motivation theory undergirded 60% ($n = 9$) of *JAAL* articles. This number is relatively large compared to those found in *RT* (20%, $n = 12$), which may be due to the increased focus on autonomy in the upper grades, as students strive to become independent thinkers who are less reliant on teacher assistance [102]. Alternately, DCT was somewhat influential for vocabulary learning in early schooling, but only underlay recommendations in 13% ($n = 2$) of *JAAL* articles. We noted that the vocabulary instructional practices published in *JAAL* were more abstract in nature; once again, this could be attributed to the focus on content instruction in the upper grades. However, many recently-published content areas textbooks for older learners contain visuals [144], so teachers must not assume that students are going to make the verbal–nonverbal connection naturally [57,144]. Direct, explicit, and scaffolded instruction is required. Practices guided by DCT could assist in concretizing the abstract and allowing students to connect verbal representations to context-appropriate visuals.

Articles were also coded for the desired outcome (productive or receptive) focused on. Our review noted that the majority of recommendations sought to increase receptive vocabulary; whereas 68% ($n = 50$) of articles provided recommendations for developing receptive vocabulary, only 34% ($n = 26$) focused on productive. Much like our other findings, recommendations for both outcomes were primarily driven by social constructivism/sociocultural theories (Receptive 84%, $n = 43$; Productive 92%, $n = 24$) and schema theories (Receptive 76%, $n = 39$; Productive 73%, $n = 19$). Strategies for productive vocabulary were more frequently derived from motivation theory (65%, $n = 17$) than those focusing on receptive vocabulary (37%, $n = 19$).

The fact that productive vocabulary has been largely overlooked was unexpected, especially considering the recent emphasis in vocabulary literature on active word use across a variety of contexts [14]. Vocabulary instruction should not end at an assessment of understanding or a recall of words, but should instead consider if students are able to use the new words they have acquired. Kelley et al. assert that integrating writing activities into vocabulary instruction is essential, because including new words within writing indicates a true understanding of their meaning [134]. However, the use of writing for vocabulary development was reported in very few of the articles in *RT* and *JAAL*. Those that did ask students to write only required a few sentences, such as writing within semantic graphic organizers or creating sentences with new words [68,79]. Only articles that included journaling activities called for students to write multiple paragraphs using new words [97,107], indicating that writing and vocabulary are seldom paired.

3.3. Research Question Three

In research question three, we sought to determine the differences and similarities between the underlying theories within empirical vocabulary research and practitioner-oriented vocabulary articles. More than half ($n = 20$) of the practices coded by Wright and Cervetti intersected with practices identified in our coding scheme, allowing us to easily code the underlying theory [5]. For the remaining 11 practices, our team of coders met and reached a consensus on how they should be coded. Through comparing the empirical research articles in Wright and Cervetti to our findings, we sought to discover what vocabulary instructional strategies, if any, were identified in empirical journals but not in practitioner-oriented articles, and vice versa. By highlighting such strategies, we could guide future researchers towards practices that warrant further investigation.

Schema theory was found to guide 48% ($n = 15$) of the research interventions reviewed by Wright and Cervetti, suggesting that schema theory exerts an important influence in practitioner and empirical research [5]. Interestingly, strategies that are encouraged within practitioner journals, such as the Frayer Model [68], were absent within the intervention studies reviewed by Wright and Cervetti [5]. This may suggest that strategies to develop content-area vocabulary are not often emphasized, despite promising evidence that the integration of literacy strategies within content instruction is an effective way to increase students' achievement [145].

Social constructivism and sociocultural theories were found to underlie 32% ($n = 10$) of the interventions reported by Wright and Cervetti [5]. The prevalence of social constructivism and sociocultural theories indicate that both empirical and practitioner-oriented research are pushing for the use of interactive learning activities, such as "think-pair-share" [67].

Nine of the instructional practices included in Wright and Cervetti were frequently recommended within *RT* and *JAAL* over the past decade [5]. The only practice that was seldom suggested for use in the classroom was *syntactic feature analysis*, which requires teachers to draw attention to different forms of the target word, and how they relate to certain parts of speech [144]. Knowledge of a word extends beyond its *meaning* to its *form* and *use*, which includes its grammatical functions [18]. Given our findings, it is reasonable to conclude that recommendations for vocabulary instruction published in *RT* and *JAAL* focus primarily on activities to develop *meaning* and *form*, with little acknowledgment of *use* [146]. Future research could investigate the benefits of incorporating grammar and discourse in vocabulary instruction and suggest evidence-based practices for practitioners.

Only 18% (*n* = 4) of studies were directed by motivation theory within Wright and Cervetti [5]. Suggestions grounded in motivation theory, such as the use of real-life experiences, the development of self-efficacy, and games based on student interests, seem to appear more frequently within practitioner journals than in empirical studies. Other underpinnings of motivation theory, such as goal setting and the development of autonomy [147], should be examined for their ability to increase breadth and depth of word knowledge, particularly with struggling learners and ELLs. Additionally, researchers may want to consider how traditional constructs of motivation impact diverse student populations, as varying cultural beliefs and goals may require different types of motivational interventions [148].

Much like in the present review, intervention studies based on DCT were scarce within Wright and Cervetti, with only 6% (*n* = 2) guided by this theory [5]. It seems that within both practitioner and research journals, the use of DCT-based strategies for vocabulary learning is uncommon. Interestingly, in reviewing Wright and Cervetti, we noted the overall lack of influence that DCT has had on vocabulary instruction research during 1965–2006. Out of the 31 strategies included by Wright and Cervetti, none outside of Türk and Erçetin and Levin, Levin, Glasman, and Nordwall were guided by DCT [149,150]. One possible explanation for this is made by Sadoski and Paivio themselves [57]. They stated that DCT started as a theory of memory and cognition in the 1970s, continued to focus on memory and cognition in the 1980s and 1990s, extended to explain literacy-related issues (i.e., reading comprehension and composition) in the 1990s, and was finally declared as a unified theory of literacy at the beginning of the new millennium [57] (p. 886). Further research could dig deeper into this matter and provide additional explanations for why DCT has gained popularity in the past decade.

4. Conclusions

4.1. Summary of Findings

In the present content trend analysis, we sought to investigate the salient theories on which vocabulary instructional recommendations made by practitioner-oriented articles are founded. We also examined how theories underlying recommendations for vocabulary instruction varied across grade levels, student populations, and desired learning outcome. Finally, we parallel-coded our findings with those of Wright and Cervetti, who reviewed empirical vocabulary research [5].

Our analysis showed that a combination of theories guided most strategy recommendations: Social constructivism and sociocultural theories, schema and psycholinguistic theories, motivation theory, and dual coding theory. Social constructivism and sociocultural theories were the most influential, guiding 88% of vocabulary instructional recommendation in *RT* and *JAAL*. Schema and psycholinguistic theories also commonly influenced recommendations for vocabulary instruction, guiding 76% of vocabulary instructional recommendation in *RT* and *JAAL*. Forty-seven percent of vocabulary instructional recommendations in *RT* and *JAAL* were rooted in motivation theory, and 32% in DCT.

Our findings are similar to those of another content analysis that focused on the underlying theories guiding instructional recommendations for science literacy in *JAAL* [25]. Wright et al. examined 22 articles and found that 77% were guided by social constructivism and sociocultural theories, 36% by DCT, 27% by schema theory, and 18% by motivation theory [25]. The predominance of social constructivism and sociocultural theories in both content analyses indicate that practitioner-oriented articles are pushing for interactive learning environments in which inquiry, collaboration, dialogue, and active participation are encouraged. By contrast, of the 14 articles in Wright et al. that focused on vocabulary, most were guided by DCT and schema theory [25]. As only 32% of strategies in the present review were rooted in DCT, we can postulate that strategies based on DCT may be more common for teaching science or other content-area vocabulary, and with older students.

Another finding from the present study is that very few theories were explicitly referenced within *RT* and *JAAL* (12%, *n* = 9), which was also reported by Wright et al. (23%, *n* = 5) [25]. We posit that explicitly stating the theoretical underpinnings of instructional recommendations is essential for increasing teachers' awareness of the link between theory and practice, particularly as this relationship may not be transparent to teachers [36]. The process of turning theories into practice requires explicit discussions and can be problematic if theories are misunderstood. Perhaps this issue is what led Jagger and Yore, who analyzed theories underlying science literacy recommendations, to conclude that 56% of the instructional recommendations were atheoretical [151].

The present review also examined the grade levels addressed, target student populations, and desired outcome. In terms of theories guiding recommendations for ELLs and struggling readers, most were rooted in social constructivism, sociocultural, and schema theories. It is noteworthy, however, to acknowledge that very few articles addressed struggling readers. More research is needed to help this population of students advance their word knowledge. The majority of reviewed articles targeted elementary students, with similar theoretical foundations; social constructivism, sociocultural, and schema theories were the most common. Few articles suggested practices for middle-school students and very few targeted high schoolers. More research addressing vocabulary instruction for middle- and high-school students is needed, particularly because vocabulary is essential for comprehending the abstract and domain-specific vocabulary found in content-area textbooks [152].

Most of the instructional recommendations in the present review targeted receptive vocabulary and were guided by social constructivism, sociocultural, and schema theories. Future researchers could investigate how to incorporate productive vocabulary practices in classrooms, particularly as it relates to using new words within writing.

The parallel coding of our content analysis with the literature review by Wright and Cervetti revealed a similar pattern between practices in empirical and practitioner-oriented research [5]. The combination of theories that guided the majority of instructional recommendations in Wright and Cervetti were schema theory (48%), social constructivism and sociocultural theories (32%), motivation theory (18%), and DCT (6%) [5].

4.2. Limitations and Directions for Future Research

Our study was constrained by several limitations, which point to several directions for future research. Due to the nature of a content analysis, we were unable to examine a critical issue underlying our research, which is how teacher knowledge of theories impacts their implementation [25]. Additionally, we had not anticipated that recommendations for vocabulary instruction would be less common for ELLs, struggling readers, and students in middle and high school, or that DCT and motivation theories would be so underrepresented. This could be because we were only able to review two practitioner journals, *RT* and *JAAL*. It is possible that other journals would have provided a more theoretically diverse range of recommendations and/or targeted different populations of students. Future content analyses could examine all literacy journals geared towards practitioners to extend the findings of this study.

Our study makes a unique contribution to the field, in that no other research has investigated the theories driving vocabulary instruction in K–12 schools. In this content analysis, we have theorized that knowledge of underlying theories of vocabulary instructional practices helps teachers to focus on the big picture within vocabulary lessons, to manipulate and modify their vocabulary instructional practices according to students' need and characteristics of word, to reflect upon their practices and self-evaluate their performance, and most importantly to justify their choice of practice. Our findings can be used by educators as a guide to what theories are important for understanding how to provide effective vocabulary instruction.

Individuals interested in literacy can use our findings as a guide for future directions in vocabulary research. Our content analysis can be considered as phase 1 of an exploratory sequential design mixed method study. In such a design [153], qualitative data are initially gathered to explore a certain phenomenon or to identify themes. Then, these findings are used to help future researchers determine questions, variables, and samples for the follow-up quantitative phase. One suggestion for future researchers would be to empirically investigate whether knowledge of theories has an impact on teachers' performance and/or students' achievement in word knowledge and reading comprehension measures. It is possible that such research could provide the foundation for how to approach theory and vocabulary instruction in pre-service teacher preparation programs, professional development, and vocabulary research.

Author Contributions: Conceptualization, L.-J.K.; Methodology, S.M., X.H., and M.J.; Software, X.H.; Validation, X.H.; Formal Analysis, X.H.; Investigation, S.M., X.H., M.J., Z.X., and S.L.; Resources, S.M.; Data Curation, X.H.; Writing-Original Draft Preparation, S.M., X.H., M.J., Z.X., and S.L.; Writing-Reviewing & Editing: S.M. and M.J.; Supervision, S.M. and L.-J.K.; Project Administration, S.M.

Funding: This research received no external funding.

Conflicts of Interest: The authors declare no conflict of interest.

References

1. National Reading Panel (US), National Institute of Child Health and Human Development (US). *Teaching Children to Read: An Evidence-Based Assessment of the Scientific Research Literature on Reading and Its Implications for Reading Instruction*; National Institute of Child Health and Human Development, National Institutes of Health: Rockville, MD, USA, 2000.
2. Ricketts, J.; Nation, K.; Bishop, D.V. Vocabulary is Important for Some, but Not All Reading Skills. *Sci. Stud. Read.* **2007**, *11*, 235–257. [CrossRef]
3. Sénéchal, M.; Ouellette, G.; Rodney, D. The misunderstood giant: On the predictive role of early vocabulary to future reading. In *Handbook of Early Literacy Research*; Guilford Press: New York, NY, USA, 2006; Volume 2, pp. 173–182.
4. Thorndike, E.L. Reading as Reasoning: A Study of Mistakes in Paragraph Reading. *J. Educ. Psychol.* **1917**, *8*, 323–332. [CrossRef]
5. Wright, T.S.; Cervetti, G.N. A Systematic Review of the Research on Vocabulary Instruction that Impacts Text Comprehension. *Read. Res. Q.* **2017**, *52*, 203–226. [CrossRef]
6. Ford-Connors, E.; Paratore, J.R. Vocabulary Instruction in Fifth Grade and Beyond: Sources of Word Learning and Productive Contexts for Development. *Rev. Educ. Res.* **2015**, *85*, 50–91. [CrossRef]
7. Goswami, U. Early phonological development and the acquisition of literacy. In *Handbook of Early Literacy Research*; Guilford Press: New York, NY, USA, 2001; Volume 1, pp. 111–125.
8. Hemphill, L.; Tivnan, T. The importance of Early Vocabulary for Literacy Achievement in High-Poverty Schools. *JESPAR* **2008**, *13*, 426–451. [CrossRef]
9. McDowell, K.D.; Lonigan, C.J.; Goldstein, H. Relations among Socioeconomic Status, Age, and Predictors of Phonological Awareness. *JSLHR* **2007**, *50*, 1079–1092. [CrossRef]
10. Rasinski, T.; Padak, N.; Newton, J. The Roots of Comprehension. *Literacy* **2017**, *74*, 41–45.
11. Kuo, L.J.; Anderson, R.C. Morphological Awareness and Learning to Read: A Cross-Language Perspective. *Educ. Psychol.* **2006**, *41*, 161–180. [CrossRef]
12. Nagy, W. Why vocabulary instruction needs to be long-term and comprehensive. In *Teaching and Learning Vocabulary, Bringing Research to Practice*; Hiebert, E.H., Hamil, M.L., Eds.; Routledge: Mahwah, NJ, USA, 2005; pp. 27–44.
13. Snow, C. *Reading for Understanding: Toward an R&D Program in Reading Comprehension*; Rand Corporation: Santa Monica, CA, USA, 2002.
14. Beck, I.L.; McKeown, M.G.; Kucan, L. *Bringing Words to Life: Robust Vocabulary Instruction*; The Guilford Press: New York, NY, USA, 2013.
15. Bowers, P.N.; Kirby, J.R.; Deacon, S.H. The Effects of Morphological Instruction on Literacy Skills: A Systematic Review of the Literature. *Rev. Educ. Res.* **2010**, *80*, 144–179. [CrossRef]
16. Moran, E.E.; Moir, J. Closing the Vocabulary Gap in Early Years: Is 'Word Aware' a Possible Approach? *Educ. Child Psychol.* **2018**, *35*, 51–64.
17. Ganske, K. *Word Sorts and More: Sound, Pattern, and Meaning Explorations K–3*, 2nd ed.; The Guilford Press: New York, NY, USA, 2018.

18. McKeown, M.G.; Crosson, A.C.; Moore, D.W.; Beck, I.L. Word Knowledge and Comprehension Effects of an Academic Vocabulary Intervention for Middle School Students. *Am. Educ. Res. J.* **2018**, *55*, 572–616. [CrossRef]

19. National Center for Education Statistics. Available online: http://nces.ed.gov/programs/coe/indicator_cnb.asp (accessed on 8 October 2017).

20. Chiu, Y.H. Computer-Assisted Second Language Vocabulary Instruction: A Meta-Analysis. *Br. J. Educ. Tech.* **2013**, *44*, E52–E56. [CrossRef]

21. Hairrell, A.; Rupley, W.H.; Simmons, D. The State of Vocabulary Research. *Lit. Res. Instr.* **2011**, *50*, 253–271. [CrossRef]

22. Marulis, L.M.; Neuman, S.B. How vocabulary interventions affect young children at risk: A meta-analytic review. *J. Res. Educ. Eff.* **2013**, *6*, 223–262. [CrossRef]

23. Nagy, W.; Townsend, D. Words as Tools: Learning Academic Vocabulary as Language Acquisition. *Read. Res. Q.* **2012**, *47*, 91–108. [CrossRef]

24. Cain, K.; Parilla, R. Introduction to the Special Issue. Theories of Reading: What We Have Learned from Two Decades of Scientific Research. *Sci. Stud. Read.* **2014**, *18*, 1–4. [CrossRef]

25. Wright, K.L.; Franks, A.D.; Kuo, L.J.; McTigue, E.M.; Serrano, J. Both Theory and Practice: Science Literacy Instruction and Theories of Reading. *Int. J. Sci. Math. Educ.* **2016**, *14*, 1275–1292. [CrossRef]

26. Merk, S.; Rosman, T.; Rueß, J.; Syring, M.; Schneider, J. Pre-Service Teachers' Perceived Value of General Pedagogical Knowledge for Practice: Relations with Epistemic Beliefs and Source Beliefs. *PLoS ONE* **2017**, *12*, e0184971. [CrossRef] [PubMed]

27. Bondy, E.; Ross, D.; Adams, A.; Nowak, R.; Brownell, M.; Hoppey, D.; Stafford, L. Personal Epistemologies and Learning to Teach. *TESE* **2007**, *30*, 67–82. [CrossRef]

28. Sjølie, E. The Role of Theory in Teacher Education: Reconsidered from a Student Teacher Perspective. *J. Curric. Stud.* **2014**, *46*, 729–750. [CrossRef]

29. Joram, E. Clashing Epistemologies: Aspiring Teachers', Practicing Teachers', and Professors' Beliefs about Knowledge and Research in Education. *Teach. Teach. Educ.* **2007**, *23*, 123–135. [CrossRef]

30. Koenig, J.; Blömeke, S.; Klein, P.; Suhl, U.; Busse, A.; Kaiser, G. Is Teachers' General Pedagogical Knowledge a Premise for Noticing and Interpreting Classroom Situations? A Video-Based Assessment Approach. *Teach. Teach. Educ.* **2014**, *38*, 76–88. [CrossRef]

31. Bråten, I.; Ferguson, L.E. Beliefs about Sources of Knowledge Predict Motivation for Learning in Teacher Education. *Teach. Teach. Educ.* **2015**, *50*, 13–23. [CrossRef]

32. McVee, M.B.; Dunsmore, K.; Gavelek, J.R. Schema Theory Revisited. *Rev. Educ. Res.* **2005**, *75*, 531–566. [CrossRef]

33. Cunningham, A.E.; Stanovich, K.E. Early Reading Acquisition and its Relation to Reading Experience and Ability 10 Years Later. *Dev. Psychol.* **1997**, *33*, 934–945. [CrossRef] [PubMed]

34. Heilman, A.W.; Blair, T.R.; Rupley, W.H. *Principles and Practices of Teaching Reading*; CE Merrill Books: Columbus, OH, USA, 1961.

35. Stahl, K.A.D.; Bravo, M.A. Contemporary Classroom Vocabulary Assessment for Content Areas. *Read. Teach.* **2010**, *63*, 566–578. [CrossRef]

36. Beck, I.L.; McKeown, M.G.; Omanson, R.C. The effects and uses of diverse vocabulary instructional techniques. In *The Nature of Vocabulary Acquisition*; McKeown, M.G., Curtis, M.E., Eds.; Lawrence Erlbaum Associates, Inc.: Hillsdale, NJ, USA, 1987; pp. 147–163.

37. Giroir, S.; Grimaldo, L.R.; Vaughn, S.; Roberts, G. Interactive Read-Alouds for English Learners in the Elementary Grades. *Read. Teach.* **2015**, *68*, 639–648. [CrossRef]

38. Metros, S.E. The Educator's Role in Preparing Visually Literate Learners. *Theor. Pract.* **2008**, *47*, 102–109. [CrossRef]

39. Sadoski, M. A Dual Coding View of Vocabulary Learning. *Read. Writ. Q.* **2005**, *21*, 221–238. [CrossRef]

40. Lane, H.B.; Allen, S.A. The Vocabulary-Rich Classroom: Modeling Sophisticated Word Use to Promote Word Consciousness and Vocabulary Growth. *Read. Teach.* **2010**, *63*, 362–370. [CrossRef]

41. Abrams, S.S.; Walsh, S. Gamified Vocabulary. *J. Adolesc. Adult Lit.* **2014**, *58*, 49–58. [CrossRef]

42. Brabham, E.; Buskist, C.; Henderson, S.C.; Paleologos, T.; Baugh, N. Flooding Vocabulary Gaps to Accelerate Word Learning. *Read. Teach.* **2012**, *65*, 523–533. [CrossRef]

43. Kozdras, D.; Joseph, C.; Schneider, J.J. Reading Games. *Read. Teach.* **2015**, *69*, 331–338. [CrossRef]

44. Labbo, L.D.; Love, M.S.; Ryan, T. A Vocabulary Flood: Making Words "Sticky" with Computer-Response Activities. *Read. Teach.* **2007**, *60*, 582–588. [CrossRef]

45. Unrau, N.J.; Alvermann, D.E. Literacies and their investigation through theories and models. In *Theoretical Models and Processes of Reading*; Alvermann, D.E., Unrau, N.J., Ruddell, R.B., Eds.; International Reading Association: Newark, DE, USA, 2013; pp. 47–90.

46. Vygotsky, L. Interaction between learning and development. In *Mind and Society*; Harvard University Press: Cambridge, MA, USA, 1978; pp. 34–41.

47. Vygotsky, L.S. *Thought and Language, Revised ed.*; MIT Press: Cambridge, MA, USA, 1986.

48. Wood, D.; Bruner, J.S.; Ross, G. The Role of Tutoring in Problem Solving. *JCPP* **1976**, *17*, 89–100. [CrossRef] [PubMed]

49. Adams, P. Exploring Social Constructivism: Theories and Practicalities. *Education* **2006**, *34*, 243–257. [CrossRef]

50. Zhang, D.; Fan, Y.B.; Du, W. Sociocultural Theory Applied to Second Language Learning: Collaborative Learning with Reference to the Chinese Context. *Int. Educ. Stud.* **2013**, *6*, 165–174. [CrossRef]

51. Donato, R. Collective scaffolding in second language learning. In *Vygotskian Approaches to Second Language Research*; Ablex Publishing Corp: Norwood, MA, USA, 1994.

52. Swain, M.; Lapkin, S. Interaction and Second Language Learning: Two Adolescent French Immersion Students Working Together. *Mod. Lang. J.* **1998**, *82*, 320–337. [CrossRef]

53. Anderson, J.R. *The Architecture of Cognition*; Psychology Press: New York, NY, USA, 2013.

54. Carrell, P.L.; Eisterhold, J.C. Schema Theory and ESL Reading Pedagogy. *TQ* **1983**, *17*, 553–573. [CrossRef]

55. Little, D.C.; Box, J.A. The Use of a Specific Schema Theory Strategy-Semantic Mapping-to Facilitate Vocabulary Development and Comprehension for At-Risk Readers. *Read. Improv.* **2011**, *48*, 24–32.

56. Burgoyne, K.; Whiteley, H.E.; Hutchinson, J.M. The Role of Background Knowledge in Text Comprehension for Children Learning English as an Additional Language. *J. Res. Read.* **2013**, *36*, 132–148. [CrossRef]

57. Sadoski, M.; Paivio, A. A Dual Coding Theoretical Model of Reading. In *Theoretical Models and Practices of Reading*; 5th ed.; Ruddell, R.B., Unrau, N.J., Eds.; International Reading Association: Newark, DE, USA, 2004; pp. 1329–1362.

58. Dalton, B.; Grisham, D.L. eVoc Strategies: 10 Ways to Use Technology to Build Vocabulary. *Read. Teach.* **2011**, *64*, 306–317. [CrossRef]

59. Sadoski, M. Dual Coding Theory and Reading Poetic Text. In *The Journal of the Imagination in Language Learning and Teaching*; Coreil, C., Ed.; Bastos Educational Books: Woodside, NY, USA, 2002; p. 82.

60. Guthrie, J.T.; Wigfield, A.; Perencevich, K.C. *Motivating Reading Comprehension: Concept-Oriented Reading Instruction*; Routledge: Mahwah, NJ, USA, 2004.

61. Hodges, T.S.; Feng, L.; Kuo, L.J.; McTigue, E. Discovering the Literacy Gap: A Systematic Review of Reading and Writing Theories in Research. *Cogent Educ.* **2016**, *3*, 1228284. [CrossRef]

62. Becker, M.; McElvany, N.; Kortenbruck, M. Intrinsic and Extrinsic Reading Motivation as Predictors of Reading Literacy: A Longitudinal Study. *J. Educ. Psychol.* **2010**, *102*, 773. [CrossRef]

63. Huang, Y.M.; Huang, S.H.; Wu, T.T. Embedding Diagnostic Mechanisms in a Digital Game for Learning Mathematics. *ETRD* **2014**, *62*, 187–207. [CrossRef]

64. Yang, X.; Kuo, L.J.; Ji, X.; McTigue, E. A Critical Examination of the Relationship among Research, Theory, and Practice: Technology and Reading Instruction. *Comput. Educ.* **2018**, *125*, 62–73. [CrossRef]

65. Akkus, R.; Gunel, M.; Hand, B. Comparing an Inquiry-Based Approach Known as the Science Writing Heuristic to Traditional Science Teaching Practices: Are There Differences? *Int. J. Sci. Educ.* **2013**, *29*, 1745–1765. [CrossRef]

66. Ellery, V. How Do We Teach Reading as a Strategic, Decision-Making Process? *Read. Teach.* **2010**, *63*, 434–436. [CrossRef]

67. Feezell, G. Robust Vocabulary Instruction in a Readers' Workshop. *Read. Teach.* **2012**, *66*, 233–237. [CrossRef]

68. Adams, A.E.; Pegg, J. Teachers' Enactment of Content Literacy Strategies in Secondary Science and Mathematics Classes. *J. Adolesc. Adult. Lit.* **2012**, *56*, 151–161. [CrossRef]

69. Baumann, J.F.; Ware, D.; Edwards, E.C. "Bumping Into Spicy, Tasty Words That Catch Your Tongue": A Formative Experiment on Vocabulary Instruction. *Read. Teach.* **2007**, *61*, 108–122. [CrossRef]

70. Beauchat, K.A.; Blamey, K.L.; Walpole, S. Building Preschool Children's Language and Literacy One Storybook at a Time. *Read. Teach.* **2009**, *63*, 26–39. [CrossRef]

71. Blamey, K.L.; Beauchat, K.A. Word Walk: Vocabulary Instruction for Young Children. *Read. Teach.* **2011**, *65*, 71–75.

72. Boulware-Gooden, R.; Carreker, S.; Thornhill, A.; Joshi, R. Instruction of Metacognitive Strategies Enhances Reading Comprehension and Vocabulary Achievement of Third-Grade Students. *Read. Teach.* **2007**, *61*, 70–77. [CrossRef]

73. Boyd, F.B.; Sullivan, M.P.; Popp, J.S.; Hughes, M. Vocabulary Instruction in the Disciplines. *J. Adolesc. Adult. Lit.* **2012**, *56*, 18–20. [CrossRef]

74. Briceño, A. Vocabulary and Sentence Structure in Emergent Spanish Literacy. *Read. Teach.* **2016**, *69*, 611–619. [CrossRef]

75. Bromley, K. Nine Things Every Teacher Should Know about Words and Vocabulary Instruction. *J. Adolesc. Adult. Lit.* **2007**, *50*, 528–537. [CrossRef]

76. Ciechanowski, K.M. "A Squirrel Came and Pushed Earth": Popular Cultural and Scientific Ways of thinking for ELLs. *Read. Teach.* **2009**, *62*, 558–568. [CrossRef]

77. Crosson, A.C.; Lesaux, N.K. Connectives. *Read. Teach.* **2013**, *67*, 193–200. [CrossRef]

78. Dashiell, J.; DeBruin-Parecki, A. Supporting Young Children's Vocabulary Growth Using FRIENDS Model. *Read. Teach.* **2014**, *67*, 512–516. [CrossRef]

79. Donnelly, W.B.; Roe, C.J. Using sentence frames to develop academic vocabulary for English learners. *Read. Teach.* **2010**, *64*, 131–136. [CrossRef]

80. Fisher, D.; Frey, N. Content Area Vocabulary Learning. *Read. Teach.* **2014**, *67*, 594–599. [CrossRef]

81. Flanigan, K.; Greenwood, S.C. Effective Content Vocabulary Instruction in the Middle: Matching Students, Purposes, Words, and Strategies. *J. Adolesc. Adult Lit.* **2007**, *51*, 226–238. [CrossRef]

82. Flanigan, K.; Templeton, S.; Hayes, L. What's in a Word? Using Content Vocabulary to Generate Growth in General Academic Vocabulary Knowledge. *J. Adolesc. Adult Lit.* **2012**, *56*, 132–140. [CrossRef]

83. Flynt, E.S.; Brozo, W.G. Developing Academic Language: Got Words? *Read. Teach.* **2008**, *61*, 500–502. [CrossRef]

84. Gallagher, M.; Anderson, B.E. Get All 'Jazzed Up' for Vocabulary Instruction: Strategies that Engage. *Read. Teach.* **2016**, *70*, 273–282. [CrossRef]

85. Ganske, K. SAIL: A Framework for Promoting Next Generation Word Study. *Read. Teach.* **2016**, *70*, 337–346. [CrossRef]

86. Gill, S.R. Learning About Word Parts with Kidspiration. *Read. Teach.* **2007**, *61*, 79–84. [CrossRef]

87. Gillanders, C.; Castro, D.C.; Franco, X. Learning Words for Life. *Read. Teach.* **2014**, *68*, 213–221. [CrossRef] [PubMed]

88. Gillis, V. Talking the talk. *J. Adolesc. Adult Lit.* **2014**, *58*, 281–287. [CrossRef]

89. Goodwin, A.P.; Perkins, J. Word Detectives. *Read. Teach.* **2015**, *68*, 510–523. [CrossRef]

90. Goodwin, A.P.; Cho, S.; Nichols, S. Ways to WIN at Vocabulary Learning. *Read. Teach.* **2016**, *70*, 93–97. [CrossRef]

91. Goodwin, A.; Lipsky, M.; Ahn, S. Word Detectives: Using Units of Meaning to Support Literacy. *Read. Teach.* **2012**, *65*, 461–470. [CrossRef]

92. Grant, M.; Lapp, D.; Fisher, D.; Johnson, K.; Frey, N. Purposeful Instruction: Mixing Up the "I", "we", and "you". *J. Adolesc. Adult Lit.* **2012**, *56*, 45–55. [CrossRef]

93. Graves, M.F.; Watts-Taffe, S. Words, Words Everywhere, but Which Ones Do We Teach? *Read. Teach.* **2008**, *62*, 185–193. [CrossRef]

94. Green, J.D. Language Detectives. *Read. Teach.* **2015**, *68*, 539–547. [CrossRef]

95. Greenwood, S.C.; Flanigan, K. Overlapping Vocabulary and Comprehension: Context Clues Complement Semantic Gradients. *Read. Teach.* **2007**, *61*, 249–254. [CrossRef]

96. Griffith, P.L.; Ruan, J. Story Innovation: An Instructional Strategy for Developing Vocabulary and Fluency. *Read. Teach.* **2007**, *61*, 334–338. [CrossRef]

97. Hall, A.H. Filling toolboxes. *Read. Teach.* **2016**, *69*, 429–434. [CrossRef]

98. Harmon, J.M.; Wood, K.D.; Hedrick, W.B.; Vintinner, J.; Willeford, T. Interactive Word Walls: More than Just Reading the Writing on the Walls. *J. Adolesc. Adult Lit.* **2009**, *52*, 398–408. [CrossRef]

99. Helman, L.A.; Burns, M.K. What Does Oral Language Have to Do With It? Helping Young English-Language Learners Acquire a Sight Word Vocabulary. *Read. Teach.* **2008**, *62*, 14–19. [CrossRef]

100. Hendrix, R.A.; Griffin, R.A. Developing Enhanced Morphological Awareness in Adolescent Learners. *J. Adolesc. Adult Lit.* **2017**, *61*, 55–63. [CrossRef]
101. Hernández, A.C. Using Spanish–English Cognates in Children's Choices Picture Books to Develop Latino English Learners' Linguistic Knowledge. *Read. Teach.* **2016**, *70*, 233–239. [CrossRef]
102. Kieffer, M.J.; Lesaux, N.K. Breaking down Words to Build Meaning: Morphology, Vocabulary, and Reading Comprehension in the Urban Classroom. *Read. Teach.* **2007**, *61*, 134–144. [CrossRef]
103. Kesler, T. Shared Reading to Build Vocabulary and Comprehension. *Read. Teach.* **2010**, *64*, 272–277. [CrossRef]
104. Kindle, K.J. Vocabulary Development During Read-Alouds: Primary Practices. *Read. Teach.* **2009**, *63*, 202–211. [CrossRef]
105. Kucan, L. What is most important to know about vocabulary? *Read. Teach.* **2012**, *65*, 360–366. [CrossRef]
106. LaBrocca, R.; Morrow, L.M. Embedding Vocabulary Instruction into the Art Experience. *Read. Teach.* **2016**, *70*, 149–158. [CrossRef]
107. Larson, S.C. Using a Generative Vocabulary Matrix in the Learning Workshop. *Read. Teach.* **2014**, *68*, 113–125. [CrossRef]
108. Manyak, P. Character Trait Vocabulary: A Schoolwide Approach. *Read. Teach.* **2007**, *60*, 574–577. [CrossRef]
109. Manyak, P.C. Vocabulary instruction for English learners: Lessons from MCVIP. *Read. Teach.* **2010**, *64*, 143–146. [CrossRef]
110. Manyak, P.C.; Bauer, E.B. English Vocabulary Instruction for English Learners. *Read. Teach.* **2009**, *63*, 174–176. [CrossRef]
111. Manyak, P.C.; Gunten, H.V.; Autenrieth, D.; Gillis, C.; Mastre-O'Farrell, J.; Irvine-McDermott, E.; Blachowicz, C.L.Z. Four Practical Principles for Enhancing Vocabulary Instruction. *Read. Teach.* **2014**, *68*, 13–23. [CrossRef]
112. McGee, L.M.; Schickedanz, J.A. Repeated Interactive Read-Alouds in Preschool and Kindergarten. *Read. Teach.* **2007**, *60*, 742–751. [CrossRef]
113. McKeown, M.G.; Crosson, A.C.; Artz, N.J.; Sandora, C.; Beck, I.L. In the Media: Expanding Students' Experience with Academic Vocabulary. *Read. Teach.* **2013**, *67*, 45–53. [CrossRef]
114. Mountain, L. Synonym Success—Thanks to the Thesaurus. *J. Adolesc. Adult Lit.* **2007**, *51*, 318–324. [CrossRef]
115. Neuman, S.B.; Roskos, K. More Than Teachable Moments: Enhancing Oral Vocabulary Instruction in Your Classroom. *Read. Teach.* **2012**, *66*, 63–67. [CrossRef]
116. Picot, C.J. Using Academic Word Lists to Support Disciplinary Literacy Development. *Read. Teach.* **2017**, *71*, 215–220. [CrossRef]
117. Pierce, M.E.; Fontaine, L.M. Designing Vocabulary Instruction in Mathematics. *Read. Teach.* **2009**, *63*, 239–243. [CrossRef]
118. Pollard-Durodola, S.; Pollard-Durodola, S.; Gonzalez, J.E.; Gonzalez, J.E.; Simmons, D.C.; Simmons, D.C.; Walichowski, M.N. Using Knowledge Networks to Develop Preschoolers' Content Vocabulary. *Read. Teach.* **2011**, *65*, 265–274. [CrossRef]
119. Putman, S.M.; Kingsley, T. The Atoms Family: Using Podcasts to Enhance the Development of Science Vocabulary. *Read. Teach.* **2009**, *63*, 100–108. [CrossRef]
120. Rasinski, T.V.; Padak, N.; Newton, J.; Newton, E. The Latin–Greek Connection. *Read. Teach.* **2011**, *65*, 133–141. [CrossRef]
121. Rodgers, E. Scaffolding Word Solving While Reading: New Research Insights. *Read. Teach.* **2017**, *70*, 525–532. [CrossRef]
122. Savino, J.A. The Shakespeare in All of Us: A Monumental, Multitudinous, Premeditated Approach to Vocabulary Instruction. *J. Adolesc. Adult Lit.* **2011**, *54*, 445–453. [CrossRef]
123. Snell, E.K.; Hindman, A.H.; Wasik, B.A. How Can Book Reading Close the Word Gap? Five Key Practices from Research. *Read. Teach.* **2015**, *68*, 560–571. [CrossRef]
124. Toth, A. Not Just for After Lunch. *Read. Teach.* **2013**, *67*, 203–207. [CrossRef]
125. Townsend, D. Building Academic Vocabulary in After-School Settings: Games for Growth with Middle School English-Language Learners. *J. Adolesc. Adult Lit.* **2009**, *53*, 242–251. [CrossRef]
126. Wessels, S. Promoting Vocabulary Learning for English Learners. *Read. Teach.* **2011**, *65*, 46–50.
127. Williams, C.; Phillips-Birdsong, C.; Hufnagel, K.; Hungler, D.; Lundstrom, R.P. Word Study Instruction in the K–2 Classroom. *Read. Teach.* **2009**, *62*, 570–578. [CrossRef]

128. Winters, R. Interactive Frames for Vocabulary Growth and Word Consciousness. *Read. Teach.* **2009**, *62*, 685–690. [CrossRef]
129. Wolsey, T.D.; Smetana, L.; Grisham, D.L. Vocabulary Plus Technology: An After-Reading Approach to Develop Deep Word Learning. *Read. Teach.* **2015**, *68*, 449–458. [CrossRef]
130. Wright, T.S. From Potential to Reality. *Read. Teach.* **2014**, *67*, 359–367. [CrossRef]
131. Yopp, R.H.; Yopp, H.K. Ten Important Words Plus: A Strategy for Building Word Knowledge. *Read. Teach.* **2007**, *61*, 157–160. [CrossRef]
132. Zoski, J.; Erickson, K. Morpheme-Based Instruction in Kindergarten. *Read. Teach.* **2017**, *70*, 491–496. [CrossRef]
133. Stahl, S.A. Three Principles of Effective Vocabulary Instruction. *J. Read.* **1986**, *29*, 662–668.
134. Kelley, J.G.; Lesaux, N.K.; Kieffer, M.J.; Faller, S.E. Effective Academic Vocabulary Instruction in the Urban Middle School. *Read. Teach.* **2010**, *64*, 5–14. [CrossRef]
135. Yıldız-Feyzioğlu, E.; Akpınar, E.; Tatar, N. Monitoring Students' Goal Setting and Metacognitive Knowledge in Technology-Enhanced Learning with Metacognitive Prompts. *Comput. Hum. Behav.* **2013**, *29*, 616–625. [CrossRef]
136. Harper, C.; De Jong, E. Misconceptions about Teaching English-Language Learners. *J. Adolesc. Adult Lit.* **2004**, *48*, 152–162. [CrossRef]
137. Brandes, D.R.; McMaster, K.L. A Review of Morphological Analyses Strategies on Vocabulary Outcomes with ELLs. *Insights Learn. Disabil.* **2017**, *14*, 53–72.
138. Goodwin, A.P. Effectiveness of Word Solving: Integrating Morphological Problem-Solving within Comprehension Instruction for Middle School Students. *Read. Writ.* **2016**, *29*, 91–116. [CrossRef]
139. Helman, A.L.; Calhoon, M.B.; Kern, L. Improving Science Vocabulary of High School English Language Learners with Reading Disabilities. *Learn. Disabil. Q.* **2015**, *38*, 40–52. [CrossRef]
140. Usher, E.L.; Pajares, F. Sources of Self-Efficacy in School: Critical Review of the Literature and Future Directions. *Rev. Educ. Res.* **2008**, *78*, 751–796. [CrossRef]
141. Doménech-Betoret, F.; Abellán-Roselló, L.; Gómez-Artiga, A. Self-Efficacy, Satisfaction, and Academic Achievement: The Mediator Role of Students' Expectancy-Value Beliefs. *Front. Psychol.* **2017**, *8*, 1–12. [CrossRef] [PubMed]
142. Leacox, L.; Jackson, C.W. Spanish Vocabulary-Bridging Technology-Enhanced Instruction for Young English Language Learners' Word Learning. *J. Early Childhood Lit.* **2014**, *14*, 175–197. [CrossRef]
143. Chilton, M.W.; Ehri, L.C. Vocabulary Learning: Sentence Contexts Linked by Events in Scenarios Facilitate Third Graders' Memory for Verb Meanings. *Read. Res. Q.* **2015**, *50*, 439–458. [CrossRef]
144. Slough, S.W.; McTigue, E.M.; Kim, S.; Jennings, S.K. Science Textbooks' Use of Graphical Representation: A Descriptive Analysis of Four Sixth Grade Science Texts. *Read. Psychol.* **2010**, *31*, 301–325. [CrossRef]
145. Draper, R.J. School Mathematics Reform, Constructivism, and Literacy: A Case for Literacy Instruction in the Reform-Oriented Math Classroom. *J. Adolesc. Adult Lit.* **2002**, *45*, 520–529.
146. Nation, I.S. *Learning Vocabulary in another Language*; Cambridge University Press: Cambridge, UK, 2001.
147. Su, Y.; Reeve, J. A Meta-Analysis of the Effectiveness of Intervention Programs Designed to Support Autonomy. *Educ. Psychol. Rev.* **2011**, *23*, 159–188. [CrossRef]
148. Urdan, T.; Bruchmann, K. Examining the Academic Motivation of a Diverse Student Population: A Consideration of Methodology. *Educ. Psychol.* **2018**, *53*, 114–130. [CrossRef]
149. Türk, E.; Erçetin, G. Effects of Interactive Versus Simultaneous Display of Multimedia Glosses on L2 Reading Comprehension and Incidental Vocabulary Learning. *Comput. Assist. Lang. Learn.* **2014**, *27*, 1–25. [CrossRef]
150. Levin, J.R.; Levin, M.E.; Glasman, L.D.; Nordwall, M.B. Mnemonic Vocabulary Instruction: Additional Effectiveness Evidence. *Contemp. Educ. Psychol.* **1992**, *17*, 156–174. [CrossRef]
151. Jagger, S.L.; Yore, L.D. Mind the Gap: Looking for Evidence-Based Practice of Science Literacy for All in Science Teaching Journals. *J. Sci. Teach. Educ.* **2012**, *23*, 559–577. [CrossRef]

152. Barton, M.L.; Heidema, C.; Jordan, D. Teaching Reading in Mathematics and Science. *Educ. Leader.* **2002**, *60*, 24–28.

153. Creswell, J.W.; Clark, V.L.P. *Designing and Conducting Mixed Methods Research*; Sage Publications: Thousand Oaks, CA, USA, 2017.

Commentary

When Complexity Is Your Friend: Modeling the Complex Problem Space of Vocabulary

Amanda P. Goodwin [1,*], Yaacov Petscher [2], Dan Reynolds [3], Tess Lantos [1], Sara Gould [1] and Jamie Tock [2]

1 Teaching and Learning, Peabody College, Vanderbilt University, Peabody #230, 230 Appleton Place, Nashville, TN 37203-5721, USA; Tess.lantos@vanderbilt.edu (T.L.); Sara.a.gould@vanderbilt.edu (S.G.)
2 Florida Center for Reading Research, Florida State University; 2010 Levy Ave., Suite 100, Tallahassee, FL 32310, USA; ypetscher@fcrr.org (Y.P.); Jamie.tock@fsu.edu (J.T.)
3 Department of Education and School Psychology, John Carroll University; 1 John Carroll Boulevard, University Heights, OH 44118, USA; danielereynolds@gmail.com
* Correspondence: amanda.goodwin@vanderbilt.edu; Tel.: +1-305-710-6257

Received: 1 September 2018; Accepted: 20 September 2018; Published: 15 October 2018

Abstract: The history of vocabulary research has specified a rich and complex construct, resulting in calls for vocabulary research, assessment, and instruction to take into account the complex problem space of vocabulary. At the intersection of vocabulary theory and assessment modeling, this paper suggests a suite of modeling techniques that model the complex structures present in vocabulary data in ways that can build an understanding of vocabulary development and its links to instruction. In particular, we highlight models that can help researchers and practitioners identify and understand construct-relevant and construct-irrelevant aspects of assessing vocabulary knowledge. Drawing on examples from recent research and from our own three-year project to develop a standardized measure of language and vocabulary, we present four types of confirmatory factor analysis (CFA) models: single-factor, correlated-traits, bi-factor, and tri-factor models. We highlight how each of these approaches offers particular insights into the complex problem space of assessing vocabulary in ways that can inform vocabulary assessment, theory, research, and instruction. Examples include identifying construct-relevant general or specific factors like skills or different aspects of word knowledge that could link to instruction while at the same time preventing an overly-narrow focus on construct-irrelevant factors like task-specific or word-specific demands. Implications for theory, research, and practice are discussed.

Keywords: vocabulary; methods; confirmatory factor analysis

1. Introduction

Vocabulary, "the body of words in a given language" [1] is a deceptively complex concept. The term 'vocabulary' can describe the words an individual recognizes (i.e., receptive vocabulary), the words an individual can produce and use (i.e., productive vocabulary), the words that are being learned (i.e., vocabulary learning), as well as the words outside of an individual's understanding. It can describe a broad group of words (i.e., general vocabulary) or a more specific set of words (i.e., academic vocabulary;) or a further specific domain of words (i.e., discipline-specific academic words like those used in science) or even a specific group of words (i.e., weather vocabulary). It can be described from a strength perspective (i.e., considering bilinguals' full range of word knowledge) or from a more deficit-based perspective (i.e., vocabulary gaps). Vocabulary can also describe word-specific knowledge (i.e., definitions, synonyms, antonyms, etc.) or word-general understandings and skills (i.e., metalinguistic awareness, morphological awareness, context clue skills, and word-problem solving). Given this variability, it is no surprise that a century of research has resulted in calls for vocabulary research, assessment, and instruction to take into account the complex problem space of vocabulary (see [2] for an overview). At the core, these conceptual papers call for considering what words, word knowledge, and tasks (i.e., written, oral, decontextualized, and embedded) are being used to explore vocabulary.

The current paper builds on this work of identifying the above complexities to argue that how we model the complexities matters in important ways. This is because innovative modeling techniques allow us to model complex structures that can help researchers and practitioners understand construct-relevant and construct-irrelevant aspects of assessing vocabulary knowledge. These different aspects have important consequences for understanding both how vocabulary develops in children and what is instructionally relevant versus less generative (i.e., construct-irrelevant). An example might be modeling vocabulary consisting of general vocabulary knowledge, specific types of knowledge (e.g., definitional, relational, etc.), and knowledge of either a specific task related to words (e.g., multiple choice vs completing a sentence) or a specific set of words (e.g., a group of words in a story). In terms of understanding a child's vocabulary, modeling vocabulary in this way highlights the bigger picture, allowing one to parse a child's overall vocabulary knowledge from how comfortable they are performing certain cognitive tasks or how well they know a specific word or set of words. When thinking about links to instruction, a teacher might be encouraged to focus on broader construct-relevant components (i.e., building general vocabulary knowledge and doing this through designing activities that build specific types of knowledge like definitions or word relationships), but avoid over-focusing on tasks (e.g., teaching students to successfully figure out multiple choice questions) or on smaller sets of words (e.g., teaching the bold words from a story in the text).

As such, the goal of this paper is to present a modeling framework that can be used to separate out these various components of vocabulary knowledge. We begin by linking to the theory on why studying vocabulary is important. This identifies a rationale for modeling vocabulary in an accurate and detailed manner. Next, we highlight some of the complexities in the vocabulary problem space that such models help us to parse. We then explain how these models fit within the larger statistical landscape. Lastly, we present a set of models to consider when modeling vocabulary. We argue that modeling in this way can build an understanding of vocabulary and sort out construct-relevant structures (i.e., vocabulary relevant) from construct-irrelevant structures (i.e., those more specific to certain cognitive tasks or specific to certain words). For each model, we provide an illustration from the research that shows how such models help us in studying vocabulary. We finish by discussing how such models were pivotal in supporting our work developing a standardized, gamified measure of language and vocabulary for middle schoolers, which we call Monster, PI.

1.1. Why Vocabulary as It Relates to Language and Literacy

Theories of reading and writing agree on one thing: language provides the foundation for literacy [3]. Vocabulary, albeit narrowly, has often been used a proxy for language because both language and vocabulary emphasize the importance of meaning. Many broader language skills (i.e., phonology, syntax, morphology, and semantics) either are directly related to vocabulary (i.e., semantics and morphology) or can be found in models exploring vocabulary. For example, Perfetti's lexical quality hypothesis [4] argues that the properties of the quality of a lexical representation (i.e., what is stored in one's lexicon about a word) include phonological and syntactical information as well as information about meaning. This is why when models of reading highlight the strong role of language, they are usually highlighting the importance of vocabulary in reading as well.

Examples of the role for vocabulary and language in models of reading can be seen across theoretical camps. For example, the Simple View of Reading [5] describes reading as the product of word decoding and linguistic comprehension where linguistic comprehension is defined as "the process by which given lexical (i.e., word) information [vocabulary], sentences and discourses are interpreted" [5] (p. 7). A competing model similarly places language in a central role with Goodman [6] describing reading as "a psycholinguistic guessing game [that] involves an interaction between thought and language" [6] (p. 2). Theorists suggest different reasons regarding how vocabulary knowledge supports reading comprehension. For example, the instrumentalist hypothesis suggests integrating the word meanings themselves is critical whereas the knowledge hypothesis posits that by knowing a word's meaning, one likely knows more about that topic area, leading to improved comprehension [7]. Importantly, for this paper, the theories and research consistently show a relationship between vocabulary and reading [2]. Thus, we believe that it is important to deepen our understanding of this relationship and determine what is relevant and irrelevant when modeling vocabulary. We argue that modeling techniques can help us build this deeper understanding of vocabulary and its relationship to reading.

1.2. Components of the Vocabulary Problem Space

Snow and Kim [8] argue that vocabulary presents a challenging problem space as compared with other literacy learning tasks (particularly decoding) for readers. Similarly, Pearson, Hiebert, and Kamil [2] argue that acknowledging and modeling the complexities of the problem space is necessary to building out understandings that can lead to improvements in both conceptualizations and understandings of links to instruction. In their seminal piece, they write,

> "if we are going to teach it more effectively and if we are going to better understand how it is implicated in reading comprehension, we must first address the vexing question of how we assess vocabulary knowledge and, even more challenging, vocabulary growth. In this essay, we argue that vocabulary assessment is grossly undernourished, both in its theoretical and practical aspects—that it has been driven by tradition, convenience, psychometric standards, and a quest for economy of effort rather than a clear conceptualization of its nature and relation to other aspects of reading expertise, most notably comprehension." [2] (p. 282)

So what does that complicated problem space look like and how is it related to the models we propose? First, it may be helpful to think of vocabulary through dichotomies. These comparisons allow us to hone in on different aspects of vocabulary by explaining differences in the ways we use words. Vocabulary is often contrasted as either written or oral, productive or receptive; additionally, vocabulary knowledge is construed as either broad or deep, word-specific or word-general. These parameters allow us to think about vocabulary as a component of reading and listening, as well as writing and speaking. They also help demonstrate the fact that vocabulary can be a single measurable construct, while also representing a combination of a number of different aspects or components. We discuss a few of these components below.

1.2.1. Cognitive Demand

When thinking about vocabulary, it is helpful to think about the cognitive work involved and its impact on the size and depth of one's vocabulary. Importantly, people have different vocabularies across different cognitive contexts. Generally, receptive vocabulary involves less cognitive demand, meaning that children often score higher on receptive measures compared to productive measures. In other words, most people understand more words through reading and listening than they can produce through speech or writing.

1.2.2. Task Demands

Related, it is also important to consider the demands of vocabulary tasks. Here, Read [9] specified three key concepts for understanding vocabulary assessments: their embeddedness with comprehension, their selection of words to assess, and their tasks' provision of context. Additional test-taking literature highlights differences in item properties such as multiple choice vs. open response, etc. Understanding these three properties of assessments helps inform how our models try to separate construct-relevant variance—that is, students' vocabulary knowledge, from construct-irrelevant variance—that is, how good students are at certain kinds of test-taking tasks.

1.2.3. Breadth vs. Depth

Additionally, when describing vocabulary knowledge, researchers commonly distinguish between breadth and depth. Breadth of vocabulary knowledge refers simply to the quantity of words known, whereas depth of vocabulary knowledge refers to the richness of the understanding of those known words (e.g., [7,10]). While breadth is understood as a numerical quantity (i.e., we can count the number of words that a student knows), depth is thought of as a continuum of understanding, ranging from some recognition of a word to complete understanding of a word's various meanings and how to use it appropriately in a variety of contexts. Depth of vocabulary knowledge includes knowledge of multiple related meanings, including shades of meaning, knowledge of semantically related words including subordinates and superordinates, and the syntactic and pragmatic knowledge of whether and how to use a word in a given context (see later discussion).

1.2.4. Domain of Words

Another thing to consider is which words to assess and what performance on a certain set of words means. There are more than 200,000 words that readers might encounter in academic texts [11]. Recent work indicates there are a core group of words present in these texts (i.e., 2451 morphological families making up 58% of the 19,500 most frequent words in text [12] and we also know there are a larger set of academic words that students tend to encounter in their school learning [13–15]. We further know that words are learned in networks, including conceptual groups [16] and in morphological families [17]. This suggests that overall word knowledge likely matters more than knowledge of a specific word or set of words, unless that set of words represents a larger instructionally relevant principle (such as a concept or skill like learning words in morphological families).

1.2.5. Word-Specific vs. Word-General

Another distinction in vocabulary knowledge is often made between word-specific knowledge and word-general knowledge [18]. Word-specific knowledge includes breadth and depth of knowledge of individual word meanings. Word-general knowledge, on the other hand, involves metalinguistic knowledge about words and their meanings. One component of word-general knowledge is morphological awareness [19]. Morphology is the system by which smaller meaningful units, such as affixes and roots, are combined to form complex words. These units of meaning contribute to both the overall meaning and the syntactic function of the word, making them an important word-generative understanding. Another component of word-general knowledge is students' skill in using context to provide information about word meanings, or their contextual sensitivity [19].

1.2.6. Word Characteristics

Yet another distinction relates to how not all words are created equal in terms of word learning. Vocabulary assessments need to consider the characteristics of words and how those characteristics relate to word learning. We identify these characteristics below in Table 1 and refer readers to a discussion of these characteristics [12]. The point, though, of emphasizing word characteristics is that these differences in words make it even more important to get at construct-relevant and construct-irrelevant variance.

Table 1. Key Word Characteristics.

Word Length	Meaning (Semantics and Syntax)	Frequency/Familiarity	Orthographic Representation
	• Polysemy	• Word family; root(s)	• Regularity of grapheme to phoneme correspondence
• # Letters	• Conceptual complexity	• Concreteness	• Transparency at syllable and morpheme levels
• # Syllables	• Domain specificity	• Age of acquisition	• Irregular spellings
• # Morphemes	• Syntactic/grammatical roles	• Morphemic composition/transparency	
		• Word origin	

1.2.7. Aspects of Word Knowledge

Perhaps the most important consideration within the larger problem space related to studying vocabulary is considering what is known about word knowledge, and this relates to the discussion of depth above. Here, we highlight Nagy and Scott's [20] principles of (1) incrementality, which specifies that word knowledge is not a dichotomous known–unknown state but a continuous spectrum of understanding; (2) polysemy, which notes that words often have multiple meanings; (3) multidimensionality, suggesting that word knowledge includes different kinds of knowledge such as denotation, connotation, or collocation; (4) interrelatedness, that is, word knowledge is linked to conceptually related understandings; and (5) heterogeneity indicating that a word's meaning is dependent on its function and structure. The reason these categories are so important is that these five properties of word knowledge inform the types of factors that might be modeled. We go into further detail regarding each of these aspects of word knowledge later.

A common-sense idea holds that word knowledge is incremental. A low amount of knowledge might involve merely recognizing a familiar word whereas much more knowledge is required to have a subtle and nuanced understanding of a word's multiple uses. In fact, as researchers have noted, incremental knowledge of word meaning is similar to vocabulary depth (explained previously), which has been shown to be crucial from early childhood through college age and adulthood [21,22]. Beyond incremental knowledge, words also have multiple meanings—that is, they are polysemous. In fact, common words such as "set" and "run" have hundreds of meanings [1], ranging from everyday to quite specialized. Notably, Logan and Kieffer [23] found that seventh-grade students' knowledge of the particular academic meanings of words (that is, the polysemy of their vocabulary) uniquely predicted their comprehension, even when controlling for vocabulary breadth, awareness of everyday meanings of words, and decoding skills.

The third principle, multidimensionality, links to the idea of Perfetti's lexical quality hypothesis [4]: word knowledge is not just the semantics, but the orthographic, phonological, morphological, syntactic, and pragmatic aspects of its practical use. Nagy and Scott [20] point out that one student might recognize a word's orthographic form but be unable to use it in speech, while others might use a word in the proper academic register but misuse its denotation. This leads to the principle of interrelatedness, which notes that words exist in conceptual relation to other words. That is, "a person who already knows the words hot, cold, and cool has already acquired some of the components of the word *warm*" [20] (p. 272). Fitzgerald, Elmore, Kung, and Stenner [16] argue that, especially in science learning, the development of complex networks of interrelated vocabulary knowledge co-develops with children's understandings of complex concepts about the world around them. This is important because the goal of vocabulary growth is not an end, but a means of supporting students in communicating effectively with a myriad of audiences. The final principle, heterogeneity, posits that word knowledge includes knowledge of functional use. Here, word knowledge does not exist in isolation but as multifarious sources that can be used as tools to enable communication, with particular features for academic communication [13]. These principles show that a word's semantic knowledge is far more complex than knowledge of a single definition would imply and inform our view of possible construct-relevant factors to model within vocabulary.

Overall, the problem space related to vocabulary is clearly complex. Innovative vocabulary assessments that attend to the complexities of the vocabulary problem space are needed, as well as modeling techniques that can use these complexities as an asset rather than a hindrance. Next, we suggest some possible frameworks to use that take advantage of these complexities when modeling. These techniques can be used to unravel construct-relevant from construct-irrelevant variance. Note that the important part of these frameworks is that they attend to multiple complexities within the vocabulary problem space.

2. Potential Frameworks

As an introduction to our presentation of models, it is important to revisit a few *hows* and *whys* of statistical modeling. Statistical modeling maintains goals of prediction and explanation [24]. Within the explanatory mechanism, the latent variable modeling approach of confirmatory factor analysis (CFA) estimates how well a hypothesized model can fit, or partition well, the variance–covariance matrix to a set of user-specified latent factors indicated by manifest variables. Here, the researcher can compare models with different hypothesized structures, and the extent to which a specified model fits well according to combinations of incremental, comparative, or absolute fit indexes allows a researcher to begin identification of construct-relevant or construct-irrelevant sources of variance [25].

Consider the example of reading comprehension. In many assessment situations, students are administered multiple passages to read followed by a set of comprehension questions. Researchers will often simply sum the scores across the items without considering that the items have important contextual factors. One contextual factor that is frequently ignored is that items exist within passages; passages can be expository or narrative. Ignoring the potential influence of expository or narrative text on students' performance might limit our understanding of individual differences in students' reading comprehension and impact instructional implications. Another contextual factor is that across a set of passages there may be items within each passage that are designed to measure instructionally relevant skills, such as the author's purpose, selecting the main idea, or vocabulary. Here too, simply summing the items across the passages to obtain a global reading comprehension score not only limits the utility of the score but could provide misinformation about a student's ability.

CFA affords a number of modeling choices that surpass the simple summing of scores, and these modeling choices maintain inherent flexibility to include, among other attributes, single or multiple latent variables, simple or complex loading solutions, and correlated or uncorrelated constructs. One of the most well-known expressions of a CFA is a single-factor, or unidimensional, model whereby one latent construct is specified to be indicated by one or more measured variables. When more than one latent construct is specified, the CFA is known as a multidimensional or correlated trait model. Within this multidimensional model, each of the two or more constructs are indicated by respective, or sometimes cross-loading, measured variables and the constructs are typically estimated to correlate with each other. More complex CFAs can be readily specified, but for the purposes of this paper we focus on four types: (1) the single-factor model, (2) the correlated trait model, (3) the bi-factor model, and (4) the tri-factor model.

Beyond single factor and correlated trait models, a bi-factor model [26] hypothesizes that the measured variables simultaneously indicate two latent variables: A global construct designed to measure construct-relevant variance, and one or two or more latent constructs (i.e., sometimes referred to as *specific constructs*) that measure structures within and uniquely separable from the global construct. These specific constructs can be construct-relevant (e.g., skills like author's purpose, selecting the main idea, etc) or construct-irrelevant (e.g., multiple choice vs. cloze responses). The specific construct(s) are indicated by a subset of items whereas the global construct is indicated by items across the specific constructs. For example, when students read multiple reading comprehension passages, the item-level responses to questions may include information that loads simultaneously on a global latent variable of reading comprehension as well as a specific latent variable that is specific to the passage to which the item belongs [27]. An example of construct-relevant variance might be the global latent variable of reading comprehension and an example of construct-irrelevant variance would be the latent variables associated with passage effects. The global reading comprehension factor, in this case, would be malleable for teachers to instruct on (i.e., construct-relevant variance), and the specific passage effects would be nuisance constructs (i.e., construct-irrelevant variance [28]). Latent factors in the bi-factor model are typically set to be uncorrelated as the theory of bi-factor models is that the covariance among measured variables is not best explained by latent correlations for specific constructs but instead represented by a global construct. An example of a bi-factor model in language research is Goodwin et al. [29] who found that a bi-factor model was best for representing morphological knowledge data.

A tri-factor model is an extension of a bi-factor where measured variables would simultaneously indicate three latent variables. This model has not been frequently used within educational research; however, psychology researchers have used it to unpack variance attributions to theoretical constructs, maternal raters, and paternal raters [30]. With these exemplary CFA model-types in mind, our framework building approach described below is focused on identifying construct-relevant and construct-irrelevant variance with the idea of modeling vocabulary in ways that lead to deeper understandings of vocabulary development and links to instruction.

3. Proposed Models

3.1. Model 1: Single Factor Model

We begin by thinking about how to measure what students know about words in general. We first consider vocabulary as a single, albeit complex, construct. Here, we draw on the consistent findings that vocabulary is related to reading comprehension (i.e., usually correlations between 0.6 and 0.8 between reading comprehension and vocabulary [2]) and in general, people who have strong vocabularies tend to know a lot about words. The fact that a reader does not know a specific low-frequency word or even piece of word knowledge (i.e., a specific meaning) is unlikely to affect reading in general [31]. The single factor model (i.e., unidimensional model, see Figure 1) uses multiple measures of vocabulary, but conceptualizes these measures as overlapping. In other words, what is measured by one vocabulary measure might be slightly different from the other vocabulary measure, but both measures assess a broader vocabulary construct (i.e., what students know about words). Here, a single construct is modeled and, when presenting with significant variance or loadings, would be assumed to have construct-relevant variance.

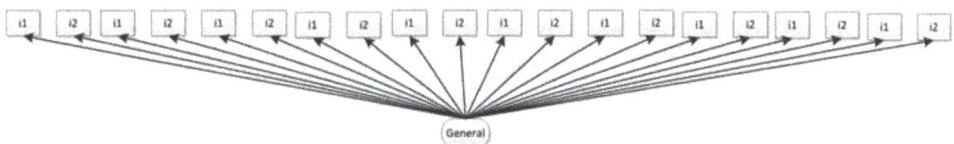

Figure 1. Model 1: Single Factor Model.

Conceptualizing vocabulary as unidimensional tends to be a default perspective in terms of modeling vocabulary for much of educational research (see [2,19] for explanations). It is also one of the first steps when exploring whether modeling additional complexities makes sense within a researcher's vocabulary data. For example, Kieffer and Lesaux [19] explored whether vocabulary was best modeled as a single (i.e., unidimensional) factor or a multidimensional construct (i.e., correlated trait model). Here, sixth graders were assessed on thirteen reading-based vocabulary measures with the goal of better understanding vocabulary knowledge. These measures assessed knowledge of synonyms, multiple meanings, context clues, and morphological knowledge, with all assessments assessing different words. Confirmatory factor analysis suggested that a single factor model for this data was not as good of a fit to the data as a multidimensional model (i.e., correlated trait model), providing evidence of the importance of modeling these structures within vocabulary data.

3.2. Model 2: Correlated Trait Model

A primary finding of the research reviewed above is that there are different aspects of word knowledge that are key to the development of children's vocabulary and which likely link to how words are instructed. Correlated trait models (see Figure 2) can model these different aspects as unique and related. Here, the key principle is to measure multiple aspects of word knowledge (e.g., definitional, relational, and incremental), with the expectation that the measures will group together as a means of conveying construct-relevant structures. The way in which the measures group together inform how a person's lexicon (i.e., vocabulary) develops. With that said, the components usually are hypothesized as meaningful to the larger construct and therefore, again, the correlated trait model conceptualizes components as construct-relevant, largely ignoring construct-irrelevant structures.

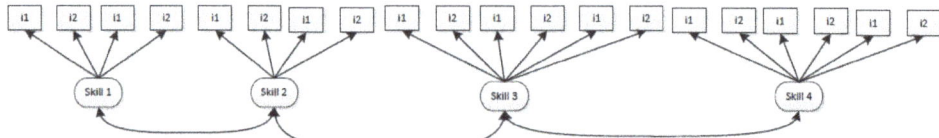

Figure 2. Model 2: Correlated Trait Model.

An example of this can be found in Kieffer and Lesaux's study [19] described previously. Use of the correlated trait model showed the vocabulary data best fit this multidimensional model and showed how the different measures of word knowledge might come together within one's lexicon (i.e., aspects of word knowledge that one might know about words). The results indicated the best fitting model consisted of three highly related, but distinct dimensions, which the authors termed breadth, contextual sensitivity, and morphological awareness. Breadth was made up of assessments where students had to provide synonyms, multiple meanings, and semantic associations for given words. Contextual sensitivity was made up of assessments of students' success at using context clues to determine word meanings. Morphological awareness was made up of real-world decomposition tasks and nonword suffix tasks. This model held for both fluent English students and dual language learners who spoke a language other than English at home, suggesting its robustness and importance in future vocabulary modeling. In this study, the correlated trait model was able to identify specific aspects of vocabulary knowledge (i.e., groupings of vocabulary tasks) that helped the researchers understand how vocabulary knowledge developed for fluent English students as compared to students who were developing multiple languages (i.e., spoke a language other than English at home). Linking to the larger vocabulary literature, the three dimensions of vocabulary knowledge modeled appear to represent different aspects of word knowledge, skills (context clue use), and linguistic awareness (morphological awareness) that could be used to figure out word meanings and build vocabulary.

The benefit of using correlated trait models when modeling vocabulary is that researchers can begin to identify structures present in vocabulary knowledge, or important aspects of word knowledge to model. Here, the individual factors are assumed to maintain construct–relevant variance. Additionally, in correlated-traits models, the constructs are estimated to correlate with each other, and often do to a high level. Those high correlations could be hiding a different source of variance that is not modeled which could be better captured by a general factor (see description of next model). For example, in the study described previously [19], the correlations between vocabulary breadth and contextual sensitivity were high ($r = 0.85$). This correlation may be indicative of variance that could be captured by a general factor of vocabulary knowledge. This leads us to our next model.

3.3. Model 3: Bi-Factor Model

While dimensionality findings establish related but distinct dimensions of vocabulary knowledge (i.e., multiple aspects of word knowledge), these models do not address how the factors overlap and how they might be separate from the larger construct. Here, we argue that while these constructs are indeed distinct, the relationships between them represent meaningful overlap such that it is best modeled as a higher level construct. In other words, the measured variables are best represented by a bi-factor model (see Figure 3) with an overarching global construct that stems from the overlap of all items as well as specific latent constructs that measure underlying structures within and uniquely separable from this global construct.

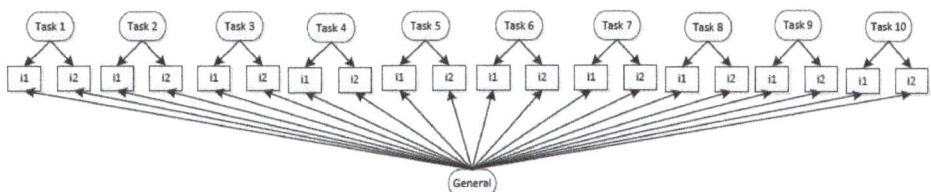

Figure 3. Model 3: Bi-factor Model.

Two recent publications show the importance and power of using bi-factor models when modeling vocabulary. First, when modeling morphological knowledge, Goodwin, Petscher, Carlisle, and Mitchell [29] showed that performance on seven morphological knowledge tasks for middle schoolers was best represented by a bi-factor model consisting of a general factor of morphological knowledge and specific factors representing differences in how tasks assessed different facets of morphological knowledge. For example, some tasks assessed morphological knowledge related to decoding while another assessed morphological knowledge as applied to determining word meanings. While tasks have been mentioned in the literature review as representing construct-irrelevant variance, in this study, variance related to tasks is construct-relevant because the task conveys a skill that is potentially instructionally relevant (e.g., applying morphological understandings to figuring out a word's meaning) rather than a cognitive action (e.g., choosing amongst answers in a multiple choice task) that is unrelated to the larger construct. These researchers showed different predictive relationships to larger literacy constructs between the general and specific factors identified. For example, the general factor and the specific factor of morphological meaning processing were positively related to standardized reading comprehension and vocabulary, whereas the specific factor of generating morphologically related words was only positively associated with standardized vocabulary knowledge.

Another example of a bi-factor model is Kieffer, Petscher, Proctor, and Silverman's [32] analysis of language skills. Here, two different studies presented in this single paper showed multiple supports for conceptualizing language as a bi-factor model. In these studies, language was made up of a general factor and specific factors of morphological awareness and vocabulary and in one study, syntax. The main idea related to assessing vocabulary is that assessments of vocabulary likely tap into general vocabulary, which is itself important to language and literacy performance. Assessments of vocabulary similarly tap knowledge of specific aspects of vocabulary which themselves represent unique pieces of knowledge or skills that are likely instructionally relevant. In the two studies described, the general and specific factors were conceptualized as construct-relevant, but bi-factor models can also identify construct-irrelevant variance (i.e., tasks) depending on design. For example, in the Goodwin et al. study [29], the specific factors related to tasks represented meaningful ways that morphological skills were applied to different literacy tasks. Alternatively, the tasks could have been related to specific cognitive skills rather than morphological skills, which would allow for modeling the construct-irrelevant variance discussed. The challenge is to have enough measures to capture all these structures, and for that, we turn to our next model, the tri-factor model.

3.4. Model 4: Tri-Factor Model

The tri-factor model (see Figure 4) models additional structures; it extends the bi-factor model to include three latent variables (a general factor, specific factors related to one structure like the aspects of word knowledge described above, and specific factors related to a different structure like task differences described above). As mentioned in our discussion of these statistical models, tri-factor models are rarely used in educational research. Still, given the layers of complexity involved in assessing vocabulary, they may be useful when researchers have enough assessments to model various structures. Factors, then, can be modeled as latent variables that are potentially construct-relevant or construct-irrelevant. Based on the vocabulary literature, a way that tri-factor models may be useful when modeling vocabulary is that the first latent variable type would include tasks. This conceptualization of tasks is, at the lowest level, representing different cognitive actions (e.g., multiple choice vs. sentence completion) that are construct-irrelevant such that an educator would not want to instruct how to complete the specific tasks because the latent skills, not the tasks, are what matters. In other words, the educator would not want to instruct students how to complete a multiple choice assessment, instead teaching the content or skills being assessed. The second latent variable type includes skills or components of knowledge. These are the components that other models have found (e.g., building definitions, understanding interrelatedness, using context clues, and unraveling heterogeneity) that are construct-relevant and instructionally relevant such that a teacher would want to instruct these larger skills. Here, for example, an educator might teach how to use units of meaning like root words or affixes to determine the meaning of an unfamiliar word (i.e., the skill of applying principles of morphology to determining meaning of words). The third latent variable type is the global trait, here vocabulary knowledge, which represents overall ability on the larger construct. An educator or researcher might use this information to determine overall performance and, in the case of vocabulary, evaluate whether building vocabulary is something that needs to be targeted intensely for example if a student scored low or whether it could be used to support other literacy skills if the student scored well. To the best of our knowledge, work has not been published in this area, but the problem space of vocabulary suggests it might be a helpful modeling tool. Initial analyses of our morphology data from our three years of development of a standardized gamified language assessment (Monster, PI to be discussed later) indicates this structure fits best. Here, 15 piloted tasks are best fit by a general factor of morphological knowledge (construct-relevant), four skills representing specific factors or specific components of morphological knowledge (construct-relevant), and specific factors related to each task used to measure morphological knowledge (construct-irrelevant). Because we had multiple tasks assessing each skill, the tri-factor model allowed us to separate the construct-relevant variance related to skills from the construct-irrelevant variance related to the cognitive skills needed to do each task. This clarifies structures that are usually ignored without such modeling techniques.

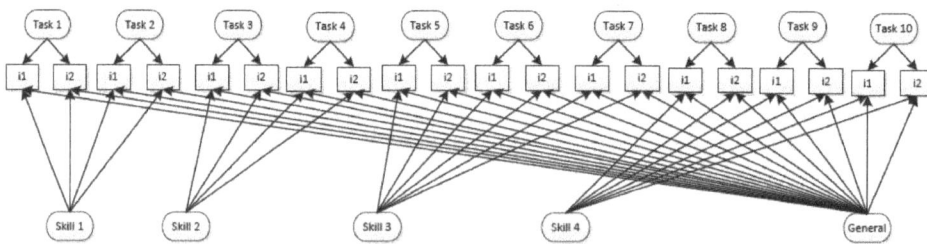

Figure 4. Model 4: Tri-factor Model.

The potential power of understanding the relationships between tasks and skills is that it offers teachers concrete examples of what a particular skill looks like. More importantly, it has the potential to show teachers multiple ways to support students' vocabulary learning. For example, an assessment which gives teachers information about each of the ten tasks might be hard to translate into instruction, as the tasks themselves might not translate into instructional activities. Equally challenging to use might be an assessment which gives teachers information about a single dimension of vocabulary knowledge (e.g., morphology); teachers might struggle to break that large problem space into instructional activities. Grouping the tasks into clearly articulated subskills, however, might offer both a stronger rationale for teaching these skills as well as presenting teachers with multiple examples of activities and assessments that tap those skills. These examples could be starting points for teachers who are themselves learning about the complexity of vocabulary knowledge.

Another example of how the tri-factor model could help sort construct-relevant from construct-irrelevant variance includes models that allow for specifying specific factors for the specific words studied. Although dimensionality related to individual words has been shown in work using other models [17,33], tri-factor models allow for constructing three latent variables: one representing general knowledge, one representing skills, and one representing words. Here, at the lowest level, the latent factors representing each word reflects knowledge of each specific word, which tends to be construct-irrelevant because knowledge of a single word or even a single set of words is unlikely to support larger literacy efforts. In other words, knowledge of weather vocabulary only supports literacy endeavors that include those specific words in texts, and, therefore, the goal is to teach large networks of words rather than word-by-word. The second latent variable type includes skills or components of word knowledge, similar to that described above. Here, performance is construct-relevant because this involves larger principles of word instruction such as highlighting the polysemous nature of words. The third latent variable represents general vocabulary knowledge, which again provides educators with an overall understanding of the students' understandings of words in general. Our work in developing the Monster, PI language assessment, highlighted later, indicates the tri-factor model was the best fitting model for our vocabulary data. In our data, the skills represented performance in definition, word relation, verbal analogy, and polysemy tasks, and these skills were separable from performance on each specific word. Linking to theory and instruction, it is likely that general vocabulary knowledge and students' different aspects of word knowledge are important factors in their language and literacy efforts (i.e., construct-relevant), but that their performance on a specific word is less relevant and less in need of instruction (i.e., construct-irrelevant).

3.5. Development of a Standardized Language Assessment

The models described previously were critical in our work developing a standardized, gamified middle school language assessment, which we call Monster, PI. This assessment assesses student understandings of written language, specifically of morphology, vocabulary, and syntax. Because it is a computer adaptive test (CAT), students start by taking a set of items and then take harder or easier items depending on their performance. How these items are delivered is based on which of the structures described above fits bests. Items continue to be delivered until a stable score is determined that represents a student's abilities. The items are embedded in a game format as 'puzzles' that students solve to earn clues to capture a monster who is wreaking havoc on the city. Crucial here is that we used these models to figure out the best structures to represent our constructs and data, resulting in a valid and reliable assessment.

We began by considering language and each construct within language (i.e., morphology, vocabulary, and syntax) as potentially multidimensional. We then identified different sources of construct-relevant and construct-irrelevant variance to consider. Informed by the models above, we considered various tasks and words in which skills could be embedded such that if the structures fit accordingly, we could separate out skill performance from task performance and/or performance on specific words. At the same time, we could also look across performance on all skills to identify general construct performance, allowing Monster, PI to convey general written language ability as well as ability in morphology, vocabulary, and syntax.

Identifying and choosing tasks and then matching them with skills was challenging, but because our work was informed by the models above, we designed and assessed multiple measures for each word, skill, and construct allowing the complexity of the problem space of language and vocabulary to serve as supports in building our assessment. Our hypothesized models often had to be adjusted based on our combination of theory and statistics, and this family of models ultimately provided a structure to our data that we could then convey to teachers in a meaningful way.

An advantage to our final model was the ability to sort out construct-relevant from construct-irrelevant data as both our morphology and vocabulary models ultimately fit best as tri-factor models where the construct-relevant latents were the general factors (i.e., general vocabulary and general morphological knowledge) and the skills being assessed. For vocabulary, skills included the ability to determine (1) definitions, (2) word relations like antonyms and synonyms, (3) polysemous meanings, and (4) verbal analogies. For morphology, skills identified included (1) identification of units of meaning, (2) use of suffixes, (3) application to meaning, and (4) reading and spelling of morphologically complex words. Scores showing performance in these skills are construct relevant because an educator could design instruction around each of these skills. The construct-irrelevant latents represented specific knowledge of words (i.e., for vocabulary) or tasks (i.e., for morphology). As mentioned, these are construct-irrelevant because teaching a single word or set of words would be unlikely to build general vocabulary and similarly, teaching a certain task like multiple choice or fill in the blank would not build the desired understandings related to vocabulary. For each model, we initially hypothesized additional tasks that were ultimately not retained because they did not explain additional construct-relevant variance. Lessons here indicate that development of vocabulary assessments must include multiple tasks and then must consider whether each task contributes meaningfully to the larger model. Additionally, for both constructs, we originally hypothesized an additional skill which ultimately did not fit our data, suggesting that these models can be helpful in identifying potentially relevant skills for instruction and eliminating others. These models have supported us in developing a reliable and valid standardized, gamified, computer adaptive assessment of language. This assessment will serve both researchers and practitioners in developing understandings of what students know and considering possible instructional interventions for better supporting developing readers.

4. Discussion

Empirical research and theory development in vocabulary paint a complex picture of vocabulary. Researchers continue to grapple with how to best model complexities related to vocabulary. In this paper, we have presented a family of models that can capitalize on many of the complexities identified within the larger vocabulary literature to model structures that build an understanding of children's vocabulary development and links to instruction. Specifically, we argue that these structures can help researchers model construct-relevant variance vs. construct-irrelevant variance. Such distinctions are critical to obtaining accurate understandings that can move the field forward.

The various modeling strategies suggested offer different insights for vocabulary research. Single factor vs multidimensional models can help researchers understand their own data in light of what the larger field is suggesting: that vocabulary is multidimensional in various ways. There is a use for single factor models, though. A researcher may be interested in one aspect of vocabulary or may find that some of the dichotomies suggested within the literature (e.g., breadth vs. depth) do not stand when tested in these models or may even vary for learners at different ages or who are considering different sets of words. As such, single factor models can serve to highlight similarities and overlap within the larger vocabulary landscape. Multidimensional models, in contrast, can serve to highlight potentially important similarities and differences. Correlated trait models identify unique, but often correlated factors. Bi-factor models offer a larger understanding, exploring structures for these more specific factors but also modeling a larger general factor. Bi-factor and tri-factor models help us model additional structures that can be important to moving the field forward. Here, distinctions between construct-relevant and construct-irrelevant variance take center stage. These models allow for modeling a general factor and specific instructionally relevant skills while at the same time separating out noise that may be distracting from these more important understandings. This noise might be related to how students perform on a particular task or a particular word or set of words.

Limitations

One thing to keep in mind is that these models are just a starting point, and also have their challenges as well. First, these models require extensive data collection (e.g., 13 different measures of vocabulary [19]) and detailed assessment design (e.g., our work with Monster, PI, which examined and tested more than 20 tasks over three years). Additionally, replication studies are important as models are likely to vary when considering student differences such as those related to language background or age. While some of the studies contained students from diverse language backgrounds (e.g., [17,19]), consistent attention to the nuances of vocabulary remains essential, including how students' local and vernacular English vocabulary intersects with the principles of academic English. In addition, all of the studies described here focus on students' vocabulary learning at the crucial ages of upper elementary through the end of middle school (i.e., grades 4–8). How might these models translate to learners across the developmental spectrum? Furthermore, while these studies offer exciting insights into the complex problem space of vocabulary, it can be difficult to translate the insights of these models into instructional practice. Developing teacher-friendly ways to discuss the implications of these models could be a way for this research to better impact students.

Overall, the models described here are a sampling of choices one may use when exploring the richness of complexity related to vocabulary. Beyond these sets of models, other emerging analytics assist researchers with simultaneously modeling the relation between person-level attributes and word-level attributes in understanding individual differences related to word-level performance [17,34,35]. These models are known by a variety of names including generalized linear mixed models, cross-classified models, and explanatory item response models. The framework of these methods involves parsing and explaining variance in item-level responses that are due to individual differences and that are due to item differences [36]. Such models take into account the fact that different readers learn different words differently and hence might be useful next steps. An additional step is to model interactions with instruction [17] as word learning is often dependent on instruction.

5. Conclusions

The models suggested in this paper mark an important first step in modeling complexities related to vocabulary, including construct-relevant vs. construct-irrelevant variance. Such models can be helpful when designing a vocabulary assessment and when modeling vocabulary more broadly. It is our hope that illustrating and comparing these models might inform future study designs that can capitalize rather than struggle with the complexity of vocabulary. We hope this discussion will support others in selecting the appropriate analytical models to enrich theory and practice.

Funding: This research was funded by the Institute of Educational Sciences, grant number R305A150199.

Conflicts of Interest: The authors declare no conflict of interest.

References

1. Vocabulary. In Oxford Dictionaries. 2018. Available online: https://en.oxforddictionaries.com/definition/vocabulary (accessed on 1 September 2018).
2. Pearson, P.D.; Hiebert, E.H.; Kamil, M.L. Vocabulary Assessment: What We Know and What We Need to Learn. *Read. Res. Q.* **2007**, *42*, 282–296. [CrossRef]

3. Dickinson, D.K.; Golinkoff, R.M.; Hirsh-Pasek, K. Speaking out for Language: Why Language is Central to Reading Development. *Educ. Res.* **2010**, *39*, 305–310. [CrossRef]

4. Perfetti, C. Reading Ability: Lexical Quality to Comprehension. *Sci. Stud. Read.* **2007**, *11*, 357–383. [CrossRef]

5. Gough, P.B.; Tunmer, W.E. Decoding, Reading, and Reading Disability. *Rem. Spec. Educ.* **1986**, *7*, 6–10. [CrossRef]

6. Goodman, Y.M. *Reading Miscue Inventory: Alternative Procedures*; Richard C. Owen Publishers: New York, NY, USA, 1987.

7. Anderson, R.C.; Freebody, P. Vocabulary knowledge. In *Comprehension and Teaching: Research Reviews*; Guthrie, J.T., Ed.; International Reading Association: Newark, DE, USA, 1981; pp. 77–117.

8. Snow, C.E.; Kim, Y.-S. Large Problem Spaces: The Challenge of Vocabulary for English Language Learners. In *Vocabulary Acquisition: Implications for Reading Comprehension*; Wagner, R.K., Muse, A.E., Tannenbaum, K.R., Eds.; Guilford Press: New York, NY, USA, 2007; pp. 123–139.

9. Read, J. *Assessing Vocabulary*; Cambridge University Press: Cambridge, UK, 2000.

10. Stahl, S.A.; Nagy, W.E. *Teaching Word Meanings*; Routledge: Hoboken, NJ, USA, 2006.

11. Nagy, W.E.; Anderson, R.C. How Many Words are there in Printed School English? *Read. Res. Q.* **1984**, *19*, 304–330. [CrossRef]

12. Hiebert, E.H.; Goodwin, A.P.; Cervetti, G.N. Core Vocabulary: Its Morphological Content and Presence in Exemplar Texts. *Read. Res. Q.* **2018**, *53*, 29–49. [CrossRef]

13. Nagy, W.; Townsend, D. Words as Tools: Learning Academic Vocabulary as Language Acquisition. *Read. Res. Q.* **2012**, *47*, 91–108. [CrossRef]

14. Snow, C.E.; Lawrence, J.F.; White, C. Generating Knowledge of Academic Language among Urban Middle School Students. *J. Res. Educ. Eff.* **2009**, *2*, 325–344. [CrossRef]

15. Uccelli, P.; Galloway, E.P.; Barr, C.D.; Meneses, A.; Dobbs, C.L. Beyond Vocabulary: Exploring Cross-Disciplinary Academic-Language Proficiency and Its Association with Reading Comprehension. *Read. Res. Q.* **2015**, *50*, 337–356. [CrossRef]

16. Fitzgerald, W.J.; Elmore, J.; Kung, M.; Stenner, A.J. The Conceptual Complexity of Vocabulary in Elementary-Grades Core Science Program Textbooks. *Read. Res. Q.* **2017**, *52*, 417–442. [CrossRef]

17. Goodwin, A.P.; Cho, S.J. Unraveling Vocabulary Learning: Reader and Item-Level Predictors of Vocabulary Learning within Comprehension Instruction for Fifth and Sixth Graders. *Sci. Stud. Read.* **2016**, *20*, 490–514. [CrossRef]

18. Nagy, W.E. Metalinguistic Awareness and the Vocabulary-Comprehension Connection. In *Vocabulary Acquisition: Implications for Reading Comprehension*; Wagner, R.K., Muse, A.E., Tannenbaum, K.R., Eds.; Guilford: New York, NY, USA, 2007; pp. 52–77.

19. Kieffer, M.J.; Lesaux, N.K. Direct and Indirect Roles of Morphological Awareness in the English Reading Comprehension of Native English, Spanish, Filipino, and Vietnamese Speakers. *Lang. Learn.* **2012**, *62*, 1170–1204. [CrossRef]

20. Nagy, W.E.; Scott, J.A. Vocabulary Processes. *Handb. Read. Res.* **2000**, *3*, 269–284.

21. Binder, K.S.; Cote, N.G.; Lee, C.; Bessette, E.; Vu, H. Beyond Breadth: The Contributions of Vocabulary Depth to Reading Comprehension among Skilled Readers. *J. Res. Read.* **2017**, *40*, 333–343. [CrossRef] [PubMed]

22. Hadley, E.B.; Dickinson, D.K. Measuring Young Children's Word Knowledge: A Conceptual Review. *J. Early Child. Lit.* **2018**, in press.

23. Logan, J.K.; Kieffer, M.J. Evaluating the Role of Polysemous Word Knowledge in Reading Comprehension among Bilingual Adolescents. *Read. Writ.* **2017**, *30*, 1687–1704. [CrossRef]

24. Shmueli, G. To Explain or to Predict? *Stat. Sci.* **2010**, *25*, 289–310. [CrossRef]

25. Morin, A.J.; Arens, A.K.; Marsh, H.W. A Bifactor Exploratory Structural Equation Modeling Framework for the Identification of Distinct Sources of Construct-Relevant Psychometric Multidimensionality. *Struct. Equ. Model.-Multidiscip. J.* **2016**, *23*, 116–139. [CrossRef]

26. Reise, S.P. The rediscovery of Bifactor Measurement Models. *Multivar. Behav. Res.* **2012**, *47*, 667–696. [CrossRef] [PubMed]

27. Petscher, Y.; Foorman, B.R.; Truckenmiller, A.J. The Impact of Item Dependency on the Efficiency of Testing and Reliability of Student Scores From a Computer Adaptive Assessment of Reading Comprehension. *J. Res. Educ. Eff.* **2017**, *10*, 408–423. [CrossRef]

28. Wainer, H.; Bradlow, E.T.; Wang, X. *Testlet Response Theory and Its Applications*; Cambridge University Press: Cambridge, UK, 2007.

29. Goodwin, A.P.; Petscher, Y.; Carlisle, J.F.; Mitchell, A.M. Exploring the Dimensionality of Morphological Knowledge for Adolescent Readers. *J. Res. Read.* **2017**, *40*, 91–117. [CrossRef] [PubMed]

30. Bauer, D.J.; Howard, A.L.; Baldasaro, R.E.; Curran, P.J.; Hussong, A.M.; Chassin, L.; Zucker, R.A. A Trifactor Model for Integrating Ratings across Multiple Informants. *Psychol. Methods* **2013**, *18*, 475–493. [CrossRef] [PubMed]

31. Perfetti, C.A.; Hart, L. The Lexical Bases of Comprehension Skill. In *On the Consequences of Meaning Selection: Perspectives on Resolving Lexical Ambiguity*; Gorfien, D.S., Ed.; American Psychological Association: Washington, DC, USA, 2001; pp. 67–86.

32. Kieffer, M.J.; Petscher, Y.; Proctor, C.P.; Silverman, R.D. Is the Whole Greater than the Sum of Its Parts? Modeling the Contributions of Language Comprehension Skills to Reading Comprehension in the Upper Elementary Grades. *Sci. Stud. Read.* **2016**, *20*, 436–454. [CrossRef]

33. Cho, S.J.; Goodwin, A.P. Modeling Learning in Doubly Multilevel Binary Longitudinal Data Using Generalized Linear Mixed Models: An Application to Measuring and Explaining Word Learning. *Psychometrika* **2017**, *82*, 846–870. [CrossRef] [PubMed]

34. Cho, S.J.; Gilbert, J.K.; Goodwin, A.P. Explanatory Multidimensional Multilevel Random Item Response Model: An Application to Simultaneous Investigation of Word and Person Contributions to Multidimensional Lexical Quality. *Psychometrika* **2013**, *78*, 830–855. [CrossRef] [PubMed]

35. Goodwin, A.P.; Gilbert, J.K.; Cho, S.J.; Kearns, D.M. Probing Lexical Representations: Simultaneous Modeling of Word and Person Contributions to Multidimensional Lexical Representations. *J. Educ. Psychol.* **2014**, *106*, 448–468. [CrossRef]

36. De Boeck, P.; Wilson, M. A Framework for Item Response Models. In *Explanatory Item Response Models*; Springer: New York, NY, USA, 2004; pp. 3–41.

Article

An Analysis of the Features of Words That Influence Vocabulary Difficulty

Elfrieda H. Hiebert [1,*], Judith A. Scott [2], Ruben Castaneda [3] and Alexandra Spichtig [4]

1   TextProject, Santa Cruz, CA 95060, USA
2   Education Department, University of California-Santa Cruz, Santa Cruz, CA 95064, USA; jascott@ucsc.edu
3   National Board of Osteopathic Medical Examiners, Chicago, IL 60631, USA; rcastaneda@nbome.org
4   Research Department, Reading Plus, Winooski, VT 05404, USA; alex@readingplus.com
*   Correspondence: hiebert@textproject.org

Received: 24 September 2018; Accepted: 18 December 2018; Published: 3 January 2019

Abstract: The two studies reported on in this paper examine the features of words that distinguish students' performances on vocabulary assessments as a means of understanding what contributes to the ease or difficulty of vocabulary knowledge. The two studies differ in the type of assessment, the types of words that were studied, and the grade levels and population considered. In the first study, an assessment of words that can be expected to appear with at least moderate frequency at particular levels of text was administered to students in grades 2 through 12. The second study considered the responses of fourth- and fifth-grade students, including English learners, to words that teachers had identified as challenging for those grade levels. The effects of the same set of word features on students' vocabulary knowledge were examined in both studies: predicted appearances of a word and its immediate morphological family members, number of letters and syllables, dispersion across content areas, polysemy, part of speech, age of acquisition, and concreteness. The data consisted of the proportion of students who answered an item correctly. In the first study, frequency of a word's appearance in written English and age of acquisition predicted students' performances. In the second study, age of acquisition was again critical but so too were word length, number of syllables, and concreteness. Word location (which was confounded by word frequency) also proved to be a predictor of performance. Findings are discussed in relation to how they can inform curriculum, instruction, and research.

Keywords: vocabulary; student learning; word features

1. An Analysis of the Features of Words That Influence Vocabulary Difficulty

Vocabulary has long been recognized as a strong predictor of comprehension [1]. Furthermore, without strong vocabulary instruction, student performance tied to socioeconomic status is perpetuated [2]. Yet the words chosen for vocabulary instruction in school are not necessarily ones that ameliorate this gap. Historically, the criteria for choosing words for instruction have been ill defined. Gates [3] established that second-graders knew over 80% of target words prior to instruction. Almost 30 years later, Stallman et al. [4] found that the pattern reported by Gates for second-graders also applied to fifth-graders. In the Stallman et al. study, overall mean scores for both second- and fifth-grade cohorts were above 75% for grade-level words and over 70% for the "new" words that had not yet been presented.

Both the Gates [3] and Stallman et al. [4] analyses are dated but a comparison of the target words chosen for vocabulary instruction in the 1965 and 2013 copyrights of a core reading program [5] showed that the focus words for the two points in time were similar in frequency of appearance in written language, age of acquisition, and utility in different content areas. The words differed on two features—length and concreteness. In both cases, the focus words in the 2013 program were shorter and more concrete, features that have been shown to make words easier for students to learn. These patterns suggest that core reading programs—and perhaps elementary vocabulary instruction in general—lack an underlying framework for word selection.

To identify the most salient words for instruction, information is needed on students' existing vocabulary knowledge. What features distinguish words that students know from those that they do not? Do the features of known and unknown words vary over students' developmental trajectory? A relatively new and potentially critical source for gaining insight into which words are known or unknown by students lies in databases that have become available as a result of digitized vocabulary assessments. Digitization of texts has also resulted in a flourishing of knowledge about vocabulary from corpora linguistics [6]. This work has resulted in new knowledge about language use [7] and in numerous analytic tools [8]. Little of this work has been applied to the study of school vocabulary assessments or vocabulary instruction.

In this paper, we present two separate studies that explore a common set of word features, identified through previous research, as factors that may contribute to students' vocabulary performance. The purpose of this research is to contribute to the conversation about the selection of words that merit instructional focus. The first study looks at students' knowledge of words that are predicted to appear in texts at different grade levels. The second study uses the same methodology and examines the same features, but the target words are those identified by teachers as challenging for students at a specific grade band—fourth and fifth grades—rather than the span of grades 2 through 12 in the first study. Furthermore, the second study includes a large number of students who were classified as English language learners, a group that is overrepresented among the students who score at basic levels and below on the National Assessment of Educational Progress (NAEP) [9].

2. Review of Research

What it means to know a word is complex [10], and there is no consensus about how to measure the complexity of word knowledge [11–13]. However, there does appear to be consensus that vocabulary knowledge is multi-dimensional and that various features of words can potentially influence students' knowledge of vocabulary. In considering multiple features of words that merit instruction, we use the theoretical framework of Nagy and Hiebert [14] to identify features that may contribute to the ease or difficulty of knowing the meanings of words. Their framework addresses the role of words in four dimensions of language and instruction: language, the lexicon, knowledge, and the lesson (see Table 1). The description that follows describes three of these four dimensions. The final cluster in the Nagy and Hiebert's word-selection framework addresses the centrality of words in particular texts and in existing curricula. The goal of the present study is to provide evidence based on student performances to guide curriculum development. Consequently, this fourth cluster is not a basis for the selection of descriptive word factors.

Table 1. Factors That Are Predicted to Influence Word Learning.

	Nagy/Hiebert (2011) Criteria	Study Measure
Role in Language	Frequency: How often does this word occur in text?	•Frequency •Polysemy •Part of speech
Role in the Lexicon	Dispersion: How does the frequency of a word differ by genre, topic, or subject area?	•Dispersion (Domain specificity)
	Morphological relatedness: What is the size of the morphological family?	•Size of morphological family
	Semantic relatedness: How is this word related to other words that students know or need to know?	

Table 1. *Cont.*

Role in Students' Existing Knowledge	Familiarity: Is this word already known to students and, if so, to what degree? Conceptual difficulty: To what extent can the meaning of this word be explained to students in terms of words, concepts, and experiences with which they are already familiar?	•Age of acquisition •Length in letters and syllables •Concreteness–Abstractness

2.1. Role in Language

Some words are ubiquitous in written language, especially those that connect ideas in discourse (e.g., *of, and, or*) but most words carry nuanced or specialized meanings and appear infrequently in English texts (e.g., *scurry, lurch*). Moreover, some words appear in texts across a wide array of topics and content areas (e.g., *sharp, flat*), while other words are specific to a particular domain (e.g., *concerto, metronome*). Nagy and Hiebert [14] referred to these two dimensions of the role that words play in written language as frequency and domain specificity.

Frequency. It is to be expected that students who read more texts are exposed to the words that appear with moderate to high frequency in written language to a greater degree than students who read less text. This effect of exposure means that frequency of words influences virtually all word recognition tasks [15]. Frequency counts are compiled by computers based on the number of occurrences of the word in a corpus. They are given for a particular orthographic form of the word (e.g., *sleep, sleeps,* and *sleepless* all have different frequency counts). As the section on Morphological Relatedness (below) explains, evidence indicates that the frequency of the inflectional and derivational relatives of a word also influence the speed of word recognition [16].

The role of word frequency in students' knowledge of words is not as clear-cut as its role in word recognition. Both frequency and morphological family frequency counts fail to distinguish among multiple meanings of words or polysemy [17]. Even among words with the same etymological history, differences in meanings can be substantial (e.g., *milk* as a liquid and *milk* as taking advantage of someone). The second meaning of the word may occur less frequently than the first meaning but, even so, uses of the word in the second meaning contribute to the overall frequency count.

Cervetti, Hiebert, Pearson, and McClung [18] found that polysemy was a significant factor in the vocabulary knowledge of second and third-graders, both independent of and as a result of instruction. Sullivan [19] found that acquiring a secondary sense of a word accounts for a significant amount of growth in vocabulary knowledge between Grade 3 and Grade 12. Often, as the illustration of meanings associated with the word *milk* suggests, secondary word senses are associated with changes in parts of speech. The degree to which the different meanings of words are associated with variations in parts of speech can add a degree of challenge for readers, especially beginning and struggling students [20].

Domain specificity. Domain specificity refers to the degree to which words appear in texts on different topics and in different subject areas. One measure of domain specificity comes from a measure that Carroll, Davies, and Richman [21] identified as dispersion. Words that appear across all subject areas receive a dispersion index of 1 (e.g., *a, that, with*), while words that appear in esoteric or specialized topics receive a dispersion index of <0.01 (e.g., *copperplate, rotogravure, platen*). Measures of dispersion can be connected to polysemy, as words often take specific secondary meanings within disciplines. For instance, the words *force* and *energy* have specific secondary meanings in physics. Cervetti et al. [18] found no significant effect for dispersion in their study of second- through fourth-graders' knowledge of science vocabulary, in contrast to Dockerall et al. [22] who found such an effect with 5- and 6-year-olds. Additional consideration of dispersion and domain specificity seems warranted.

2.2. Role in the Lexicon

Factors related to the lexicon refer to the relationship among the meanings of words. Two types of relationships are especially relevant in understanding a word's connections to the meanings of other words within the lexicon: semantic and morphological.

Semantic relatedness. Knowledge of a word's meaning is not isolated to simply one word. Rather, a word's meaning is embedded in networks of relationships to the meanings of other words. Researchers have explored various ways to group words into semantic networks. Marzano and Marzano [23], for example, applied a hierarchical semantic scheme establishing superclusters (e.g., feelings and emotions), clusters containing words with semantic ties close to the concepts (e.g., *fear: fright, startle, afraid*), and mini-clusters where words have synonymous meanings (e.g., *startle: scare, frighten, terrify*). Research indicates that semantic networks may influence word learning, although the complexity of the concept depicted by the word is an important consideration when conceptualizing semantic relatedness as a factor [24,25]. In addition, there is contradictory evidence regarding whether teaching semantically related words interferes with or enhances word learning [26,27].

Morphological relatedness. English is a morphophonemic language [28], which means that the sounds and spellings of words are influenced by the morphemes or meaning units of English. For example, at the expense of grapheme-phoneme-correspondences, the spelling of *health* conveys the link to its morphological family (i.e., the root word *heal* and other family members such as *healing, healed, healthy, healthful, unhealthy*), making it more likely that students will consider these words as a family rather than as separate lexical units when encountering them in a text. In identifying 88,500 as the number of word families in written English that students are likely to encounter over their school careers, Nagy and Anderson [29] estimated that there are, on average, one to three additional related words for every word that students encounter after the initial stages of reading acquisition.

Aspects of the morphological structure of words also contribute to the challenge of word learning. The speed of accessing a word's meaning is affected by the morphological structure, including the transparency and frequency of the root word, inflected endings, and derivations [30].

2.3. Role in Students' Existing Knowledge

Students' existing vocabularies and background knowledge can also influence how well and how quickly they remember or learn words. Nagy and Hiebert [14] identified two aspects of students' knowledge that influence the challenge of reading and learning words: (a) their familiarity with the words and concepts and (b) the conceptual complexity that the words represent.

Familiarity. Familiarity refers to students' prior experience with and exposure to words and their associated concepts. Familiarity and frequency are related, but some words that appear with similar frequency in written texts can differ substantially in familiarity. For example, the words *silly, slide,* and *resistance* all have U function values of 25 [31], indicating that they appear with similar frequency in English texts, but elementary students' familiarity with these words is likely to vary considerably.

Typical analyses of familiarity involve adults [32] and older school-aged children [33]. Because no large-scale database exists of children's ratings of words, a more useful index of schoolchildren's familiarity with words appears to be age of acquisition (AoA) data, an indicator of the age at which a word is typically understood or used in oral language [8]. The age at which words are acquired in oral language appears to affect word recognition performance beyond correlated variables such as word frequency [34].

Familiarity in reading also requires students to be able to associate a word's meaning with the graphic form of the word. This act, in common parlance, is what it means to "read a word." Length, as measured in number of syllables or letters, has been shown to be a reliable predictor of word recognition [35] and of recognition of word meaning [36].

Conceptual complexity. Conceptual complexity has often been established by identifying empirically how many students at a given age are able to identify a word's meaning correctly [37,38]. Even though related, conceptual challenge and AoA are likely different characteristics. Efforts such as

Latent Semantic Analysis [39], HAL [40], and WordNet [41] attempt to identify numbers and kinds of links between ideas, but, as yet, data are not available that establishes the relative difficulty of large numbers of specific concepts for school-age students at different developmental levels.

The one aspect of the operationalization of conceptual complexity that can be established with relative ease is concreteness. The concreteness of a word refers to how readily readers can summon a mental image of the concept. Researchers have shown that concreteness (or conversely, abstractness) and imageability [42] influence variables such as speed of lexical processing [43] and vocabulary knowledge [44]. Consequently, this construct has been prominent in models of conceptual development and cognitive processing [45].

Taken together, the three categories identified by Nagy and Hiebert [14]—the role of words in language, their role in the lexicon, and aspects that represent students' existing knowledge—provide a theoretically and empirically grounded framework for identifying words that are known or unknown by students at particular points in development. We examined how most features identified by Nagy and Hiebert—word length, number of syllables, parts of speech, frequency, morphological family frequency, dispersion, polysemy, AoA and concreteness—predict students' vocabulary knowledge. The construct of conceptual complexity was restricted to concreteness. Furthermore, a measure of semantic relatedness was not included. At the present time, measures of conceptual complexity (other than concreteness) and semantic relatedness have yet to be validated and are open to interpretation.

The two studies reported on in this paper examine how well the identified variables predict students' knowledge of words on two assessments that differ in substantial ways including population, basis for selection of target words, and task. The types of words in the two studies differ but the underlying goal of both studies is directed at answering the same question: What factors predict the ease or difficulty of students' understanding of word meaning in text? Answers to this question are critical if school time is to be directed at strengthening students' vocabularies. Relatively large databases of students' performances on vocabulary assessments, we believe, offer the opportunity to gain evidence to address this question.

3. Study One: Words on an Assessment of Core Vocabulary

In typical vocabulary assessments, words are not chosen to represent the lexicon in any systematic way. Rather words are selected based on psychometric analyses. Words known by most students are eliminated, leaving words where performances vary. Such assessments give an indication of individuals' standing in relation to a norm group, but they provide little understanding of what types of words are known by students at different points in their development as readers. The perspective of the vocabulary assessment in this study takes a different direction. It aims to establish how students do with the words that form a core vocabulary. We use the term core vocabulary to refer to words that account for a substantial percentage of the words in texts.

The topic of which words occur frequently in texts has had a long history of study. In the first book of words for teachers, Thorndike [46] organized words in frequency bands (10 for the first 10,000 words), based on an analysis of approximately 4.75 million words that came from 41 sources (primarily the Bible and English classics but also some schoolbooks and children's trade books). The initial version was followed by two additional summaries: the 20,000 most frequent words [47] and 30,000 most frequent words [48]. Gray [49] and Gates [50] used the lists for designating words in basal reading programs. Thorndike's word frequency analyses were apparent in assessments such as the Gray Oral Reading Test and the Gates–MacGinitie Reading Tests [51]. However, the analyses of word frequency do not appear to have been the basis for vocabulary assessments in any systematic fashion.

Thorndike [46] did not describe the distribution of groups of words in text but, shortly thereafter, Zipf [52] hypothesized that the frequency of any word is inversely proportional to its rank in a frequency list. Thus, the most frequent word, *the*, accounts for roughly 7% of all words and the next most frequent word, *of*, accounts for approximately 3.5%. Zipf predicted that 135 words would account for half of the words in a large sample.

The verification of what came to be called Zipf's [52] law in large vocabulary corpora occurred with the advent of computers. Kučera and Francis's [53] analysis was the first to take advantage of digitization. Their corpus, however, consisted only of texts for adults and from a single year. It would be the work of Carroll et al. [21] that would provide insight into the distribution of words in school text. Their analysis consisted of five million words from schoolbooks covering grades 3 through 9 and a comprehensive selection of content areas. They identified the U function, which predicted the appearances of a word per million words of text as adjusted for a word's distribution across content areas. This measure made it possible to provide an indication of which words accounted for particular portions of school text. They showed that, as Zipf had predicted, 135 words accounted for roughly 50% of the total words in schoolbooks.

The effort to describe the distribution of vocabulary in texts was expanded considerably by Zeno et al. [31] in the *Educator's Word Frequency Guide* (EWFG), which was based on over 17 million words of texts that represented school content areas and grade levels from first through college. Several substantial efforts have produced ranks of vocabulary in large corpora of text [54,55] but the Zeno et al. analysis remains the last systematic, published database of the distribution of vocabulary in school text. The Zeno et al. work further verified Zipf's [52] hypothesis about the distribution of words in the corpus. Of the 154,941 words in the Zeno et al. database, 87% of the words are predicted to appear less than once per million (and more than half of this group is predicted to occur approximately once in every 10 million words).

Hiebert [56] set out to establish a parsimonious vocabulary for school instruction. If only a limited number of words can be taught in school, Hiebert reasoned, the words that account for substantial portions of texts should be given priority in vocabulary instruction. The interest in identifying such a vocabulary goes much beyond the Dolch [57] words or even the 1000 most frequent words that Fry [58] emphasized. In particular, Hiebert was interested in identifying what she called a "core vocabulary" that accounts for 90% of the words in typical texts read by students in elementary through high school. The 90% level was chosen because leading literacy scholars [59,60] have proposed this level of word recognition as sufficient for comprehension.

In that success in third-grade reading has received considerable attention in policy beginning with the Reading Excellence Act [61], Hiebert [56] examined third-grade texts on norm-referenced tests, state tests, and oral reading assessments to determine the number of complex words per 100 words of text. Complex words were defined as those that were multi-syllabic or did not appear among the first 1000 words in the EWFG [31]. On average, the six assessments in the sample had 4.8 complex words per 100. The state assessments were the most challenging (6 complex words per 100) and the norm-referenced tests were the least challenging (3.5 complex words per 100).

Hiebert's [56] use of single-syllable words as a criterion for word complexity lacks nuance in describing students' familiarity and exposure to words. For example, third-graders are likely to know *breath* but not *swath*, even though both are single-syllable words. Subsequently, Hiebert [62] identified the words that accounted for 90% of total words in fourth-grade assessments of three states and the NAEP. For this analysis, Hiebert identified eight word zones from the EWFG's [31] predictions of word appearances in a million words of text. The eight word zones and the number of words in each are as follows: (1) U = 68,006 to 1000 (n = 107); (2) U = 999 to 300 (n = 203); (3) U = 299 to 100 (n = 620); (4) U = 99 to 30 (n = 1676); (5) U = 29 to 10 (n = 2980); (6) U = 9 to 4 (n = 4052); (7) U = 3 to 1 (n = 9830); and (8) 0.999 and below (n = 135,473). Hiebert found that 90% of the total words on all assessments were accounted for by the words in zones 1 through 5: words that are predicted to have 10 or more appearances per million words of text.

Subsequently, Hiebert [63] analyzed excerpts from the 168 exemplar texts identified by developers of the Common Core State Standards (CCSS) [64]. In texts for grades 2–3, 92.5% of the total words were from word zones one through five. The percentage decreased to 88% for the texts at the grades

11–College and Career Ready (CCR) level. Hiebert's [63] conclusion was that the 5586 words in word zones one through five in the EWFG could be regarded as an essential or parsimonious vocabulary for success in school reading, particularly at the elementary grades. An assessment that progressively evaluates students' facility with the meanings of words in these word zones seemed to be a worthy endeavor. Consequently, the vocabulary component of the InSight assessment [65] was based on the word zone model. The focus was on coordinating words within a particular word zone with a developmental level at which those words are predicted to appear in texts with at least moderate frequency. Information on the factors that influence students' performances on words from particular word zones can contribute to the underlying research question of this study: What factors influence the ease or difficulty of students' knowledge of word meanings?

3.1. Method

3.1.1. The Assessment

The vocabulary component of the InSight assessment [65] had 12 levels with two forms, each consisting of 20 items. The 480 words on the assessment (12 levels x 2 forms x 20 items) were derived from the first seven word zones established by Hiebert [63]. The eighth word zone that encompasses words with frequencies less than 1 in the EWFG was not included in the assessment.

The assessment was intended to span the school grades of 1–12. The aim was to address word zones 1 through 3 in levels 1 through 3 of the assessment; word zone 4 in levels 4 to 6; word zone 5 in levels 7 to 9, word zone 6 in levels 10 to 11, and word zone 7 in Level 12. The words from word zone 1 were not used after results from an initial pilot test indicated that most students knew these words. Where one or more grades shared a word zone, the words were parsed into an equivalent number of sub-zones.

The goal of creating two forms of the assessment, each with 20 items, meant that words were chosen in pairs. Each set of words assigned to a grade level was divided into 20 groups. The first 2 items of a grade-level assessment came from the first group, the second pair of items from the second group, and so on. Words were sorted within a group for length, grade at which a word was known on the Living Word Vocabulary [38], and part of speech. To the degree possible, words were also matched on morphological family size and concreteness. As evident in Table 2, the features of words at the 12 levels of the final forms of the assessment show that, on the primary features of frequency, morphological frequency, and AoA, a progression of movement from easy to hard was maintained across the levels of the assessment. Differences across levels are not as distinctive on the concreteness feature.

Table 2. Means (and Standard Deviations) of Features of Words on the 12 Levels of InSight Vocabulary Assessment and on the Vocabulary Assessment Study in Education (VASE) [66].

Assess. Level	U	Morph. Family Size	Dispersion	Word Length (Letters)	Word Length (Syllables)	Polysemy	Parts of Speech	A of A	Concreteness	Example
InSight 1	449.10 (468.80)	742.7 (339.3)	0.90 (0.01)	5.48 (0.71)	1.68 (0.71)	8.8 (8.5)	1.88 (0)	5.21 (1.2)	3.15 (0.19)	words
InSight 2	222.40 (6.36)	428.58 (360.91)	0.90 (0.10)	5.90 (0.71)	1.85 (0)	12.13 (0.75)	1.80 (0)	6.40 (0.52)	3.06 (0.01)	strong
InSight 3	134.68 (36.06)	229.74 (254.79)	0.89 (0.04)	7.28 (0)	2.60 (0.71)	6.90 (12.0)	1.40 (0.71)	7.56 (0.69)	2.65 (0.12)	minutes
InSight 4	80.83 (22.63)	189.05 (139.90)	0.86 (0.16)	6.53 (2.12)	2.28 (0)	6.53 (0.71)	1.45 (0)	7.90 (1.53)	2.72 (0.03)	private
InSight 5	52.43 (25.46)	205.64 (42.87)	0.86 (0.01)	7.28 (2.12)	2.50 (0.71)	6.93 (6.36)	1.60 (0.71)	8.56 (2.91)	2.49 (1.43)	opinion
InSight 6	35.10 (9.19)	141.83 (1.43)	0.87 (0.06)	8.33 (1.41)	2.8 (0)	5.98 (2.83)	1.35 (0.71)	8.60 (2.40)	2.46 (0.57)	selection
InSight 7	24.30 (9.89)	90.37 (80.20)	0.83 (0.17)	8.73 (1.41)	3.1 (0.71)	5.43 (0.71)	1.25 (0.71)	9.63 (0.84)	2.46 (0.94)	challenge
InSight 8	16.23 (3.54)	60.13 (0.06)	0.82 (0.06)	8.30 (1.41)	2.93 (0.71)	4.1 (3.92)	1.23 (0.71)	9.49 (0.27)	2.51 (0.28)	isolated

Table 2. *Cont.*

InSight 9	10.30 (8.49)	54.23 (148.58)	0.80 (0.14)	8.33 (0)	2.78 (1.41)	4.50 (4.24)	1.38 (0.71)	9.98 (2.84)	2.28 (0.04)	literally
InSight 10	7.83 (8.49)	34.39 (10.98)	0.74 (0.08)	8.65 (2.12)	3.00 (1.41)	3.80 (1.41)	1.28 (0.71)	10.41 (3.01)	2.43 (0.02)	corporate
InSight 11	4.95 (6.36)	37.84 (3.97)	0.67 (0.18)	8.80 (0.71)	3.18 (0.71)	3.80 (1.41)	1.3 (0)	11.11 (0.47)	2.15 (0.41)	magnitude
InSight 12	2.14 (1.76)	9.30 (15.73)	0.63 (0.25)	9.05 (0.71)	3.23 (0.71)	2.93 (0)	1.13 (0)	11.96 (0.44)	2.12 (0.66)	negotiate
VASE	20.64 (40.62)	79.21 (126.27)	0.65 (0.20)	7.79 (2.14)	2.60 (0.97)	3.75 (3.42)	1.35 (0.54)	9.4 (1.82)	3.12 (0.92)	sequence

Item format. The assessment required students to identify a synonym for a highlighted word in a sentence. Seven categories of distractors were identified where words had: (a) an alternate meaning of the word that is not applicable in the context, (b) a thematically related but inappropriate meaning, (c) a potential miscue, (d) an opposite meaning, (e) frequently used in an expression with the highlighted word, (f) shared prefixes or suffixes, and (g) an unrelated meaning. In that the format had four distractors, all distractor types were not used for every item.

The stems for items were short (an average of 6 words) and were intended to reveal nothing about the target word except its part of speech. An illustration of an item is: *I read the entire book.* The correct response was *whole* and distractors were *not broken, enter, large*, and *part*. The words in the stems, distractors, and correct responses had approximately the same or more frequent U functions as the target word, as indicated in the information from Zeno et al. [31] following each word: *I* (4443), *read* (436), *the* (68,006) *entire* (89), *book* (290), *whole* (270), *not* (4356) *broken* (106), *enter* (66), *large* (597), and *part* (694). Only one word in this example—the distractor *enter*—had a U function that was less than the target word, but even this difference is not a substantial one.

3.1.2. Variables for Analysis

The set of variables used in analyzing the features of words associated with student performances was the same in both studies. A description of the nine variables follows.

Length. The length of the word was the number of letters as calculated by the Word Zone Profiler [67].

Syllables. The number of syllables was calculated using the syllabication breakdown found in the first line of the definition after a Google search. Each word was entered into the Google search engine, followed by the word "meaning" to produce the dictionary definition. The word *entire*, for example, was represented as two syllables (en, tire).

Word Frequency. The EWFG frequency measure (U function) provided the data for the frequency variable [31].

Frequency of Morphological Family. This variable captures the frequency of the members of a word's morphological family. Frequencies for all members of a word family were obtained from the EWFG database [31]. Becker, Dixon & Anderson-Inman's [68] morphological database was used to determine which words in the EWFG were morphologically related.

Dispersion. The EWFG [31] provides data on dispersion as the level of a word's use across texts from different content areas. We used this D factor data for the words in the studies.

Concreteness. A word's concreteness was based on the norms developed by Brysbaert, Warriner, and Kuperman [69], which indicate levels of concreteness from 1 (very abstract; e.g., *charity*) to (very concrete; e.g., *chair*).

AoA. This variable captures the age at which students typically understand or can use a word in oral language. We used the calculations from the database of Kuperman et al. [8].

Part of Speech. This variable captures the number of possible parts of speech for each word according to the WordNet [42] database. For example, the word *zone* could be both a noun and a verb for a score of 2.

Polysemy. This variable was calculated as the sum of all meanings of a word from all possible parts of speech according to WordNet [42].

All 480 words in the InSight assessment were coded according to the nine features (as was also the case with the 172 words in the VASE assessment in the second study). Descriptive statistics of the word features at the 12 levels of the InSight assessment are provided in Table 2.

3.2. Sample of Students

The InSight vocabulary assessment was administered to 28,901 students in grades 2 through 12 from 2469 schools across 46 states in the U.S. Of the 2247 schools for which demographic data were available, schools were distributed over three contexts: urban (27.5%), suburban (33%), and small town and rural (39.6%) and across four regions of the U.S: Northeast (4%), Midwest (12%), South (63%), and West (21%).

The 28,901 students were distributed across grade bands as follows: Grades 2–3, 1929; grades 4–5: 7472; grades 6–8: 13,731; and grades 9–12: 5769. For the 17,919 students for whom gender data were available, 51% were female and 49% were male. Racial/ethnicity (available for 14,133 students) was distributed as follows: American-Indian/Alaska Native/Native Hawaiian/Pacific Islander (0.81%), Asian-American (2.5%), African-American (42.4%), European-American (31.5%), Hispanic-American (21.7%), and two or more races (1.1%).

The data collection was part of the end-of-the-year assessment of students who had participated in the Reading Plus program over the academic year. The assessment is administered digitally in groups in either classroom or laboratory settings. The InSight assessment is adaptive. Students are first assigned the form for their grade level. If students' scores fall below 70% correct on the grade-level form, they are given the form for the adjacent lower level, and so forth until they perform at 70% or higher or until they have reached the first level of the assessment. If students' performances on the grade-level form are above 70%, they receive forms for subsequent grade levels until their scores fall below 70%. Across the 480 items, there was an average of 8865 responses. The dataset consisted of the proportion of correct responses to each word for four grade bands: Grades 2–3, 4–5, 6–8, and 9–12.

3.3. Data Analysis

We analyzed the data in two steps. The first involved looking at the overall performance of students on items (i.e., each of the 480 words) with word characteristics as moderator variables. This involved fitting a series of hierarchical models with words on level one and grade (of students) on level two. To fit these models, we used the R base program combined with the lmer4 package for hierarchical linear models [70,71]. Additionally, we applied a logistic transformation to the outcome variable (proportion correct) to normalize the outcome variable and apply linear regressions. The first model is an intercept only model (null model) and a random effect (variability), used as the base model to enable a likelihood ratio test in subsequent models. The second and third models include word feature variables indicating the proportion accounted for by each variable as well as the impact on the outcome variable *p*. Each model was compared to the previous model via likelihood ratio test to determine whether the additional factors account for variability.

The second step involved examining the performance of word features for each subgroup (i.e., the 4 grade groups) individually via a series of regression models. This analysis permitted an examination of which word features were important for each group level. Such an analysis is necessary because, for some variables such as word frequency, it would be expected that older students would perform better on words with lower frequencies since they have had exposure to these words over a longer period of time.

3.4. Results

3.4.1. Word Characteristics: Overall

The null model showed a large amount of variability between grades. The second model, which included word features (e.g., length, polysemy), accounted for a significant amount of variability over model 1 (see Table 3). The third model with dummy coded variables that represent student grade ranges showed that grade level accounts for a significant amount of variability beyond word characteristics alone.

Table 3. Model Fit Between Three Models.

Model Comparison	AIC	BIC	LogLike	Deviance	Chi X	df	*p*-Value
M0: Null	4047.30	4064.00	−2020.70	4041.30	-	-	-
M1: +Characteristics	3476.00	3542.70	−1726.00	3452.00	589.32	9	*p* < 0.001
M3: +Grade Level	3354.30	3437.70	−1662.20	3324.30	127.66	3	*p* < 0.001

The null model shows that a large amount of variability occurs between grades (intraclass correlation = 0.62). The grand mean γ_{00} = 1.05 indicates that, on average, students answer a word correctly exp (1.05)/1+exp (1.05) = 0.74, or 74% of the time with a grade-level variability of u_0. = 0.82. In the second model, the nine word features were included (i.e., word frequency, polysemy, etc.). The variables in model two accounted for a significant amount of variability over model one, χ^2 (9) = 589.32, $p < 0.001$ (See Table 3). Of the nine variables included in the model, only two were significant across grade levels: word frequency and AoA (See Table 4). For word frequency, the results indicate that, as the frequency of the word gets smaller, the proportion correct tends to decrease. Next, the results also indicate that students tend to fail to answer words correctly when the word has a higher AoA (i.e., known by older but not younger students).

Table 4. HLM Estimates of Main Effects.

	M0: Null Model	SE	*p*-Value	M1: +Characteristic	SE	*p*-Value	M2: +Grades	SE	*p*-Value
Fixed Effects:									
Intercept	1.0490	0.0392	<0.001	2.51	0.53	<0.001	2.3410	0.5273	<0.001
Freq	-	-	-	−0.28	0.06	<0.001	−0.2757	0.0594	<0.001
Morph	-	-	-	−0.08	0.05	0.140	−0.0740	0.0508	0.236
Disp	-	-	-	0.15	0.32	0.644	0.1352	0.3233	0.946
Length	-	-	-	0.03	0.03	0.388	0.0277	0.0316	0.495
Syllab	-	-	-	−0.09	0.07	0.218	−0.0854	0.0690	0.191
Polysem	-	-	-	−0.01	0.01	0.740	−0.0029	0.0091	0.939
Pos	-	-	-	−0.04	0.07	0.582	−0.0404	0.0712	0.341
Age	-	-	-	−0.15	0.03	<0.001	−0.1458	0.0264	<0.001
Concrete	-	-	-	0.03	0.06	0.623	0.0279	0.0576	0.767
is 4th	-	-	-	-	-	-	0.2753	0.0251	<0.001
is 6th	-	-	-	-	-	-	0.1656	0.0239	<0.001
is 9th	-	-	-	-	-	-	0.1757	0.0256	<0.001
Random Effects:									
σ2e	0.6725			0.6502			0.6505		
σ2u0	0.2625			134.6224			123.5799		

3.4.2. Word Characteristics: Grade Bands

Next, to examine the influence of word features at different grade bands, we implemented a series of regression analyses (see Table 5). These analyses test how much impact each word feature has on the proportion of items correct at each grade band. Frequency and AoA were statistically significant across all grade levels, after adjusting for multiple comparisons via Bonferroni correction (alpha/10). The influence of frequency and AoA on proportion correct at each grade level is depicted in Figures 1 and 2.

Table 5. Regression Coefficients for Word Characteristics.

Word Characteristics	Grades 2–3		Grades 4–5		Grades 6–8		Grades 9–12	
	Coef (SE)	*p*-Val	Coef (SE)	*p*-Val	Coef (SE)	*p*-Val	Coef (SE)	*p*-Val
Intercept	2.455 (0.5544)	0.000	3.0359 (0.6307)	0.000	2.5839 (0.5887)	0.000	2.4958 (0.5749)	0.000
Frequency	−0.0013 (0.0003)	0.0000	−0.0016 (0.0004)	0.0002	−0.0025 (0.0005)	0.0000	−0.0031 (0.0006)	0.0000
Morphology	−0.0002 (0.0001)	0.1100	−0.0003 (0.0002)	0.1067	−0.0002 (0.0002)	0.2120	−0.0002 (0.0002)	0.2740
Dispersion	0.1487 (0.4313)	0.7300	−0.075 (0.4576)	0.8699	0.1336 (0.3795)	0.7250	0.2209 (0.3476)	0.5250
Length	−0.0014 (0.0312)	0.9630	0.0207 (0.0353)	0.5576	0.0314 (0.0338)	0.3540	0.0222 (0.0339)	0.5130
Syllables	−0.0783 (0.0642)	0.2230	−0.0543 (0.0736)	0.4611	−0.0597 (0.0734)	0.4160	−0.0167 (0.0744)	0.8230
Polysemy	0.006 (0.0062)	0.3320	0.0122 (0.0084)	0.1480	−0.0003 (0.0103)	0.9730	−0.0048 (0.0118)	0.6820
Parts of Speech	−0.0387 (0.0558)	0.4890	−0.1512 (0.0702)	0.0318	−0.0853 (0.0765)	0.2650	−0.0343 (0.0806)	0.6710
Age of Acquisition	−0.158 (0.0261)	0.0000	−0.1767 (0.0295)	0.0000	−0.1516 (0.0284)	0.0000	−0.1459 (0.0283)	0.0000
Concreteness	−0.0003 (0.0472)	0.9950	0.0495 (0.059)	0.4012	0.0409 (0.062)	0.5100	0.0113 (0.0654)	0.8630

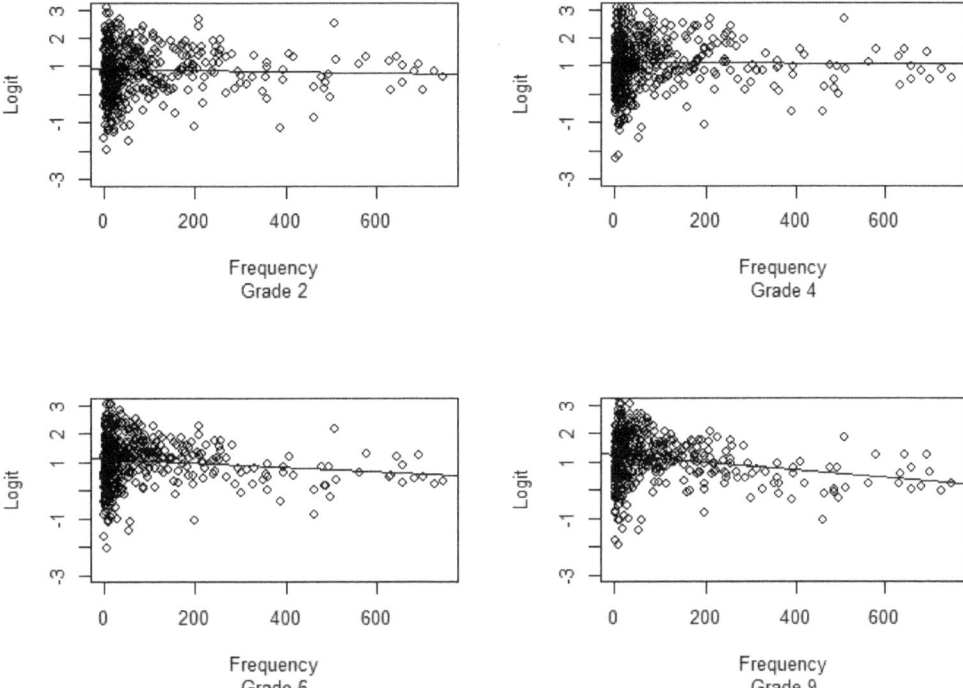

Figure 1. Scatter plots for word frequency against logit transformed proportion correct for each grade level. The regression line becomes steeper for each grade level indicating the importance of frequency for older students.

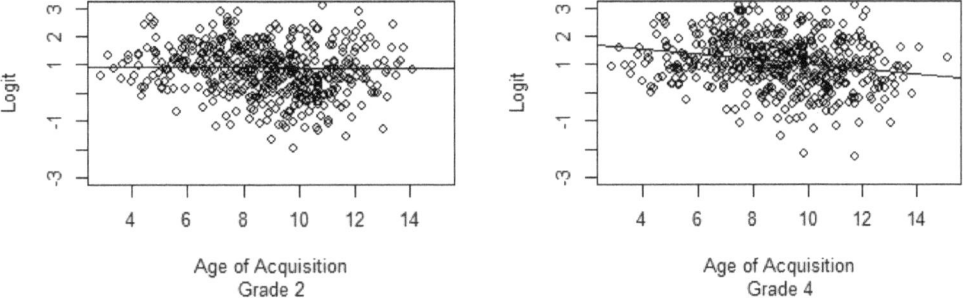

Figure 2. *Cont.*

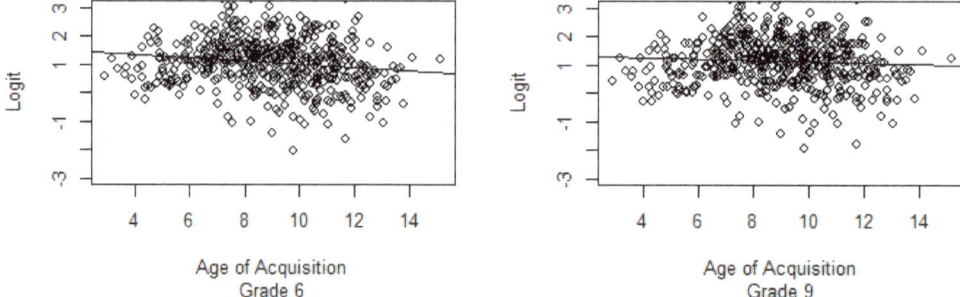

Figure 2. Scatter plots for word age of acquisition against logit transformed proportion correct for each grade level. The line remains stable across all grade groups indicating that age of acquisition has equal importance for all grade levels in predicting proportion of items correct.

3.5. Summary

The first two criteria for selecting words for the assessment were frequency and part of speech. Pairs of words, one for each of the two assessment forms, were then vetted for comparable features on word familiarity, size of morphological family, number of syllables, and concreteness. Students' performances on the vocabulary items were analyzed using measures of these criteria and, additionally, dispersion and polysemy. One of the original variables—familiarity—was assessed with a measure unique from that used in the original selection progress. In the original selection of words, grade norms from the LWV [38] were used to determine familiarity. In the current analysis, AoA [8], which was not available during the word-selection process, was used. The correlation between the grade norms of the LWV and the AoA ratings for the 480 words in the assessment was in the moderate range ($r = 0.57$). Similar to the findings of other studies [72,73], the AoA norms [8] performed robustly.

We had anticipated that morphological family size might prove to be a stronger predictor of students' performances than proved to be the case, especially considering research linking family size to word knowledge [74,75]. Rather, the most consistent and strongest predictions came from frequency and AoA. The role of frequency and AoA in students' word knowledge could be viewed as expected in that exposure to words, either in oral language and text or both, is required for acquisition. However, the finding that the average correct rate was 74% indicates that there were words that shared frequency and AoA metrics but were not known by students.

Furthermore, the strength of frequency and AoA in predicting students' word knowledge does not translate into conclusions that only frequent and familiar words should be taught. Nor do these patterns translate into conclusions that only infrequent and unfamiliar words should be taught. Rather, the patterns suggest that these variables should be considered in the selection of words for instruction. If students at particular grade bands do not know particular words that can be expected to appear with some frequency in texts, these words should be a priority. Rather than devoting instructional time to words that are already known by students, vocabulary instruction should prepare students for the words that can be anticipated to appear with frequency in current and subsequent levels of text.

At the present time, criteria of frequency and AoA do not appear to undergird the selection of vocabulary for instruction in core reading programs. Among the 685 words chosen for third-grade vocabulary instruction across three core reading programs [5], half of the words were quite frequent ($X = 57.2$) and half were quite rare ($X = 4.6$). Furthermore, half of the vocabulary had a relatively low AoA ($X = 6.7$) and half had a relatively high AoA ($X = 9.6$). If the goal is to close the vocabulary gap and expand students' vocabulary and comprehension prowess, words that are either too easy or too hard would not seem to be a good use of school time. The present findings would suggest the need to locate words within a "sweet spot" where instructed words are ones that will increase students' facility with text but are unknown by students.

4. Study Two

The first study showed that the frequency of words and AoA predicted students' knowledge of words anticipated to appear with some frequency at different developmental levels. The second study provides triangulation for the findings of the first study as it differs from the first in design, word selection, and the population involved. A question that remains is whether the same variables predict students' performances on an assessment that was not derived from a model where words were chosen for particular grade bands based on their frequency.

A second question that was not addressed by the first study is how status as a native or non-native English speaker might influence performance on the variables. In 2017, over two and a half million students (42%) in Californian schools spoke a language other than English in their homes [76], a demographic shift reflected across the nation. This second study looks explicitly at students who are English learners. They comprise a significant portion of students in today's classrooms and this population may perform differently than native English speakers on tests of English vocabulary knowledge. Scholars looking at language acquisition in a second language have examined features of words such as those explored in the first study. A review of research [77] showed that, in addition to morphological complexity and polysemy, features such as the pronounceability of words, similarity of lexical form (synformy), idiomatic expressions, and specificity of register contributed to difficulty of word knowledge among ELs. There was not, however, a clear effect for word length, part of speech or concreteness/ abstractness. In contrast, more recent research shows that ELs learn and use concrete words earlier and more easily than abstract words [78,79].

The second study uses the same methodology (logistically transformed proportions) in a non-hierarchical manner and examines the predictive nature of word features that influence student vocabulary performances. The measure used in this study, however, is unique in its representation of vocabulary knowledge—both from the measure used in study 1 and in other previous research. The VASE assessment [66] measures knowledge of individual words from students' responses to a set of questions about the words ranging from their level of confidence in knowing the word, to information about the word's semantic attributes, morphology, use in context, definition, and part(s) of speech. Word selection was based on teacher and researcher evaluation of the familiarity of selected items using words from an exhaustive review of grade-level math, science, and social studies textbooks, basal readers, Newbery Award-winning novels, and the California standards in English language arts. Furthermore, the nature of variables that predict English learners' performances were also considered in this study. The criteria for word selection, the assessment task, and the composition of the sample differed in this study from that of study 1. The research question, however, remained the same: What factors predict the ease or difficulty of students' knowledge of a word?

4.1. Method

VASE Vocabulary Assessment

The VASE assessment was developed primarily as a "proof of concept" study but has also been used to successfully assess the efficacy of the Word Learning Strategies program [80]. The VASE assessment consists of four 24-item multiple-choice tests that are each timed for 15 min. The four tests in the VASE assessment are linked using common-item equating, with four words appearing on all versions of the tests. There are two equivalent forms for fourth grade and two for fifth grade. Scores are reported on a common scale that spans the two grades, allowing for longitudinal tracking of vocabulary growth. The features of the 172 words on the various forms and tests of the VASE are summarized in Table 2.

The VASE assessment was given to 6976 fourth- and fifth-grade students in school districts across the state of California, including urban, suburban, and rural areas. Within the sample, 53% were female and 47% were male. Ethnicity was distributed as follows: Caucasian (24%), Latinx (40%), Asian (16%), African-American (7%), Filipinio (4%), and more than one ethnicity (9%).

A little over half of the sample were native English speakers (52%). The rest were classified as having different levels of English: (a) English learners (30%), (b) bilingual students deemed to be fluent in English on school entry (2%), or (c) students who had been redesignated as English Proficient in an earlier grade (16%).

The VASE assessment was developed to explore multiple dimensions of word knowledge. The six components it addresses—metacognition, semantics, morphology, syntax, definitions, and polysemy—each appear to make related but independent contributions to the richness of word knowledge [81]. Students were asked six multiple-choice questions about each word: (a) How well they know a word; (b) If they can identify a synonym related to the target word; (c) If they can identify an appropriate morphological family member; (d) If they can choose the sentence that uses the word correctly; (e) If they can choose an appropriate definition; and (f) If they can identify the part or parts of speech that could fit the word. For each question, students select one of four options. The scores reported in this study are a composite of these questions based on Thissen, Steinberg & Mooney's [82] "testlet" construct in which related items are linked to create one larger, graded item and Samejima's [83] graded IRT model.

In item response theory (the approach used for scaling the tests), reliability varies as a function of proficiency. However, it may be summarized for a test by averaging over the proficiency distribution, resulting in a single marginal reliability for the test. Marginal reliability for the VASE tests ranged from 0.91 to 0.93. The word-selection process, which drew words from typical classroom materials using the expertise of skilled fourth- and fifth-grade teachers in all stages of the assessment's development, provides a strong foundation for the validity of the VASE assessment.

Because words were selected from intact texts, they were found in various morphological forms. An algorithm was used to choose the tested words from the words selected by the teachers resulting in the use of the intact morphological form, not the root word, in the assessment. For instance, VASE presented the words *admiration* instead of *admire* and *graphs* instead of *graph*. The selected words were extensively piloted and culled to develop the final set of words for the assessment.

4.2. Analysis and Results

Descriptive statistics for the variables in study 2 are included in Table 2. The present analysis used the same factors as in study 1 but operationalized in a different fashion to predict performance on the VASE assessment. In the VASE analysis, word location was included as a predictor because VASE was a speeded test. The more frequent and easier words were at the beginning of the test, along with the linking items (words common to all four tests). Many students did not reach the words on the latter portion of the assessment, making these words inherently more difficult. Word Location ranges from 1 (first item on the test) to 24 (last item on the test) with an average of 13.69 and standard deviation of 6.58.

The estimated coefficient for location is -0.1926, and the intercept is 2.0988 (see Table 6). The back transformation to change to the proportion metric is $p = \frac{e^{(\beta 0)} * e^{(\beta x)}}{1 + e^{(\beta 0)} * e^{(\beta x)}}$. For a word in the first position, the expected proportion of passing the word (ignoring the effects of all other predictors) would be $p = \frac{e^{(2.0988)} * e^{(-0.1926*1)}}{1 + e^{(2.0988)} * e^{(-0.1926*1)}} = 0.87$. In contrast, the expected proportion of passing a word in the 12th position would be $p = \frac{e^{(2.0988)} * e^{(-0.1926*12)}}{1 + e^{(2.0988)} * e^{(-0.1926*12)}} = 0.45$.

Table 6. Beta Regression Analysis of Word Difficulty (All VASE Students).

Predictor	Coefficient	SE	Z Value	*p*-Value
(Intercept)	2.0988	0.6221	3.3740	0.0000
Word Location	−0.1926	0.0116	−16.5970	0.0000
Word Frequency	0.0008	0.0018	0.4200	0.6748
Morphology	0.0002	0.0005	0.3460	0.7293
Dispersion	0.1609	0.3910	0.4110	0.6808
Length	−0.1253	0.0561	−2.2350	0.0254
Syllables	0.3239	0.1236	2.6200	0.0000
Parts of Speech	0.1390	0.1383	1.0050	0.3150
Polysemy	−0.0352	0.0251	−1.4020	0.1608
Age of Acquisition	−0.1019	0.0360	−2.8320	0.0046
Concreteness	0.1544	0.0734	2.1040	0.0354

Note: Phi = 17.993; R^2 = 0.8677.

Table 6 shows the estimated coefficients for all VASE respondents, along with their standard errors, test statistics, and *p* values. The significant predictors of proportion passing the item are word location, word length, number of syllables, AoA, and concreteness.

Further analyses were conducted for both the native English speakers and the English learners, as seen in Tables 7 and 8. The patterns differ slightly as the role of concreteness was highly significant for the EL students, and not significant for native English speakers. Thus, the finding of significance in the overall analysis seems to be driven by the EL students.

Table 7. Beta Regression Analysis of Word Difficulty (VASE Native English Speakers).

Predictor	Coefficient	SE	Z Value	*p*-Value
(Intercept)	2.5000	0.6095	4.1010	0.0000
Word Location	−0.2046	0.0119	−17.2310	0.0000
Word Frequency	0.0011	0.0019	0.5990	0.5491
Morphology	0.0000	0.0004	−0.0090	0.9931
Dispersion	0.0748	0.3927	0.1900	0.8490
Length	−0.1221	0.0566	−2.1570	0.0310
Syllables	0.2832	0.1263	2.2420	0.0250
Parts of Speech	0.1568	0.1400	1.1200	0.2626
Polysemy	−0.0269	0.0253	−1.0620	0.2884
Age of Acquisition	−0.0836	0.0354	−2.3610	0.0182
Concreteness	0.1228	0.0752	1.6330	0.1025

Note: phi = 17.38; R^2 = 0.8670.

Table 8. Beta Regression Analysis of Word Difficulty (VASE EL Students).

Predictor	Coefficient	SE	Z Value	*p*-Value
(Intercept)	0.7095	0.6035	1.1760	0.2398
Word Location	−0.1718	0.0114	−15.1230	0.0000
Word Frequency	0.0015	0.0017	0.9310	0.3518
Morphology	0.0001	0.0005	0.1740	0.8617
Dispersion	0.4053	0.4049	1.0010	0.3168
Length	−0.1516	0.0566	−2.6800	0.0074
Syllables	0.4401	0.1262	3.4880	0.0005
Parts of Speech	0.1239	0.1343	0.9230	0.3560
Polysemy	−0.0437	0.0242	−1.8060	0.0710
Age of Acquisition	−0.1219	0.0332	−3.6700	0.0002
Concreteness	0.2748	0.0723	3.8000	0.0001

Note: Phi = 21.068; R^2 = 0.8656.

4.3. Summary

The results of the second study indicate that word location, AoA, word length, number of syllables, and concreteness were all significant word-level factors that contributed to performance on the VASE assessment. At first glance, the lack of significance in this study for word frequency may appear unexpected. This finding, however, may well represent a confound of word frequency with word location. When the VASE tests were created, there was a deliberate effort to order the words by difficulty. Since word frequency was involved in those decisions, it is likely that it is subsumed by word location in the analyses.

Like the first study, AoA was highly predictive of performance on the VASE test. However, this analysis also indicated that the graphic form of the word, as measured by the number of letters and syllables also influenced the performance of these 4th and 5th grade students. A potential explanation for the prominence of these variables in the second study but not the first study may lie in the comparative rareness of the words in the VASE assessment relative to the InSight assessment. The mean U function for the VASE was 20.64 (SD = 40.62), while the mean U function for the grades 4–5 levels of the InSight was 66.23 (SD = 16.67). The likelihood that students had encountered many of the words on the VASE previously were substantially less than for words on the InSight. Furthermore, words on the VASE were longer than those on the grades 4–5 levels of InSight: X = 7.79 (SD = 2.14) for the former and X = 6.90 (SD = 1.54) for the latter. Findings from previous studies confirm the influence of word and syllable length on students' recognition of words [35,36].

An intriguing result relates to the concreteness factor, which was highly predictive for the English learners but not significant for students whose native language was English. This finding could be partially attributed to the preponderance of nouns in VASE. We carefully constructed the test to represent four parts of speech (adverbs, adjectives, nouns, and verbs) in relative proportion to the English language. As a result, 58% of the words were nouns, with a mean of 3.12 on the BRM Concreteness Scale from 1 (abstract) to 5 (concrete) [69].

5. Overall Discussion

The two assessments that provided the data on student vocabulary knowledge differed from one another on several dimensions. First, the content that was assessed by the two assessments differed. The InSight vocabulary assessment was designed to test students' knowledge of core vocabulary, while the VASE used words that teachers had identified as likely challenging for grade-level students. Item formats of the two assessments also differed with a fairly conventional format of stems and single word responses on the InSight assessment and six questions that each queried students' knowledge of unique dimensions of word knowledge on the VASE.

Even with these differences in content and format, one variable reliably predicted students' word knowledge of the two assessments—AoA. AoA gives an indication of when words typically appear in students' oral vocabularies. This result makes sense, as it is much more difficult for students to perform well on vocabulary assessments when the words on the test are not part of their oral vocabularies. Additionally, word frequency was a critical variable on both assessments. For the InSight measure, this variable proved the strongest predictor. Although frequency did not appear to be significant in the analysis of the VASE data, word location was a significant factor. The construction of the VASE assessment was such that frequency was subsumed in the word location factor, making it likely to be a proxy for frequency. Thus, in both assessments, exposure to words in written language was a strong predictor of knowledge of word meaning. As with the finding on AoA, this result is understandable. That is, when students have opportunities to encounter words in texts, they gain knowledge about those words. These findings, of course, do not mean that only words with high frequency or high familiarity should be taught or, conversely, only words with low frequency or low familiarity. As has been discussed previously—and will be addressed in more depth in the following section on implications of the findings for curriculum design and instruction—word selection based on data on known and unknown words and their role in texts at particular grade bands can ensure that students are extending their vocabularies strategically and efficiently.

After AoA and frequency, there was divergence in the variables that accounted for students' performances on the two unique assessments. On the VASE assessment, syllabication, word length and concreteness were also salient variables. Word length and the concomitant number of syllables have been found to predict the rapidity with which students recognize words and their meanings [35]. It is likely that many students had not encountered the words on the VASE in texts previously, at least according to teachers' views. Presumably, the meanings of the words and also the structure (i.e., word length, syllabication, derivations) influenced teachers' choices and consequently the words on the VASE test.

The finding that concreteness predicted performances on the VASE assessment, especially for English learners, indicates that this could be an important and under-acknowledged factor in vocabulary learning and assessment. Others have described the role of realia and concrete nouns in English learners' instruction in English [84]. The findings of this study provide additional evidence for instruction that emphasizes concrete nouns as a way of supporting English learners in connecting known concepts to the new English orthographic and phonological forms. While ELs should not be shielded from learning academically complex vocabulary, this finding points directly to the importance of careful selection of words during instruction and on measures of assessment, especially when students are learning English.

6. Implications for Curriculum Design and Instruction

The findings that word frequency and AoA predicted students' performances could be met with the response, "Of course. Isn't that to be expected? Wouldn't that be especially anticipated when the words on the InSight assessment were chosen to represent bands according to frequency in written English?" Such an observation fails to recognize several aspects of the words in the assessments, particularly of the InSight assessment, as well as the aims of this study, which was to provide guidance for curriculum developers, publishers, and teachers in which words to choose for instruction.

First, while it is the case that the InSight assessment aimed to establish students' facility with words chosen according to frequency norms, the assessment is not a simple measure of frequency. General academic words are prominent in the InSight vocabulary corpus: 65% of all InSight words appear in Gardner and Davies's [85] Academic Vocabulary List. General academic words are already apparent in levels 1 through 3 of the InSight assessment where 51% of the words are on the Gardner and Davies list. General academic words have been identified as words that are relatively abstract and frequently not the focus of instruction in English/Language Arts or in content areas, making these words challenging for many students [86].

Second, findings that show that students are more likely to know words as a function of frequency and AoA does not translate into information as to what words are known by individual students or even groups of students. To identify the words that are known by individuals and also groups of students (as well as those words that are likely not known) requires analyses of individuals' responses to specific words. Landauer, Kireyev, and Panaccione [87] called for the individualization of vocabulary instruction but, at the time of the publication of their article, assessments based on systematic analyses of critical word features were not available. Such assessments are now available and provide the means whereby publishers and curriculum developers can create vocabulary curriculum that may address the gap in vocabulary to a greater degree than was possible in the past. The specific information on which words are likely to be known and which ones are not requires further investigation. However, the instruments to gather such information are available for publishers and curriculum designers.

Finally, we repeat our cautions regarding interpretations of the current findings as justification for emphasizing either words with high frequency and familiarity or words with low frequency and familiarity in instruction. Our rationale for this study was to direct attention of curriculum designers and publishers to the availability of data from large-scale studies that can ensure that the focus words of instruction are ones with which students are not yet facile, but which are predicted to appear in current and subsequent grade bands. That is, data from large-scale assessments can support parsimonious vocabulary instruction where students' time is spent on words that matter in texts and academic conversations and are not yet known with ease.

7. Limitations and Future Research

This project breaks ground in providing information on students' word knowledge by using data from existing vocabulary assessments. The approach of using data on students' performances on vocabulary assessment to determine features that influence word knowledge appears to be a productive direction for research. At the same time, we recognize the limitations of the project and the need for studies that replicate the approach and address unanswered questions in this study.

A question that was not addressed in either study is the degree to which these two assessments are an indication of students' ability to comprehend text. To date, data are not available on the predictive validity of the VASE on tests of reading comprehension but there is evidence that the InSight vocabulary component does predict comprehension. The InSight vocabulary measure has been found to have relatively high correlations with reading comprehension assessments of three types: a state assessment (Florida Standards Assessment): r = 0.66; a consortium assessment (Smarter Balanced Assessment Consortium): r = 0.83; and a norm-referenced assessment (GRADE): r = 0.84 [88].

Such strong relationships raise the question of whether vocabulary instruction, particularly interventions, that use data on students' knowledge of the core vocabulary could influence comprehension performances. To date, vocabulary interventions have been surprisingly ineffective in changing student performances on generalized comprehension measures [89]. One explanation is that interventions have typically not focused on the words most prominent in the lexicon at different developmental levels. English has an exceptionally large corpus of rare words [7]. If words in interventions have not been guided by the saliency of words in written English, it is not surprising that interventions have rarely closed the existing knowledge gaps between students on entering school [90]. Findings from the current study provide direction for increasing the focus and efficacy of vocabulary instruction, especially interventions. Rather than spending instructional time on words that most students already know (a pattern in historical and current core reading programs) or, alternatively, on rare words as appears to have been the case in many interventions [91], the present findings suggest that a more profitable route would be for instruction and interventions to concentrate on vocabulary that is unknown by students but can be expected to appear in students' texts [11].

An important question for both instruction and assessment is whether frequency and AoA can be used as indicators of students' reading exposure. Without extensive reading, students are unlikely to encounter critical vocabulary sufficiently to read automatically and with meaning. A trend in reading instruction, observed at both the elementary and middle to high school levels, is a reduction in the degree to which students are responsible for reading texts themselves with texts read aloud by teachers, read by peers in round-robin reading, or read by narrators on audio versions [92,93]. Linking normative amounts of reading to vocabulary learning through the frequency of words and AoA could be useful in tracking such trends and encouraging more extensive reading in classrooms.

Another question that this study does not address is whether knowledge of a word with particular frequency and AoA is indicative of knowledge of words within a similar band of frequency and AoA. Pearson et al. [12] raised this question as especially germane in establishing students' vocabulary knowledge. The present study does not clarify the issue, but it does give grist for future research that considers whether word knowledge is idiosyncratic to a particular word or whether shared features can be used to make conclusions about students' word knowledge.

In conclusion, the close examination of word features is a fruitful line of research that can yield important information for both vocabulary instruction and assessment. Two different assessments indicate that word frequency and AoA are worth consideration in the selection of words for instruction and for vocabulary assessments. Taken together, the findings from this project point to important

Educ. Sci. **2019**, *9*, 8

factors to be taken up by publishers, teachers and researchers involved in vocabulary instruction and the construction of measures of assessment.

Author Contributions: Conceptualization, E.H.H. & J.A.S., methodology, A.S., J.A.S., statistical analysis, R.C., writing, original draft preparation, E.H.H., J.A.S., writing—review & editing, E.H.H., J.A.S.

Funding: Study 2 was partially supported by IES Reading and Writing Education Research Grant: Goal 5: #R305A090550-10. The content of this manuscript is the sole responsibility of the authors and does not necessarily reflect the opinions of the U. S. Department of Education.

Acknowledgments: We gratefully acknowledge the support and the participation of students and their teachers in both projects.

Conflicts of Interest: The authors declare no conflict of interest.

References

1. Davis, F.B. Two new measures of reading ability. *J. Educ. Psychol.* **1942**, *33*, 365–372. [CrossRef]
2. Hoff, E.; Tian, C. Socioeconomic status and cultural influences on language. *J. Commun. Disord.* **2005**, *38*, 271–278. [CrossRef] [PubMed]
3. Gates, A.I. The word recognition ability and the reading vocabulary of second-and third-grade children. *Read. Teach.* **1962**, *15*, 443–448.
4. Stallman, A.; Commeyras, M.; Kerr, B.; Reimer, K.; Jimenez, R.; Hartman, D.; Pearson, P.D. Are "new" words really new? *Read. Res. Instr.* **1989**, *29*, 12–29. [CrossRef]
5. Hiebert, E.H. The words we teach, the words we don't: An examination of the taught and rare vocabularies of core reading programs. Paper Presented at the Annual Meeting of the American Educational Research Association, Philadelphia, PA, USA, 7 April 2014. Available online: https://www.academia.edu/7858492/The_Words_We_Teach_The_Words_We_Dont_An_examination_of_the_taught_and_rare_vocabularies_of_core_reading_programs (accessed on 27 November 2018).
6. Frankenberg-Garcia, A.; Flowerdew, L.; Aston, G. (Eds.) *New Trends in Corpora and Language Learning*; Bloomsbury Publishing: New York, NY, USA, 2013.
7. Mugglestone, L. (Ed.) *The Oxford History of English*; Oxford University Press: Cambridge, UK, 2012.
8. Kuperman, V.; Stadthagen-Gonzalez, H.; Brysbaert, M. Age-of-acquisition ratings for 30,000 English words. *Behav. Res. Methods* **2012**, *44*, 978–990. [CrossRef] [PubMed]
9. U.S. Department of Education. *Academic Performance and Outcomes for English Learners: Performance on National Assessments and On-Time Graduation Rates*; U.S. Department of Education: Washington, DC, USA, 2017. Available online: https://www2.ed.gov/datastory/el-outcomes/index.html (accessed on 5 December 2018).
10. Nagy, W.E.; Scott, J.A. Vocabulary processes. In *Handbook of Reading Research*; Kamil, M., Mosenthal, P., Pearson, P.D., Barr, R., Eds.; Lawrence Erlbaum Associates: Mahwah, NJ, USA, 2000; Volume 3, pp. 269–284.
11. McKeown, M.; Deane, P.; Scott, J.; Krovetz, R.; Lawless, R. *Vocabulary Assessment to Support Instruction: Building Rich Word-Learning Experiences*; Guilford Press: New York, NY, USA, 2017.
12. Pearson, P.D.; Hiebert, E.H.; Kamil, M.L. Vocabulary assessment: What we know and what we need to learn. *Read. Res. Q.* **2007**, *42*, 282–296. [CrossRef]
13. Schmitt, N. Size and depth of vocabulary knowledge: What the research shows. *Learning* **2014**, *64*, 913–951. [CrossRef]
14. Nagy, W.E.; Hiebert, E.H. Toward a theory of word selection. In *Handbook of Reading Research*; Kamil, M.L., Pearson, P.D., Moje, E.B., Afflerbach, P.P., Eds.; Longman: New York, NY, USA, 2011; Volume 4, pp. 388–404.
15. Balota, D.A.; Yap, M.J.; Cortese, M.J. Visual word recognition: The journey from features to meaning (a travel update). *Handb. Psycholinguist.* **2006**, *2*, 285–375.
16. Nagy, W.; Anderson, R.C.; Schommer, M.; Scott, J.A.; Stallman, A.C. Morphological families in the internal lexicon. *Read. Res. Q.* **1989**, *24*, 262–282. [CrossRef]
17. Nerlich, B.; Clarke, D.D. Ambiguities we live by: Towards a pragmatics of polysemy. *J. Pragmat.* **2001**, *33*, 1–20. [CrossRef]
18. Cervetti, G.N.; Hiebert, E.H.; Pearson, P.D.; McClung, N.A. Factors that influence the difficulty of science words. *J. Lit. Res.* **2015**, *47*, 153–185. [CrossRef]

19. Sullivan, J. Developing Knowledge of Polysemous Vocabulary. Ph.D. Thesis, University of Waterloo, Waterloo, ON, Canada, 2006.

20. Millis, M.L.; Bution, S.B. The effect of polysemy on lexical decision time: Now you see it, now you don't. *Mem. Cognit.* **1989**, *17*, 141–147. [CrossRef]

21. Carroll, J.B.; Davies, P.; Richman, B. *The American Heritage Word Frequency Book*; Houghton Mifflin: Boston, MA, USA, 1971.

22. Dockrell, J.E.; Braisby, N.; Best, R.M. Children's acquisition of science terms: Simple exposure is insufficient. *Learn. Instr.* **2007**, *17*, 577–594. [CrossRef]

23. Marzano, R.J.; Marzano, J.S. *A Cluster Approach to Elementary Vocabulary Instruction*; International Reading Association: Newark, DE, USA, 1988.

24. Jenkins, J.R.; Dixon, R. Vocabulary learning. *Contemp. Educ. Psychol.* **1983**, *8*, 237–260. [CrossRef]

25. Nagy, W.E.; Scott, J.A. Word schemas: Expectations about the form and meaning of new words. *Cognit. Instr.* **1990**, *7*, 105–127. [CrossRef]

26. Buchanan, T.W.; Etzel, J.A.; Adolphs, R.; Tranel, D. The influence of autonomic arousal and semantic relatedness on memory for emotional words. *Int. J. Psychophysiol.* **2006**, *61*, 26–33. [CrossRef] [PubMed]

27. Erten, İ.H.; Tekin, M. Effects on vocabulary acquisition of presenting new words in semantic sets versus semantically unrelated sets. *System* **2008**, *36*, 407–422. [CrossRef]

28. Venezky, R.L. *The American Way of Spelling: The Structure and Origins of American English Orthography*; Guilford Press: New York, NY, USA, 1999.

29. Nagy, W.E.; Anderson, R.C. How many words are there in printed school English? *Read. Res. Q.* **1984**, *19*, 304–330. [CrossRef]

30. Carlisle, J.F.; Stone, C. Exploring the role of morphemes in word reading. *Read. Res. Q.* **2005**, *40*, 428–449. [CrossRef]

31. Zeno, S.M.; Ivens, S.H.; Millard, R.T.; Duvvuri, R. *The Educator's Word Frequency Guide*; Touchstone Applied Science Associates Inc.: Brewster, MA, USA, 1995.

32. Toglia, M.P.; Battig, W.F. *Handbook of Semantic Word Norms*; Lawrence Erlbaum: Mahwah, NJ, USA, 1978.

33. Freebody, P.; Anderson, R.C. Effects of vocabulary difficulty, text cohesion, and schema availability on reading comprehension. *Read. Res. Q.* **1983**, *18*, 277–294. [CrossRef]

34. Morrison, C.M.; Ellis, A.W. Roles of word frequency and age of acquisition in word naming and lexical decision. *J. Exp. Psychol. Learn. Mem. Cognit.* **1995**, *21*, 116. [CrossRef]

35. Bergman, C.B.; Martelli, M.; Burani, C.; Pelli, D.; Zoccolotti, P. How the word length effect develops with age. *J. Vis.* **2006**, *6*, 999. [CrossRef]

36. Miller, L.T.; Lee, C.J. Construct validation of the Peabody Picture Vocabulary Test—Revised: A structural equation model of the acquisition order of words. *Psychol. Assess.* **1993**, *5*, 438. [CrossRef]

37. Biemiller, A. *Words Worth Teaching: Closing the Vocabulary Gap*; McGraw-Hill SRA: Columbus, OH, USA, 2010.

38. Dale, E.; O'Rourke, J. *The Living Word Vocabulary*; World Book-Childcraft International: Chicago, IL, USA, 1981.

39. Landauer, T.K.; Dumais, S.T. A solution to Plato's problem: The latent semantic analysis theory of acquisition, induction, and representation of knowledge. *Psychol. Rev.* **1997**, *104*, 211. [CrossRef]

40. Lund, K.; Burgess, C. Producing high-dimensional semantic spaces from lexical co-occurrence. *Behav. Res. Methods Instrum. Comput.* **1996**, *28*, 203–208. [CrossRef]

41. Miller, G. *WordNet: An Electronic Lexical Database*; MIT Press: Cambridge, MA, USA, 1998.

42. Paivio, A.; Yuille, J.; Madigan, S.A. Concreteness, imagery and meaningfulness values for 925 nouns. *J. Exp. Psychol.* **1968**, *76*, 1–25. [CrossRef]

43. Altarriba, J.; Bauer, L.M.; Benvenuto, C. Concreteness, context-availability, and imageability ratings and word associations for abstract, concrete, and emotion words. *Behav. Res. Methods Instrum. Comput.* **1999**, *31*, 578–602. [CrossRef]

44. De Groot, A.; Keijzer, R. What is hard to learn is easy to forget: The roles of word concreteness, cognate status, and word frequency in foreign language vocabulary learning and forgetting. *Lang. Learn.* **2000**, *50*, 1–56. [CrossRef]

45. Varela, F.J.; Thompson, E.T.; Rosch, E. *The Embodied Mind: Cognitive Science and Human Experience*; The MIT Press: Cambridge, MA, USA, 1991.
46. Thorndike, E.L. *The Teacher's Word Book*; Bureau of Publications, Teachers College, Columbia University: New York, NY, USA, 1921.
47. Thorndike, E.L. *A Teacher's Word Book of the 20,000 Words*; Bureau of Publications, Teachers College, Columbia University: New York, NY, USA, 1932.
48. Thorndike, E.L.; Lorge, I. *The Teacher's Word Book of 30,000 Words*; Bureau of Publications, Teachers College, Columbia University: New York, NY, USA, 1944.
49. Elson, W.H.; Gray, W.S. *The Elson Basic Readers*; Scott Foresman: Chicago, IL, USA, 1931.
50. Gates, A.I. *The Work-Play Books*; Macmillan: New York, NY, USA, 1930.
51. Hiebert, E.H.; Raphael, T.E. Psychological perspectives on literacy and extensions to educational practice. In *Handbook of Educational Psychology*; Berliner, D.C., Calfee, R.C., Eds.; Macmillan: New York, NY, USA, 1996; pp. 550–602.
52. Zipf, G.K. *The Psychology of Language*; Houghton-Mifflin: Boston, MA, USA, 1935.
53. Kučera, H.; Francis, W. *Computational Analysis of Present Day American English*; Brown University Press: Providence, RI, USA, 1967.
54. Davies, M. The 385+ million word Corpus of Contemporary American English (1990–2008+): Design, architecture, and linguistic insights. *Int. J. Corpus Linguist.* **2009**, *14*, 159–190. [CrossRef]
55. Leech, G.; Rayson, P. *Word Frequencies in Written and Spoken English: Based on the British National Corpus*; Routledge: New York, NY, USA, 2014.
56. Hiebert, E.H. Standards, assessment, and text difficulty. In *What Research Has to Say about Reading Instruction*, 3rd ed.; Farstrup, A.E., Samuels, S.J., Eds.; International Reading Association: Newark, DE, USA, 2002; pp. 337–369.
57. Dolch, E.W. A basic sight vocabulary. *Elem. Sch. J.* **1936**, *36*, 456–460. [CrossRef]
58. Fry, E.B. *The Vocabulary Teacher's Book of Lists*; Jossey-Bass: Hoboken, NJ, USA, 2004.
59. Clay, M. *Becoming Literate: The Construction of Inner Control*; Heinemann: Portsmouth, NH, USA, 1991.
60. Stahl, S.; Heubach, K. Fluency-oriented reading instruction. *J. Lit. Res.* **2005**, *37*, 25–60. [CrossRef]
61. Reading Excellence Act. 1998. Available online: www.gpo.gov/fdsys/pkg/BILLS-105hr2614eas/pdf/BILLS-105hr2614eas.pdf (accessed on 1 January 2019).
62. Hiebert, E.H. In pursuit of an effective, efficient vocabulary curriculum for the elementary grades. In *The Teaching and Learning of Vocabulary: Bringing Scientific Research to Practice*; Hiebert, E.H., Kamil, M., Eds.; LEA: Mahwah, NJ, USA, 2005; pp. 243–263.
63. Hiebert, E.H. Core vocabulary and the challenge of complex text. In *Quality Reading Instruction in the Age of Common Core Standards*; Neuman, S.B., Gambrell, L.B., Eds.; International Reading Association: Newark, DE, USA, 2013; pp. 149–161.
64. National Governors Association Center for Best Practices & Council of Chief State School Officers. *Common Core State Standards for English Language Arts & Literacy in History/Social Studies, Science, and Technical Subjects*; Appendix A; National Governors Association Center for Best Practices & Council of Chief State School Officers: Washington, DC, USA, 2010; Available online: www.corestandards.org/assets/Appendix_A.pdf (accessed on 1 January 2019).
65. Reading Plus. *InSight Assessment*; Reading Plus: Winooski, VT, USA, 2016.
66. Vocabulary Innovations in Education Consortium. Vocabulary Assessment Study in Education; August 2014. Available online: http://vineconsortium.org/vase/ (accessed on 12 August 2018).
67. Hiebert, E.H. *Word Zone Profiler*; TextProject: Santa Cruz, CA, USA, 2012.
68. Becker, W.C.; Dixon, R.; Anderson-Inman, L. *Morphographic and Root Word Analysis of 26,000 High Frequency Words*; University of Oregon Follow Through Project, College of Education: Eugene, OR, USA, 1980.
69. Brysbaert, M.; Warriner, A.B.; Kuperman, V. Concreteness ratings for 40 thousand generally known English word lemmas. *Behav. Res. Methods* **2014**, *46*, 904–911. [CrossRef] [PubMed]
70. R Core Team. *R: A Language and Environment for Statistical Computing*; R Foundation for Statistical Computing: Vienna, Austria, 2016; Available online: https://www.R-project.org/ (accessed on 1 January 2019).

71. Bates, D.; Maechler, M.; Bolker, B.; Walker, S. Fitting linear mixed-effects models Using lme4. *J. Stat. Softw.* **2015**, *67*, 1–48. [CrossRef]

72. Cortese, M.J.; Schock, J. Imageability and age of acquisition effects in disyllabic word recognition. *Q. J. Exp. Psychol.* **2013**, *66*, 946–972. [CrossRef] [PubMed]

73. Monaghan, P. Age of acquisition predicts rate of lexical evolution. *Cognition* **2014**, *133*, 530–534. [CrossRef] [PubMed]

74. Carlisle, J.F.; Katz, L.A. Effects of word and morpheme familiarity on reading of derived words. *Read. Writ. Interdiscip. J.* **2006**, *19*, 669–693. [CrossRef]

75. Dijkstra, T.; Martín, F.M.; Schulpen, B.; Schreuder, R.; Baayen, R.H. A roommate in cream: Morphological family size effects on interlingual homograph recognition. *Lang. Cognit. Process.* **2007**, *20*, 7–41. [CrossRef]

76. California Department of Education. 29 June 2018. Facts about English Learners in California. Available online: https://www.cde.ca.gov/ds/sd/cb/cefelfacts.asp (accessed on 12 August 2018).

77. Laufer, B. Why are some words more difficult than others? Some intralexical factors that affect the learning of words. *Int. Rev. Appl. Linguist.* **1990**, *28*, 293–307. [CrossRef]

78. Crossley, S.; Salsbury, T.; McNamara, D. Measuring L2 lexical growth using hypernymic relationships. *Lang. Learn.* **2009**, *59*, 307–334. [CrossRef]

79. Salsbury, T.; Crossley, S.A.; McNamara, D.S. Psycholinguistic word information in second language oral discourse. *Second Lang. Res.* **2011**, *27*, 343–360. [CrossRef]

80. Graves, M.F.; Ringstaff, C.; Li, L.; Flynn, K. Effects of teaching upper elementary grade students to use Word Learning Strategies. *Read. Psychol.* **2018**, 1–20. [CrossRef]

81. Scott, J.A.; Flinspach, S.L.; Vevea, J.L.; Castaneda, R. *Vocabulary Knowledge as a Multidimensional Concept: A Six Factor Model*; Poster at the Annual Meeting of the Society for the Scientific Study of Reading; Hapuna Beach: Waimea, HI, USA, 2015.

82. Thissen, D.; Steinberg, L.; Mooney, J. Trace lines for testlets: A use of multiple-categorical-response models. *J. Educ. Meas.* **1989**, *26*, 247–260. [CrossRef]

83. Samejima, F. The graded response model. In *Handbook of Modern Item Response Theory*; van der Linden, W.J., Hambleton, R.K., Eds.; Springer: New York, NY, USA, 1996; pp. 85–100.

84. Graves, M.F.; August, D.; Mancilla-Martinez, J. *Teaching Vocabulary to English Language Learners*; Teachers College Press: New York, NY, USA, 2012.

85. Gardner, D.; Davies, M. A new academic vocabulary list. *Appl. Linguist.* **2013**, *35*, 305–327. [CrossRef]

86. Nagy, W.; Townsend, D. Words as tools: Learning academic vocabulary as language acquisition. *Read. Res. Q.* **2012**, *47*, 91–108. [CrossRef]

87. Landauer, T.K.; Kireyev, K.; Panaccione, C. Word maturity: A new metric for word knowledge. *Sci. Stud. Read.* **2011**, *15*, 92–108. [CrossRef]

88. Gehsmann, K.M.; Spichtig, A.N.; Pascoe, J.P.; Ferrara, J.D. Comparing the construct of reading proficiency across five commonly used reading assessments: Implications for policy and practice. Paper Presented at the 67th Annual Conference of the Literacy Research Association, Tampa, FL, USA, 29 November 2017. Available online: https://www.researchgate.net/publication/321731743_Comparing_the_Construct_of_Reading_Proficiency_Across_Five_Commonly_Used_Reading_Assessments_Implications_for_Policy_and_Practice_Literacy_Research_Association_December_2017 (accessed on 1 January 2019).

89. Wright, T.S.; Cervetti, G.N. A systematic review of the research on vocabulary instruction that impacts text comprehension. *Read. Res. Q.* **2017**, *52*, 203–226. [CrossRef]

90. Ceci, S.J.; Papierno, P.B. The rhetoric and reality of gap closing: When the "have-nots" gain but the "haves" gain even more. *Am. Psychol.* **2005**, *60*, 149–160. [CrossRef]

91. Scott, J.A.; Lubliner, S.; Hiebert, E.H. Constructs underlying word selection and assessment tasks in the archival research on vocabulary instruction. In *55th Yearbook of the National Reading Conference*; Hoffman, J.V., Schallert, D.L., Fairbanks, C.M., Worthy, J., Maloch, B., Eds.; NRC: Oak Creek, WI, USA, 2006; pp. 264–275.

92. Brenner, D.; Hiebert, E.H.; Tompkins, R. How much and what are third graders reading? In *Reading More, Reading Better: Solving Problems in the Teaching of Literacy*; Hiebert, E.H., Ed.; Guilford Press: New York, NY, USA, 2009; pp. 118–140.
93. Swanson, E.; Wanzek, J.; McCulley, L.; Stillman-Spisak, S.; Vaughn, S.; Simmons, D.; Fogarty, M.; Hairrell, A. Literacy and text reading in middle and high school social studies and English language arts classrooms. *Read. Writ. Q.* **2016**, *32*, 199–222. [CrossRef]

Article

Teachers as Learners: The Impact of Teachers' Morphological Awareness on Vocabulary Instruction

Joanna Newton

George Mason University, Fairfax, VA 22030, USA; jnewton6@gmu.edu

Received: 31 July 2018; Accepted: 25 September 2018; Published: 28 September 2018

Abstract: Academic vocabulary knowledge is central to reading and academic achievement. Largely based in the lexicons of Latin and Greek, academic vocabulary comprises morphemic structures. Many teachers devote little time to focused instruction in this area because they may lack pertinent morphological and pedagogical knowledge. This article reports findings from a broader three-year longitudinal qualitative case study that explored the experiences of three elementary teachers who engaged in professional development that included study of the morphemic features of academic vocabulary and instructional techniques. This article describes changes teachers made to practice because of their deeper understanding of Latin and Greek morphology and how to teach it. Data sources included in-depth and semistructured interviews, direct observations of classroom practice, and analysis of instructional artifacts. Data analysis revealed that all three participants moved from teacher-centered, definitional approaches towards instruction that was student-centered and focused on developing metalinguistic awareness. Instructional shifts reflected participants' new understandings about metalinguistic awareness, student-directed problem-solving, and collaborative talk in vocabulary learning. Instructional shifts address metalinguistic awareness, morphology, word consciousness, and Spanish–English cognate instruction—areas that may be overlooked in many classrooms.

Keywords: academic vocabulary instruction; morphology; cognates; metalinguistic awareness; elementary classroom teachers

---

1. Introduction

Scholars agree that the ability to understand academic vocabulary is central to reading comprehension and academic achievement for all students [1–4]. Chiefly based in the lexicons of Latin and Greek, academic vocabulary comprises complex morphemic structures that generate conceptually important terminology not always heard outside the context of school [5,6]. The primary language mode in school discourse and text, academic vocabulary is also a unique linguistic system [5,7], yet its linguistic structures are independent of home discourse for many students [7–9]. Given the complexities of academic vocabulary, Scott, Nagy, and Flinspach have argued that "Learning to use academic language is one of the greatest challenges of schooling" [7] (p. 185).

A growing body of research has found evidence that explicit instruction in Latin and Greek morphology may be an effective means of helping students develop academic vocabulary knowledge [10,11]. In fact, 76% of high-frequency academic words that students learn in school share morphological roots [12]. Morphological roots provide semantic links between words, resulting in morphological word families [5]. Through analysis of these morphemic patterns, students can make connections between words that are semantically and conceptually related [11]. Moreover, familiar morphemes can generate or be present in hundreds of words [13]. Consequently, instruction in morphological analysis can not only increase definitional knowledge but also help students infer the meanings of unknown words they encounter in academic texts [10,11]. In addition to teaching the meanings of commonly occurring morphemes, scholars have recommended building metalinguistic awareness by teaching students about the structure of academic words: how morphemes—namely prefixes, suffixes, and bases—fit together to make words [14]. The development of metalinguistic awareness is a crucial component of vocabulary instruction because it can provide students with strategies to determine the meanings of unknown words independently and develop word consciousness: an awareness of and interest in words [11,12,15,16].

While this approach has long been advocated for upper-elementary students, recent research results have provided evidence as to the efficacy of this approach with primary students as well [17–19]. Furthermore, there is compelling evidence that the approach supports students from low-income and Spanish-speaking backgrounds [20]. Yet despite scholarly consensus on the critical need for consistent, purposeful, and effective vocabulary instruction, several decades of research indicate that academic vocabulary has long been undertaught across grade levels [21–27]. One reason why teachers may not adequately address vocabulary is because they themselves often lack metalinguistic and pedagogical knowledge about academic vocabulary [5]. To teach academic vocabulary effectively and develop students' metalinguistic awareness, teachers themselves must first understand the intricate linguistic features and morphological structures that comprise the academic register. To achieve these ends, teachers need opportunities to engage in extended, focused study of the linguistic and morphemic structures of academic vocabulary so that they can develop their knowledge of this instructional domain. This should be paired with opportunities to learn effective and research-based instructional techniques and consistently implement those strategies in their classrooms.

While there have been increasing calls for more pedagogical attention to academic vocabulary [5,7,28,29], to date there has been little sustained research about how to raise teachers' awareness of, and expertise in, the instruction of academic vocabulary [30–32]. This article reports findings from a longitudinal instrumental qualitative case study [33] that examined the experiences of three elementary teachers who engaged in extensive professional development that included the study of Greek and Latin morphology in addition to effective strategies for instruction of academic vocabulary [34]. The larger study was guided by several research questions that explored changes teachers made to practice as well as factors that impacted attempts to alter instruction. In addition, the broader study investigated teachers' perceptions about vocabulary instruction and the impact of professional development on their beliefs and practices. This article describes specific changes the teachers made to their vocabulary instruction over three years as a result of their deeper understanding of Latin and Greek morphology and how to teach it.

2. Materials and Methods

Since the study's objective was to describe how the participants themselves understood their professional experience, an instrumental, multiple case study design [33] was used. The participants, three elementary classroom teachers in a public Title I school in the Northeastern United States, were purposefully selected from a larger group of teachers who engaged in a yearlong site-based professional development cohort. While each participant's story was unique, analysis of their cumulative experiences generated insights about how teachers learned about and implemented vocabulary instruction.

To determine what, if any, instructional changes occurred as a result of participant experiences, the study employed a variety of data sources, including in-depth and semistructured interviews, direct observations of classroom practices, and instructional artifacts [34]. Each participant was interviewed three times throughout the course of the study, for a total of nine interviews. To learn how participants approached vocabulary instruction, direct observations of classroom instruction were conducted. Each participant's instruction was observed three times, for a total of nine classroom observations. Instructional artifacts including lesson plans and student work samples were also analyzed.

Data were analyzed from a social constructivist perspective using the constant comparative method [35]. A social constructivist approach recognizes multiple perspectives without privileging the realities of some over others [36]. This stance values the complexity of thought, experience, and social interaction from which participants' worldviews and perceptions emerged [37]. Therefore, to ensure accurate and ethical representation of each participant's experiences, descriptive narratives captured participants' own voices whenever possible.

Data analysis occurred in two stages: (1) within-case analysis and (2) cross-case analysis. The constant comparative method was used throughout both stages of data analysis. First, each case was analyzed individually. Through inductive analysis, categories were generated and a profile of each participant was constructed. Second, a cross-case analysis of categories revealed common patterns and trends that resulted in tentative findings. Third, findings were compared to the research question under scrutiny and conclusions were drawn.

To reduce researcher bias and ensure that conclusions were firmly grounded in the data, triangulation occurred through the use of multiple data sources and member checks. Several credibility strategies were employed throughout the processes of data collection, analysis, and writing to ensure that the research process was rigorous and that findings were supported by the evidence. The following credibility strategies were used: long-term involvement, analytic memos, critical friend, and intercoder reliability [38].

2.1. Context of the Study

The study was conducted at Phillis Wheatley Elementary School (PWES). (PWES is a pseudonym.) PWES is in a large public school district in the Northeastern United States, located outside a major metropolitan area. PWES serves a student population that is culturally, linguistically, and economically diverse. At the time of the study, a large percentage of students spoke languages other than English in their homes and therefore qualified as English Language Learners (ELLs).

Administrators at PWES had identified academic vocabulary knowledge as an area of need for students and requested professional development on this topic for teachers. Over the course of one academic year, teachers engaged in monthly cohort sessions in which they studied the linguistic and morphemic structures of academic vocabulary as well as instructional techniques. The researcher designed the professional development, developed the content, and facilitated all sessions. During each cohort session, participants explored morphological roots and Spanish–English cognates—the morphological origins words share across the Spanish and English lexicons [5]. The professional text *Greek and Latin Roots: Keys to Building Vocabulary* [39] was used as the primary resource for the group. Each cohort session also included opportunities for teachers to engage in collegial discourse, plan for the implementation of new techniques in their classrooms, and reflect on practice with peers.

2.2. Participants

Study participants were three veteran classroom teachers at PWES who participated in the yearlong professional development cohort. All three participants were Caucasian females. At the time of the study, two of the participants—Lisa and Kim—were third grade teachers. Lisa was in her 5th year of teaching, while Kim was in her 20th year. The third participant, Mandy, was a fourth grade teacher, also in her 5th year of teaching. All three teachers had taught at PWES for the duration of their careers; Lisa transferred to another district school during the third year of the study.

3. Results

Study results indicate that all three participants made and sustained changes to instructional practice. Two broad themes emerged: (1) the shift from a definitional approach to a metalinguistic approach, and (2) a focus on student-led problem-solving and collaborative talk in vocabulary learning.

3.1. Shift to a Metalinguistic Approach

At the onset of the study, all three participants described similar instructional routines in which they taught vocabulary by providing students with definitions of words during content area or reading instruction. There was some variance in instructional technique, ranging from asking students to look up word meanings in glossaries to teacher-provided explanations of vocabulary during reading instruction. The central focus of instruction, however, was teacher-directed presentation of individual word meanings.

Over the course of the study, participants moved from teacher-centered, definitional instructional approaches towards instruction that was student-centered and focused on developing metalinguistic awareness. These instructional shifts reflected participants' new understandings about the role of morphology, metalinguistic awareness, and student-led problem-solving in vocabulary learning.

Lisa's journey exemplifies this instructional transition. At the onset of the professional development, Lisa described her approach to vocabulary instruction as "kind of sporadic" and "spoon-feeding." She expressed frustration with this approach, feeling it did not adequately address her students' vocabulary needs, particularly as the majority of students were learning English as an additional language. Lisa depicted her instructional routine as "here, these are the words and good luck," noting that she was "giving it [definitions of words] to them. They're not being problem-solvers and trying to figure out the words."

Lisa gradually moved from a focus on providing students with word meanings to the implementation of an approach that emphasized instruction in Greek and Latin roots and word analysis skills. After completing the professional development, a driving instructional objective for Lisa was that students learn the linguistic structures of academic vocabulary and "see that there's a reason why our language was created this way." She shared that this metalinguistic approach deepened her students' understanding about words, allowing them to better decipher the meanings of unknown words. She explained, "I feel like I'm opening up a whole big chunk of words, like the prefix, like they know the meaning of the prefix! Like *re* means this or *pre* means that..." Lisa felt that this approach enabled her students to become more independent as problem-solvers and less reliant on her for support. She elaborated, "They're being problem-solvers by understanding that words are broken into parts and they can analyze the words. They're not being told, 'This word means this and then study it for a test.'"

After participating in the professional development group, Kim employed a similar instructional routine. Kim introduced the study of Greek and Latin roots as part of her content area instruction. This involved moving from content area word lists towards explicitly teaching Greek and Latin roots that frequently occurred in specific areas of study. Kim collaborated with grade level teammates, who were also participating in the cohort, to identify roots that frequently occurred in units of study. She taught these roots to her students, focusing on one or two roots per instructional unit. After introducing the root she showed students how "to break down vocabulary into meaning." This approach involved "pulling out bases and suffixes and prefixes and showing how those go together" to comprise the meaning of the word. Kim likened her new instructional approach to a code:

> It's just so different; it's almost like a code . . . it's like breaking a code, like being a detective. You know, going in and saying: 'Oh, well I can figure that out because I know what this means. Or I can at least give a good guess based on content and what I know that root means.'

All three participants observed that as they broadened their practice to include metalinguistic awareness, they noticed increased student engagement. Specifically, participants noted increased engagement and participation amongst their Spanish-speaking students who had previously struggled with academic vocabulary acquisition. They attributed this to the explicit instructional attention to Spanish–English cognates that became a regular component of their new instructional practices. Mandy, in particular, emphasized Spanish–English cognates as part of her vocabulary instruction. She explained,

> It is great for ELLs! Drawing that connection for them really helps them to not only build their vocabulary but also gives them a lot of the skills to use when they're thinking about words and their meanings. It gives them a key almost to unlock this door.

Kim noted that as a result of cognate instruction, language learning extended beyond the parameters of the classroom for her Spanish speakers. She recalled one student's spontaneous recognition of the Spanish–English cognate *parasol* while on the playground.

> When it's sunny I use a parasol because I don't like sun on me. And one day, we were walking out and one of my students said, 'Parasol—para sol? For sun?' Oh my God! It was, 'For sun!' I was like, 'Oh my God!' *Sol* is *sun* and *para* is *for*—parasol! Isn't that so cool?!

Participants' insights about the impact of their vocabulary instruction on student engagement for Spanish-speaking students who were learning English was particularly meaningful as all three participants had expressed concern about the demands of academic language on these students at the onset of the study.

3.2. Student Problem-Solving and Collaborative Talk

At the onset of the study, Lisa, Mandy, and Kim offered students few opportunities to collaborate and problem-solve about language. As they engaged in sustained professional development, participants shifted instruction to include opportunities for students to work collaboratively and apply their understanding of linguistic structures to decipher word meanings. This was a marked shift from an earlier instructional approach in which students relied on the teacher for word meanings.

Of special note was the participants' increased use of instructional time for students to talk with each other about words that either challenged or interested them. In addition, all three participants deliberately provided opportunities for students to apply their developing skills through a variety of hands-on and collaborative learning experiences, including word play activities such as student-created word spokes, webs, graffiti boards, and riddles that engaged students in peer talk. As a result of these student-centered instructional approaches, participants noted a surge in students' engagement with and enthusiasm about word learning. Lisa explained,

> I didn't realize that there would be so much student talk versus teacher talk. It's good for them to be talking about words! That was my biggest take-away: that it's okay for kids to talk about these words and it's okay for the classroom to be loud! So many times I felt like I needed to have kids diligently doing work at their desks and it doesn't need to be like that for them to learn; that might not be the best thing for them. So, what I took away was the student talk and realizing that they can be enthusiastic learners and they can be interested in where words come from and what they mean.

Building students' word awareness was an integral component of this problem-solving approach. Mandy prompted students to notice prefixes and suffixes they studied as they read and wrote: "I would have them try to be aware, as they're reading, and have them write down in their independent reading or guided reading the times when they saw that prefix and then we would share those." Mandy engaged students as word learners by "giving the students a chance to talk about things with each other and reflect on things that they've learned through conversations about words."

Mandy believed that as students became more word-aware, their engagement increased:

> I remember students being excited when they found words that they had learned, or prefixes that they had learned, in their independent reading. They would find them on their own and they would be so excited about it, so that was really cool to see!

At times, instructional shifts were difficult for the participants because it required them to alter instructional identities, moving from positions in which they assumed authority for word knowledge toward an instructional stance that allowed for ambiguity as students engaged as problem-solvers. Lisa explained that this shift required her to "step away from always wanting to be right and always wanting to have the answer." These instructional changes occurred gradually as each participant cultivated her own understanding of vocabulary teaching and learning. As participants deepened their own understandings of academic vocabulary and how to teach it, they made changes that reflected newfound insights about the value of student talk, engagement, and problem-solving in vocabulary learning.

4. Discussions

As demonstrated above, all three participants underwent significant changes to their instructional practice. These changes were generated largely by the participants' deepened understanding of the linguistic structures of academic vocabulary. As part of the professional development cohort, Lisa, Mandy, and Kim had consistently engaged in extended and focused study about the linguistic and morphemic structures of academic language. As they themselves engaged in word analysis, they developed new insights about the importance of morphology, metalinguistic awareness, and problem-solving. When Lisa, Mandy, and Kim became vocabulary students themselves, they realized that students needed more than definitions and isolated word instruction: they needed to understand how language works. Ultimately, this experience led to what Kim characterized as a "shift in thinking." This shift facilitated the changes participants made to practice.

For all participants, this experience was the first time they had ever studied the linguistic and morphemic structures of academic vocabulary. As Lisa, Mandy, and Kim acquired a deeper understanding of the role of morphology in academic vocabulary, they came to understand the concept of metalinguistic awareness. As a result, all three participants moved away from instruction that was mostly definitional and teacher-directed. They adopted student-centered instructional techniques focused on the morphemic structures of words and problem-solving strategies that enabled students to become independent and strategic word learners.

Researchers agree that the depth of a teacher's knowledge about an instructional domain significantly influences instructional practice [22,40]. Results of this study are consistent with this body of scholarship. As Lisa, Mandy, and Kim deepened their knowledge of academic vocabulary and instructional techniques they made dramatic changes in their practice from teacher-directed definitional approaches to student-directed problem-solving approaches. Furthermore, it was their new understanding of the morphological foundation of academic vocabulary that served as the catalyst for this new instructional approach. Results of this study suggest that when given sufficient instruction and time to engage in extended, focused study of the linguistic and morphemic structures of academic vocabulary, teachers can develop both their content and pedagogical knowledge of this instructional domain.

Increasingly, research has established that vocabulary instruction must address both definitional and metalinguistic word knowledge [41,42]. Similarly, to understand the complexities of academic vocabulary, teachers must provide frequent and consistent opportunities for students to learn new words in a variety of contexts, acquire a range of word-solving strategies, develop metalinguistic awareness, and become word conscious [14,42–44]. Yet, to date, a sustained focus on the development of metalinguistic awareness and word consciousness is often overlooked [24].

The instructional shifts Lisa, Mandy, and Kim made are therefore particularly important because they address metalinguistic awareness and word consciousness. As Lisa, Mandy, and Kim taught from a metalinguistic stance they observed that their students developed word consciousness [15]. Word consciousness is an important element of word learning because it increases motivation to learn about language [15]. While this study did not include a measure of students' vocabulary achievement, participants noticed that as students developed metalinguistic awareness, their engagement with academic language and word consciousness improved [34].

In addition, it is noteworthy that instruction in Spanish–English cognates appeared to be beneficial for Spanish-speaking students. Again, while this study did not include a formal measure of students' vocabulary acquisition, participants noted significant changes in their Spanish-speaking students' engagement with vocabulary and increased independence as problem-solvers when they taught from a metalinguistic approach. This finding is consistent with earlier research that suggests instruction in Spanish–English cognates may be an effective means of supporting vocabulary development for Spanish-speaking students [20,45]. Analysis of academic texts has determined that one-third of English words in academic texts have Spanish cognates [46]. Given this abundance of Spanish–English cognates in the academic register, cognate instruction may be an effective means of increasing access to academic vocabulary for all learners, but especially for those students who are familiar with Spanish.

This finding may be particularly important as research suggests that Spanish-speaking students who are learning English may be at increased risk of low academic achievement due to limited academic vocabulary knowledge [47]. Yet, while a growing number of scholars have called for increased instructional attention to cognate connections between Spanish and English [5,29,48], this appears to be an area that is currently undertaught in many classrooms [20]. It is noteworthy that prior to participation in professional development, all three participants expressed minimal awareness of Spanish–English cognates or their role in vocabulary instruction. This is concerning given that a large percentage of students at PWES spoke Spanish as a first language. Results of this study suggest that professional development that includes explicit attention to Spanish–English cognates may be one way to deepen teachers' knowledge of this important component of academic vocabulary instruction.

While earlier research has suggested that focused study of instructional content can lead to improvements in practice [49], this is the first study to explore the impact of focused study of academic vocabulary as a content area. As Lisa, Mandy, and Kim's understanding of academic vocabulary developed, each became better equipped to teach it to her students. As each teacher deepened her knowledge of academic vocabulary, she made shifts in practice, often in instructional areas that appear to be undertaught [20,24]. Results of this study suggest that teachers need time to engage in extended, focused study of the linguistic and morphemic structures of academic vocabulary so that they can develop their knowledge of this instructional domain and enrich students' experiences with academic vocabulary.

Funding: This study had no funders. Therefore, funders had no role in the design of the study; in the collection, analyses, or interpretation of data; in the writing of the manuscript, and in the decision to publish the results.

Conflicts of Interest: The author declares no conflicts of interest.

References

1. Beck, I.L.; Perfetti, C.A.; McKeown, M.G. Effects of long-term vocabulary instruction on lexical access and reading comprehension. *J. Educ. Psychol.* **1982**, *74*, 506–521. [CrossRef]
2. Biemiller, A. Teaching vocabulary: Early, direct and sequential. *Am. Educ.* **2001**, *25*, 24–28.
3. Hart, B.; Risley, T. *Meaningful Differences in the Everyday Experiences of Young American Children*; Brookes Publishing: Baltimore, MD, USA, 1995; ISBN 1-55766-197-9.
4. Stanovich, K.E. Matthew effects in reading: Some consequences of individual differences in the acquisition of literacy. *Read. Res. Q.* **1986**, *21*, 360–407. [CrossRef]
5. Hiebert, E.H.; Lubliner, S. The nature, learning and instruction of general academic vocabulary. In *What Research Has to Say about Vocabulary Instruction*; Farstrup, A.E., Samuels, S.J., Eds.; International Reading Association: Newark, DE, USA, 2008; pp. 106–129, ISBN 978-0-87207-698-3.
6. Padak, N.; Newton, E.; Rasinski, T.; Newton, R.M. Getting to the root of word study: Teaching Latin and Greek word roots in elementary and middle grades. In *What Research Has to Say about Vocabulary Instruction*; Farstrup, A.E., Samuels, S.J., Eds.; International Reading Association: Newark, DE, USA, 2008; pp. 6–31, ISBN 978-0-87207-698-3.
7. Scott, J.A.; Nagy, W.E.; Flinspach, S.L. More than merely words: Redefining vocabulary learning in a culturally and linguistically diverse society. In *What Research Has to Say about Vocabulary Instruction*; Farstrup, A.E., Samuels, S.J., Eds.; International Reading Association: Newark, DE, USA, 2008; pp. 182–210, ISBN 978-0-87207-698-3.
8. Gee, J.P. Reading as situated language: A sociocognitive perspective. In *Theoretical Models and Processes of Reading*, 5th ed.; Ruddell, R., Unrau, N., Eds.; International Reading Association: Newark, DE, USA, 2004; pp. 116–132, ISBN 0-87207-502-8.

9. Heath, S.B. *Ways with Words: Language, Life and Work in Communities and Classrooms*; Cambridge University Press: New York, NY, USA, 1983; ISBN 0-521-27319-6.
10. Kieffer, M.J.; Lesaux, N.K. Effects of academic language instruction on relational and syntactic aspects of morphological awareness for sixth graders from linguistically diverse backgrounds. *Elem. Sch. J.* **2012**, *112*, 519–545. [CrossRef]
11. Carlisle, J.F.; McBride-Chang, C.; Nagy, W.E.; Nunes, T. Effects of instruction in morphological awareness on literacy achievement: An integrative review. *Read. Res. Q.* **2010**, *45*, 464–487. [CrossRef]
12. Coxhead, A. A new academic word list. *TESOL Q.* **2000**, *34*, 213–238. [CrossRef]
13. Nagy, W.E.; Anderson, R.C.; Schommer, M.; Scott, J.A.; Stallman, A. Morphological families in the internal lexicon. *Read. Res. Q.* **1989**, *24*, 262–282. [CrossRef]
14. Blachowicz, C.L.Z.; Fisher, P. *Teaching Vocabulary in All Classrooms*, 4th ed.; Allyn & Bacon: Boston, MA, USA, 2009; ISBN 0-13-041839-0.
15. Graves, M.F. *The Vocabulary Book: Learning and Instruction*; Teachers College Press: New York, NY, USA, 2006; ISBN 0-8077-4627-4.
16. Nagy, W.E.; Beringer, V.W.; Abbott, R.D. Contributions of morphology beyond phonology to literacy outcomes of upper-elementary and middle-school students. *J. Educ. Psychol.* **2006**, *98*, 134–147. [CrossRef]
17. Biemiller, A. Size and sequence in vocabulary development: Implications for choosing words for primary grade vocabulary instruction. In *Teaching and Learning Vocabulary: Bringing Research to Practice*; Hiebert, E.H., Kamil, M.L., Eds.; Lawrence Erlbaum Associates Publishers: Mahwah, NJ, USA, 2005; pp. 223–242, ISBN 0-8058-5286-7.
18. Carlisle, J.F. Awareness of the structure and meaning of morphologically complex words: Impact on reading. *Read. Writ. Interdiscip. J.* **2000**, *12*, 169–190. [CrossRef]
19. Mountain, L. Rooting out meaning: More morphemic analysis for primary pupils. *Read. Teach.* **2005**, *58*, 742–749. [CrossRef]
20. Carlo, M.S.; August, D.; Snow, C.E. Sustained vocabulary-learning strategy instruction for English language learners. In *Teaching and Learning Vocabulary: Bringing Research to Practice*; Hiebert, E.H., Kamil, M.L., Eds.; Lawrence Erlbaum Associates Publishers: Mahwah, NJ, USA, 2005; pp. 137–153.
21. Blachowicz, C.L.Z. Vocabulary instruction? What goes on in the classroom? *Read. Teach.* **1987**, *41*, 132–137.
22. Cunningham, A.E.; Zibulsky, J.; Stanovich, K.; Stanovich, P.J. How teachers would spend their time teaching language arts: The mismatch between self-reported and best practices. *J. Learn. Disabil.* **2009**, *42*, 418–430. [CrossRef] [PubMed]
23. Durkin, D.D. What classroom observations reveal about reading comprehension. *Read. Res. Q.* **1978**, *14*, 481–533. [CrossRef]
24. Nelson, K.L.; Dole, J.A.; Hosp, J.L.; Hosp, M.K. Vocabulary instruction in K-3 low-income classrooms during a reading reform project. *Read. Psychol.* **2015**, *36*, 145–172. [CrossRef]
25. Scott, J.A.; Jamieson-Noel, D.; Asselin, M. Vocabulary instruction throughout the day in twenty-three Canadian upper-elementary classrooms. *Elem. Sch. J.* **2003**, *103*, 269–286. [CrossRef]
26. Spear-Swerling, L.; Zibulsky, J. Making time for literacy: Teacher knowledge and time allocation in instructional planning. *Read. Writ.* **2014**, *27*, 1353–1378. [CrossRef]
27. Watts, S.M. Vocabulary instruction during reading lessons in six classrooms. *J. Read. Behav.* **1995**, *27*, 399–424. [CrossRef]
28. Bravo, M.A.; Cervetti, G.N. Teaching vocabulary through text and experience in content areas. In *What Research Has to Say about Vocabulary Instruction*; Farstrup, A.E., Samuels, S.J., Eds.; International Reading Association: Newark, DE, USA, 2008; pp. 130–149, ISBN 978-0-87207-698-3.
29. Harmon, J.M.; Wood, K.D.; Hedrick, W.B. Vocabulary instruction in middle and secondary content classrooms: Understandings and directions from research. In *What Research Has to Say about Vocabulary Instruction*; Farstrup, A.E., Samuels, S.J., Eds.; International Reading Association: Newark, DE, USA, 2008; pp. 150–181, ISBN 978-0-87207-698-3.
30. Berne, J.I.; Blachowicz, C.L.Z. What reading teachers say about vocabulary instruction: Voices from the classroom. *Read. Teach.* **2008**, *62*, 314–323. [CrossRef]
31. Blachowicz, C.L.Z.; Fisher, P.; Ogle, D.; Watts-Taffe, S. Vocabulary: Questions from the classroom. *Read. Res. Q.* **2006**, *41*, 524–539. [CrossRef]

32. Konopak, B.C.; Williams, N.L. Elementary teachers' beliefs and decisions about vocabulary learning and instruction. In *43rd Yearbook of the National Reading Conference*; Kinzer, C.K., Leu, D.J., Eds.; National Reading Conference: Chicago, IL, USA, 1994; pp. 485–495. ISSN 0547-8375.

33. Stake, R.E. *The Art of Case Study Research*; Sage Publications: Thousand Oaks, CA, USA, 1995; ISBN 978-0803957671.

34. Newton, J. Teachers' Experiences with Professional Development and a Morphological Approach to Vocabulary Instruction. Ph.D. Thesis, George Mason University, Fairfax, VA, USA, May 2018.

35. Glaser, B.G.; Strauss, A.L. *The Discovery of Grounded Theory.*; Aldine Publishing Company: New York, NY, USA, 1967; ISBN 0202302601.

36. Lincoln, Y.S.; Lynham, S.A.; Guba, E.G. Paradigmatic controversies, contradictions and emerging confluences, revisited. In *The Landscape of Qualitative Research*, 4th ed.; Denzin, N.K., Lincoln, Y.S., Eds.; Sage: Thousand Oaks, CA, USA, 2013; pp. 199–265, ISBN 978-1-4522-5806-5.

37. Guba, E.G.; Lincoln, Y.S. Paradigmatic controversies, contradictions and emerging confluences. In *The SAGE Handbook of Qualitative Research*, 3rd ed.; Denzin, N.K., Lincoln, Y.S., Eds.; Sage: Thousand Oaks, CA, USA, 2005; pp. 191–215, ISBN 0761927573.

38. Merriam, S.B. *Qualitative Research and Case Study Applications in Education*; Jossey-Bass Publishers: San Francisco, CA, USA, 1998; ISBN 0-7879-1009-0.

39. Rasinski, T.V.; Padak, N.; Newton, R.M.; Newton, E. *Greek and Latin Roots: Keys to Building Vocabulary*; Shell Education: Huntington Beach, CA, USA, 2009; ISBN 978-1-4258-0472-5.

40. Desimone, L.M.; Smith, T.M.; Phillips, K.J.R. Linking student achievement growth to professional development participation and changes in instruction: A longitudinal study of elementary students and teachers in Title I schools. *Teach. Coll. Rec.* **2015**, *115*, 1–46.

41. Nagy, W.E.; Scott, J.A. Vocabulary processes. In *Handbook of Reading Research*; Kamil, M.L., Mosenthal, P.B., Pearson, P.D., Barr, R., Eds.; Lawrence Erlbaum Associates Publishers: Mahwah, NJ, USA, 2000; pp. 269–284, ISBN 0-8058-2399-9.

42. Stahl, S.A.; Fairbanks, M. The effects of vocabulary instruction: A model-based meta-analysis. *Rev. Edcu. Res.* **1986**, *56*, 72–110. [CrossRef]

43. Graves, M.F. Instruction on individual words: One size does not fit all. In *What Research Has to Say about Vocabulary Instruction*; Farstrup, A.E., Samuels, S.J., Eds.; International Reading Association: Newark, DE, USA, 2008; pp. 56–79, ISBN 978-0-87207-698-3.

44. Newton, E.; Padak, N.D.; Rasinski, T.V. *Evidence-Based Instruction in Reading: A Professional Development Guide to Vocabulary*; Pearson Education: Boston, MA, USA, 2008; ISBN 978-0-205-45631-4.

45. Kieffer, M.J.; Lesaux, N.K. The role of derivational morphology in the reading comprehension of Spanish-speaking English language learners. *Read. Writ. Interdiscip. J.* **2007**, *21*, 783–804. [CrossRef]

46. Nash, R. *NTC's Dictionary of Spanish Cognates*; NTC Publishing: Lincolnwood, IL, USA, 1997; ISBN 9780844279619.

47. Garcia, G.E. Factors influencing the English reading test performance on Spanish-speaking Hispanic students. *Read. Res. Q.* **1991**, *26*, 371–392. [CrossRef]

48. Robinson, P.J. Teaching key vocabulary in geography and science classrooms: An analysis of teachers' practices with particular reference to EAL pupils' learning. *Lang. Educ.* **2005**, *19*, 428–445. [CrossRef]

49. Strickland, D.S.; Snow, C.; Griffin, P.; Burns, M.S.; McNamara, P. *Preparing Our Teachers: Opportunities for Better Reading Instruction*; Joseph Henry Press: Washington, DC, USA, 2002; ISBN 0-309-07445-2.

Article

Observations of Vocabulary Activities during Second- and Third-Grade Reading Lessons

Nicole Sparapani [1,*], Joanne F. Carlisle [2] and Carol McDonald Connor [3]

[1]   School of Education, University of California, Davis, Davis, CA 91616, USA
[2]   School of Education, University of Michigan, Ann Arbor, MI 48109, USA; jfcarl@umich.edu
[3]   School of Education, University of California, Irvine, Irvine, CA 92697, USA; connorcm@uci.edu
*   Correspondence: njsparapani@ucdavis.edu

Received: 26 September 2018; Accepted: 7 November 2018; Published: 12 November 2018

Abstract: Vocabulary instruction is a critical component of language and literacy lessons, yet few studies have examined the nature and extent of vocabulary activities in early elementary classrooms. We explored vocabulary activities during reading lessons using video observations in a sample of 2nd- and 3rd-grade students (n = 228) and their teachers (n = 38). Teachers spent more time in vocabulary activities than has been previously observed. In the fall, 28% of their literacy block was devoted to vocabulary in 2nd grade and 38% in 3rd grade. Our findings suggest that vocabulary activities were most likely to take place prior to reading a text—teachers rarely followed-up initial vocabulary activities after text reading. Analysis of teachers' discourse moves showed more instructional comments and short-answer questions than other moves; students most frequently engaged in participating talk, such as providing short, simple answers to questions. Students engaged in significantly more talk during vocabulary activities (including generative talk such as initiating an idea) in the spring of 3rd grade than the spring of 2nd grade. These data contribute descriptive information about how teachers engage their students in vocabulary learning during the early elementary years. We discuss implications for practice and future research directions.

Keywords: vocabulary instruction; vocabulary activities; teacher discourse moves; student responses; early elementary

---

1. Observations of Vocabulary Activities during Second- and Third-Grade Reading Lessons

Across studies and over time, scholars have found that students' vocabulary knowledge is significantly associated with their achievement in reading comprehension [1–4]. This is the case for students in the early stages of learning to read as well as the middle- and high-school years [1,5,6]. The connection between vocabulary knowledge and reading comprehension achievement is both specific (that is, a large number of unfamiliar words make a text hard to understand) and general (that is, limited vocabulary is associated with limited achievement in reading comprehension [4,7–9].

Children come to school with varying funds of vocabulary knowledge that are largely attributable to the opportunities they have to learn words in their homes and communities [10]. Learning to read provides all students opportunities to learn new words, but even so, differences in vocabulary knowledge tend to persist through the elementary years [1,11]. The consensus is that instruction in vocabulary should begin when children start school, involve the development of oral and print vocabulary, and be a regular component of teachers' reading lessons [12–16].

In recent years, there has been considerable interest in determining effective methods for teaching vocabulary skills. According to Hairrell, Rupley, and Simmons [17], six reviews and two meta-analyses centered on methods of vocabulary instruction have been published between 1998 and 2009. Most recently, Wright and Cervetti [9] reviewed 36 studies that examined the effects of vocabulary instruction on reading comprehension. In theory, the extent of students' word knowledge (both depth and breadth) contributes to their comprehension of texts [4,18,19]. The number of different words they know and the depth of their knowledge further contribute to how well they grasp ideas and information in written texts. Yet, acquiring depth of knowledge about words takes time, practice, and experience [20], thus, it is not surprising that exposure to a variety of instructional methods and reinforcement of concepts through a variety of activities is one promising approach to support vocabulary development [2,9].

The National Reading Panel report [2] emphasized the value of direct instruction, repeated or multiple exposures to words, learning words in rich contexts, and students' active engagement in literacy activities. Similar recommendations are found in other reviews and meta-analyses [17]; however, recent research has shown that some methods appear to be more effective than others. Wright and Cervetti [9] reported that neither direct teaching of word meanings nor instruction in just one or two strategies has a significant effect on general measures of reading comprehension. More promising are methods that require students to participate in active processing of words and their meanings, involving a variety of different types of word-learning strategies [4].

Of considerable concern is the fact that few studies have examined the methods and time teachers actually devote to vocabulary instruction, especially in the early elementary years. As a result, we do not know whether teachers' practices conform to findings of studies that have identified effective methods of vocabulary instruction. This gap in our knowledge of early literacy instruction is important to address because 60% of fourth graders lag behind standards for proficiency in reading comprehension [21]. The RAND study group [3] highlights this issue by asking; "How does the teaching community ensure that all children have the vocabulary and background knowledge they need to comprehend certain content areas and advanced texts?"

The results of several observational studies in the early grades suggest limited attention to vocabulary instruction and a tendency to provide brief definitions or explanations of words. For example, Wright and Neuman [16] found that teachers tended to provide in-the-moment explanations of words encountered in books they read to their kindergartners. Explanation of a word's meaning was very brief, and there were no systematic efforts to reinforce students' understanding of words. Two other recent studies have used audiorecorded vocabulary instruction in early elementary classrooms to characterize the nature of teachers' discourse during vocabulary activities [22,23]. Their results confirm the frequency of the kinds of brief explanations of word meanings that Wright and Neuman [16] found in their kindergarten observations.

While there is much we need to know about vocabulary instruction in early elementary classrooms, we do know that a number of books suggesting methods of teaching vocabulary are available to teachers [20,24–26]. Most core or comprehensive reading programs include systematic vocabulary activities that teachers are advised or required to use. Teachers in Wanzek's [23] focus groups, for example, indicated that their vocabulary instruction consisted of reviewing the word list for a given text recommended by the core reading program. They also reported feeling strapped for time—not having enough instructional time to target all the vocabulary activities outlined within the core reading program. As a practical matter, educators might benefit from further studies of current practices in teaching vocabulary in early elementary classrooms, with the goal of understanding the extent to which practices meet standards and expectations derived from theories and results of empirical studies. Because student uptake of lessons is critical [27], there is value to having information about teachers' instructional practices during vocabulary activities and students' participation in these activities. This would constitute a first step toward determining whether students receive adequate opportunities to develop the vocabulary knowledge they need to comprehend increasingly challenging academic texts.

2. Teaching Vocabulary within the Context of Reading Lessons

In an effort to understand current instruction in vocabulary in the elementary years, we carried out a study in which we analyzed observations of entire reading lessons (i.e., the literacy block) in

2nd and 3rd-grade classrooms in the fall and spring. Within these lessons, we focused specifically on teachers' activities involving oral language and print vocabulary. In early elementary classrooms, studies have suggested that teachers tend to integrate instruction in various areas of reading during lessons. They might plan lessons that include any of the five foundational skills that the National Reading Panel Report considered essential components of reading instruction [2]: phonemic awareness, decoding, vocabulary, fluency, and comprehension. They also might adjust their planned lessons to meet students' needs—for example, by reviewing the meaning or pronunciation of words as students are reading and discussing a text. Thus, in our study, we examined vocabulary activities within the context of such lessons.

Teachers' integration of instruction across various areas of reading had implications for our study. One was the expectation that instruction would go beyond memorizing definitions; teachers would embrace activities that build conceptual representations, and when necessary, use discourse moves to help students integrate word meanings with their existing knowledge [9]. Another was the expectation that some vocabulary activities would be planned and others spontaneous; there are times, for example, when anything more than a brief explanation of a word would disrupt the flow of a lesson [14]. In both cases the teacher needs to help the students link the meaning of a new word to their previous knowledge or experience. The two examples below (excerpts from observations of early elementary classrooms) illustrate this. In the first example, the teacher reviews vocabulary words with her students prior to reading the text, she makes an effort to link the word's meaning to a student-friendly usage. The second example illustrates a brief exchange while reading a text in which the teacher uses the students' personal experience to help them understand the meaning of a word.

In the following example, the teacher is directing a small group of four students. She first calls the students to the carpet to review the vocabulary words that they will see in the story they are about to read.

> T: For our vocabulary words this week, we are going to talk about the words clutch and refuse. If you clutch something, you hold it tight. If you refuse something, you do not want it. S1, if you refuse to do something, are you going to do it or are you not going to do it?
> S1: Not going to do it.
> T: Right. If you refuse something, you are not going to do it. Now, I'm going to name things that you might clutch or refuse. If you think you should clutch, do this with your hands [motions with hand]. If you think you should refuse it, do this with your hands [motions with hand]. Okay? [Teacher models hand motions again]. I'm going to clutch or I'm going to refuse.
> T: Monkey bars on the playground. Clutch or refuse?
> Ss: Clutch [students chorally respond].
> T: A basketball. Are you going to clutch it or refuse it?
> S1: Let it go. You are going to clutch it at first and then let it go.
> T: Good. And if you are getting the ball away from someone else, you might clutch it. Okay. Let's go get our reading books and head to the back table. We're going to read a story called the *Great Ball Game*.

In this example the teacher uses the students' experience to help them grasp the meaning of the word "vigorously." Students have read a story on their own; now the teacher is reviewing the story with them, asking them questions. One of the students is reading a portion of the text aloud, and he stops on the word "vigorously."

> T: I am guessing you are unsure about that word, right?
> Ss: [nods in agreement]
> T: Vigorously. How many people participated in the walking club outside?
> Ss: [A number of students raise their hands]
> T: So when you are walking around the track, do you go very slowly or do you go quickly?

Ss: [several say "quickly" enthusiastically]
T: So you are going vigorously; you are doing something with energy. You are not just dragging, you are doing something vigorously. Does that make sense in the sentence you just read, S1?
S1: Yeah, it does.

Because we set out to study vocabulary instruction that involved both planned and spontaneous, in-the-moment explanations and discussion of new words, our observation study may present a somewhat different picture of vocabulary learning than has been recorded by other studies, some of which focus on older students [27]. With regard to younger students, Graves [25] and Watts [15] noted that observed vocabulary instruction largely focused on pre-reading activities that most often involved looking up and writing down definitions of words. However, we were also interested in extended lessons, those that included discussions of vocabulary during and after time spent reading a text.

With regard to the time devoted to vocabulary, Watts [15] found that 10% of the time in 4th grade reading lessons was spent on vocabulary. Several more recent observation studies in the early elementary years provide some insight into both the amount of time spent on vocabulary and teachers' preferred instructional methods. Connor, Spencer, Day and colleagues [28] observed literacy lessons in 3rd-grade classrooms and reported that students spent about 5 min on average engaged in oral language and print vocabulary activities. Wanzek [23] gathered information about "direct instruction" in vocabulary in 2nd-grade classrooms. Fourteen teachers audiorecorded their literacy instruction for three sequential days; analysis of the data showed that 8% of the core reading lesson was devoted to vocabulary (the range was 0–23 min). Direct instruction in this study included a wide range of vocabulary instructional methods; the most commonly observed were giving word definitions and providing examples of word meanings. Much less common were morphology instruction, context clue instruction, semantic instruction, and discussion.

Other studies have also characterized teachers' discourse during vocabulary activities. Michener et al. [22] audiorecorded vocabulary instruction in 31 3rd–5th grade classrooms three times during the school year to examine the relation between teachers' discourse moves and students' reading comprehension outcomes. They found that two teacher discourse moves, teacher explanations and follow-up questions, predicted students' reading comprehension.

In an observational study, Carlisle, Kelcey and Berebitsky [29] examined four particular discourse practices that teachers were likely to use during vocabulary instruction in 2nd- and 3rd-grade classrooms. The most common was asking students to read vocabulary words in sentences from workbook exercises (31.6%). This finding was seen as reflecting teachers' use of the required basal program in their schools. In about 25% of the lessons, the teacher defined words and/or asked students to examine the meaning of a word in context. Far less common were asking students to define a word (9.5%) and fostering discussion (7.6%). One finding of interest was that when a teacher employed a rarer action (e.g., asking students to define a word), he or she had a high probability of employing the more common actions as well. In another study of 2nd- and 3rd-grade vocabulary activities during reading lessons, Kelcey and Carlisle [30] noted differences between common and infrequent discourse actions; explaining words or word contexts was observed in 75% of the lessons; asking questions and providing practice in 77% and 75% of the lessons respectively. Less common were fostering discussion (40%) and giving students an opportunity to ask questions (32%).

On the basis of these observational studies, we developed expectations about the actions or "moves" that we might expect 2nd- and 3rd-grade teachers to use frequently in vocabulary activities. These included the following: telling/explaining word meanings (including student-friendly usages), asking basic questions about word meanings, and asking students to read words or words in sentences aloud. Less common would be teachers' efforts to engage students in discussion of a word's meaning or asking for students' explanation of words in context—actions that stimulate students' thinking. We expected to see more use of discourse moves that engage students' thinking in the 3rd than in 2nd grade because both teachers and reading researchers have suggested that reading presents greater challenges in 3rd grade [23,31]. We had no reason to expect differences in basic discourse moves by grade level or timing of observation (fall versus spring). The example below illustrates three types of teachers' common or basic vocabulary discourse moves. To help the students understand the new vocabulary words, the teacher explains the word meanings, asks the students basic questions about the words, and asks them to read sentences that include the vocabulary words aloud.

This 2nd-grade teacher is introducing new vocabulary words during a small group vocabulary activity.

T: Now, the next word is clamber. Does anyone know what that means?
Ss: [students nod their heads "no"]
T: Clamber means to climb up something with both hands and feet.
S2: Like a puppy! When a puppy gets up, he goes like this [student acts out puppy climbing].
T: Yes, and a panda bear might also clamber up the tree to get leaves.
Ss: [students pretend to climb up a tree like a panda bear]
T: The next word is clumsy. If you are clumsy, you might trip and fall over things sometimes. Let's read a few sentences together that have the word clumsy in them.
Ss: [Teacher and students read together]. The clumsy lamb was wobbly. The clumsy puppy took a step.

However, we were aware that observing and counting the particular vocabulary discourse moves (e.g., explaining word meanings) teachers use offers a limited view of the opportunities students have to acquire deep understanding of new words. It seemed important to go beyond teaching techniques by recording and analyzing students' response to their teachers' practices. We were particularly interested in the extent to which students gave relatively rote responses to teachers' questions, as opposed to demonstrating a deeper interest in word meanings. A number of researchers [9,14,17] note that in theory students' active processing is central to word learning. Active learning may grow out of discussion in which students explore their understanding of words. Student explanations and discussion are thought to reflect the quality of their verbal reasoning and metalinguistic development [22,32]. They need to make connections between new and known information, and they need to acquire depth of knowledge about word meanings (e.g., different meanings or ways to use a word). Discussion is one way to achieve that goal, albeit not the only way. Blachowicz and Fisher [33] proposed that for instruction to be effective, it should have the goal of immersing students in exploring word meanings, taking ownership of words as they become comfortable using them orally and in their writing.

Thus, for our observations of students' engagement in the vocabulary activities, we included a set of moves focused on their basic responses (participating talk) and a set focused on their generative/interactive responses (generative talk). Examples of participating talk are answering short-answer questions or reading aloud; examples of generative talk are sharing ideas, initiating questions, and participating in a discussion. We expected that generative responses would be greater in 3rd than 2nd grade. The example below illustrates both participating and generative talk.

This 2nd-grade teacher is introducing a new text to a small group. To make sure the students understand the title, the teachers encourages them to make connections (text-to-self) with the word, celebration. The students answer her "short-answer" questions but in doing so also share ideas.

T: What does celebrations mean?
S: It's a birthday party, like when you do something fun with cake and balloons and stuff.
T: Anyone else? Another kind of celebration?
S: We celebrate Easter.
T: Okay, what else?
S: Birthday.
S: Christmas.
T: That is definitely a celebration. So our story this week is called "City Celebrations." How

could a city celebrate? What do you think it might do that? City celebrations? Have you ever heard of anything?

S: Fourth of July.

T: Could a city have a birthday?

Ss: Yes [chorally respond].

Experts in vocabulary instruction argue that students need to have a chance to experience the use and meaning of words in different contexts and have opportunities to use words. To achieve this goal, researchers suggest that learning unfamiliar words depends in large on repeated exposures [34]. Beck and McKeown [35] and Coyne et al. [36] found that extended, rich vocabulary instruction led to better learning than instruction that was rich but of relatively short duration. Thus, we expected vocabulary activities to take place at different times, relative to engagement in reading and discussing a text—that is, before reading, while reading, or after reading a text. At least some teachers were likely to carry out vocabulary activities, both before and after text reading in order to provide extended opportunities to engage in understanding unfamiliar words [35].

To summarize, our study was designed to contribute descriptive information about how teachers engage their students in vocabulary learning. One particular interest is the ways that teachers include vocabulary activities in reading lessons, as it is apparent they also use considerable portions of the literacy block to help students acquire foundational reading skills. This includes examining the duration of time teachers engage their students in oral language and print vocabulary activities as well as the timing of their instruction—whether vocabulary activities preceded and/or followed text reading within the lesson. A second interest is the nature and extent of both teachers' moves and students' participation, evaluating the frequency and types of talk teachers and students used during vocabulary activities. Information pertaining to these aspects of vocabulary instruction in the early elementary years should help guide future research designed to examine the effects of these practices on students' reading comprehension. Our overarching research question is: what do classroom observations tell us about vocabulary instruction within early elementary reading lessons? We outline our four research questions below.

1. What percentage of the reading lesson is designated to vocabulary activities, and does this vary for 2nd- and 3rd-grade students?
2. What discourse moves (those that involve basic instruction of word meanings and those that involve discussion of meanings) are teachers using during vocabulary activities, and are there differences between 2nd and 3rd grade?
3. How often are students exhibiting participating and generative talk during vocabulary activities, and are there differences between 2nd and 3rd grade?
4. When are teachers delivering vocabulary instruction during reading lessons? More specifically, what is the probability that vocabulary activities precede and/or follow text reading during the reading lesson?

3. Methods

3.1. Participants

Our study included students in second ($n = 114$) and third grade ($n = 114$) and their teachers ($n = 19$ 2nd grade; 19 3rd grade) across five schools who were drawn from a longitudinal study of reading comprehension instruction in the early elementary years between 2009 and 2011 [37]. Participating teachers and families provided informed consent after all study procedures, potential risks, and benefits were disclosed prior to the start of the study, and Institutional Review Board approval was maintained throughout the longitudinal study. Participating teachers were 96% female; 95% identified as White. They reported an average of 16 ($SD = 8.87$) years of teaching experience. Eighteen percent of the teachers reported having an M.A or M.S. degree, and 5% reported having an M.Ed. As part of the larger study, six students were randomly selected from each classroom based on their reading ability, selecting two higher achieving, two typical, and two lower-achieving students per classroom.

3.2. Procedures

All 2nd- and 3rd-grade teachers followed a 90-min district-mandated block of time devoted to literacy instruction. During this time, teachers used the district-mandated curriculum, Harcourt Trophies, and other reading materials (e.g., trade books with narrative and expository texts). As part of the larger project, reading lessons (i.e., the literacy block) were video-recorded three times across the school year, once in the fall, winter, and spring. However, the current study only utilized observations from the fall and spring of the school year. Trained research assistants coded the reading lessons using the observation system, Individualized Student Instruction (ISI) [37,38], which is a multi-dimensional observation tool that describes student-level classroom reading activities. In addition, teachers' discourse moves and students' responses were coded during teacher-managed literacy activities that centered on text-based topics using the observation system, Creating Opportunities to Learn from Text (COLT) [39]. The video observations were coded using Noldus Observer® Video-Pro Software (Noldus Information Technology, Leesburg, VA, USA, 2010). The teacher and the six target students per classroom were coded with the COLT system. Both the ISI and COLT observation systems have good reported interrater agreement, with a Cohen's Kappa coefficient score of 0.72 for ISI and scores ranging between 0.78–0.90 for COLT.

Vocabulary Activities. We analyzed the amount of time that teachers and students spent in two types of vocabulary activities (oral language and print vocabulary) during reading lessons in the fall and the spring. We also examined the frequency of teachers' discourse moves and students' responses during vocabulary activities. As outlined in the ISI observation system, oral language activities focus on increasing students' oral vocabularies (i.e., their ability to access a word's meaning upon hearing it) and/or listening and speaking skills when print or text is not present, whereas, print vocabulary activities focus on increasing students' ability to access a word's meaning upon seeing its written form. All activities outlined in the ISI observation system last at least 15 s; thus the system detects even minimal times that teachers spend teaching vocabulary as well as how they may move in and out of vocabulary activities during the reading lesson. Finally, we coded vocabulary activities without regard to grouping arrangement (whole-class and small-group sessions) because instruction did not always conform to a single format. For example, the teacher might start with the whole class, have students work in small groups for a short time, and then reconvene the whole group.

Teacher Discourse Moves and Student Responses. Our conceptualization of teachers' discourse moves and students' responses were adapted from the COLT Observation system to identify and measure teacher discourse moves that support student reading comprehension gains within early elementary classrooms. Appendix A provides a list and description of the teacher discourse moves and student responses. Full manuals are available from the authors upon request.

The COLT system outlines discourse moves that have been identified as key components in the process of teaching reading comprehension, such as efforts to extend students' talk and promote higher-order thinking. In the current study, we describe two broad categories of teacher discourse moves that, based on the research literature, we might expect 2nd- and 3rd-grade teachers to use during vocabulary activities. Basic Instruction in Word Meanings includes a set of commonly observed discourse moves, such as reading aloud to students, providing explanations, and asking short-answer questions. Discussion/Elaboration of Word Meanings includes less common moves that engage students' thinking, such as facilitating sharing of ideas, asking follow-up questions, and challenging students to reason.

We also adapted student responses from the COLT system, outlining two dimensions of student talk that represent key aspects of vocabulary teaching and learning. Participating talk, students' responses that show active involvement in learning activities, includes such responses as answering simple questions, choral responding, and reading text aloud. Generative talk, talk that focuses on cognitive engagement in which students construct or generate new information, includes such responses as answering questions that require thinking, sharing ideas, and participating in discussions.

4. Results

4.1. Data Preparation

It is important to note that 2nd- and 3rd-grade classrooms were included in the analyses only if they had both fall and spring classroom observations. We summed the total number of responses of the six students in each classroom and reported the average of the summed responses. The median of students' choral responses, in which teachers asked the students to respond together, were used rather than summing. Distribution properties were examined through descriptive statistics for each of the teacher discourse moves and student responses. We identified one outlier for the teacher discourse moves (asking short-answer questions) in the spring of 2nd grade and one in the fall of 3rd grade. We also identified two outliers for student responses in the fall of 2nd grade (choral responding and taking notes to dictation). We then combined the variables to comprise two categories of teacher discourse moves (Basic Instruction in Word Meanings and Discussion/Elaboration of Word Meanings) and two categories of student responses (participating talk and generative talk) for both 2nd and 3rd grade separately—all of which were normally distributed (skewness < 2).

4.2. Vocabulary Activities in 2nd and 3rd Grade

RQ1. What percentage of the reading lesson is designated to vocabulary activities, and does this vary for 2nd- and 3rd-grade students?

Time Spent on Vocabulary Activities. We examined the amount of time that teachers spent teaching oral language and print vocabulary activities during their designated literacy block, using time metrics; from the duration of time and proportion metrics we derived a percentage score reflecting time on vocabulary activities out of the total reading lesson (literacy block). The literacy block in 2nd grade ranged from 120 min in the fall to 121 min in the spring. In 3rd grade it ranged from 103 min in the fall to 93 min in the spring. In the fall of 2nd grade, teachers spent an average of 31 min ($SD = 26$), 28% of their reading lesson, on vocabulary activities. This dropped to 24 min ($SD = 16$), 21%, in the spring although the length of the literacy block was consistent from fall to spring. Teachers designated 38 min ($SD = 23$) or 39% of their reading lesson to vocabulary activities in the fall of 3rd grade and 29 min ($SD = 18$), 30%, in the spring. These means might suggest that time spent on vocabulary was greater in 3rd than 2nd grade, but we did not statistically examine this because of differences in the time designated to literacy blocks in the two grades.

4.3. Teacher Discourse Moves

RQ2. What discourse moves (those that involve basic instruction of word meanings and those that involve discussion of meanings) are teachers using during vocabulary activities, and are there differences between 2nd and 3rd grade?

Types of Discourse Moves. Count metrics were used to provide information on the total number of occurrences that teachers used discourse moves in both categories, Basic Instruction in Word Meanings (basic) and Discussion/Elaboration of Meanings (discussion). We first calculated the total number of occurrences for each discourse move and then combined these and calculated the average number of occurrences by category. See Table 1 for means and standard deviations of each teacher discourse move and each category. Overall, 2nd-grade teachers used 58.42 ($SD = 48.99$) basic discourse moves on average in the fall and 29.63 ($SD = 27.29$) in the spring. We observed a similar pattern in 3rd grade, with teachers using 63.79 ($SD = 41.64$) basic moves in the fall and 47.47 ($SD = 38.64$) in the spring of the school year. Consistent with the current literature, we observed less frequent use of discussion moves in 2nd grade ($M = 5.84$; $SD = 8.60$) than 3rd grade ($M = 8.00$; $SD = 6.72$)—both fall and spring of the school year.

Differences between 2nd and 3rd Grade. Using multivariate analysis of variance (MANOVA), we did not observe significant differences in basic or discussion moves between 2nd and 3rd grade.

Table 1. Teacher discourse moves in vocabulary activities.

Teacher Discourse Moves	Grade 2 Fall M (SD)	Grade2 Spring M (SD)	Grade 3 Fall M (SD)	Grade 3 Spring M (SD)
Basic Instruction in Word Meanings	58.42 (48.99)	29.63 (27.29)	63.79 (41.64)	47.47 (38.64)
Reading aloud to students	1.66 (3.47)	1.11 (2.16)	1.84 (3.86)	0.37 (1.17)
Asking students to read aloud	0.79 (1.91)	1.05 (2.48)	0.74 (1.94)	0.16 (0.50)
Instructional comments	15.89 (15.62)	12.32 (10.60)	19.89 (14.12)	16.53 (15.47)
Nonverbal responses	1.89 (3.55)	0.47 (0.77)	5.63 (6.48)	2.74 (4.03)
Short-answer questions	24.66 (32.13)	14.68 (16.35)	35.68 (28.56)	27.68 (24.40)
Discussion/Elaboration of Meanings	5.84 (8.60)	4.53 (5.97)	8.00 (6.72)	6.82 (8.40)
Facilitating sharing of ideas	1.32 (2.04)	1.47 (2.29)	1.95 (2.61)	2.05 (2.99)
Asking follow-up questions	3.26 (4.88)	2.11 (3.16)	3.21 (3.07)	2.21 (2.44)
Challenging to reason	1.42 (2.50)	0.89 (1.60)	1.00 (1.25)	2.42 (4.78)

Notes. Means and standard deviations are provided for each teacher discourse category in addition to individual teacher discourse moves. Providing Explanations/Instructional Comments (Instructional comments); Asking questions that require non-verbal responses (Non-verbal responses); Asking short-answer questions (Short answer questions); Challenging students to reason (Challenging to reason).

4.4. Student Participation

RQ3. How often are students exhibiting participating and generative talk during vocabulary activities, and are there differences between 2nd and 3rd grade?

Types of Student Responding. Count metrics were used to provide information on the total number of occurrences that students exhibited participating and generative talk during the vocabulary activities. Similar to teacher discourse moves, we first calculated the total number of occurrences for each student response and then combined these and calculated the average number of occurrences by category. See Table 2 for means and standard deviations of each student response and each category. On average, 2nd-grade students exhibited 25.53 ($SD = 28.49$) participating and 3.68 ($SD = 4.93$) generative responses in the fall. In the spring, students in 2nd grade exhibited 13.00 ($SD = 15.13$) participating and 2.16 ($SD = 2.27$) generative responses. In 3rd grade, students exhibited 45.10 ($SD = 29.69$) participating responses and 7.95 ($SD = 6.98$) generative responses on average in the fall; they exhibited 28.42 ($SD = 21.23$) participating and 2.79 ($SD = 5.99$) generative responses in the spring.

Differences between 2nd and 3rd Grade. Using MANOVA, we next evaluated whether significant differences in participating and generative talk existed between 2nd and 3rd grade. The results indicated that differences in students' responses between grades in the fall of the school year were not statistically significant. However, we did find differences in the spring, with students exhibiting significantly more participating talk, F (1) 36 = 5.57, $p = 0.024$, and more generative talk, F (1) 36 = 7.012, $p = 0.012$, in 3rd grade than in 2nd grade.

Table 2. Student responses during vocabulary activities.

Student Responses	Grade 2 Fall M (SD)	Grade2 Spring M (SD)	Grade 3 Fall M (SD)	Grade 3 Spring M (SD)
Participating Talk Total	25.53 (28.49)	13.00 (15.13)	45.10 (29.69)	28.42 (21.23)
Answering nonverbal questions	6.79 (6.12)	3.42 (3.88)	11.26 (7.49)	6.58 (5.09)
Answering short-answer questions	6.00 (5.50)	3.47 (4.62)	14.26 (13.33)	12.37 (10.56)
Choral responding	6.11 (12.78)	3.05 (5.91)	6.58 (8.33)	2.47 (2.53)
Reading text silently	1.05 (3.21)	0.32 (0.82)	2.11 (5.22)	0.63 (1.92)
Choral reading	0.21 (0.92)	1.22 (3.26)	0.47 (1.43)	0.37 (1.61)
Reading text aloud	3.53 (6.72)	3.35 (1.88)	3.16 (4.25)	2.16 (4.43)
Taking notes/writing to dictation	1.84 (4.86)	1.61 (4.36)	5.00 (9.61)	1.84 (6.22)
Generative Talk Total	3.68 (4.93)	2.16 (2.27)	7.95 (6.98)	12.74 (15.42)
Answering thinking questions	1.11 (1.79)	0.32 (0.75)	1.58 (2.29)	2.79 (5.99)
Initiating a new idea	1.53 (1.74)	1.42 (1.74)	3.21 (3.35)	6.79 (10.61)
Asking short-answer questions	0.32 (0.82)	0.05 (0.23)	0.26 (0.65)	0.42 (0.69)
Using text to justify a response	0.26 (1.15)	0	0	0.05 (0.23)
Writing questions and responses	0.21 (0.71)	0.16 (0.50)	1.47 (2.74)	0.58 (1.81)
Reading self-generated text	0	0	0.32 (0.67)	0.79 (3.44)
Participating in a discussion	0.16 (0.69)	0.05 (0.23)	0.11 (0.46)	1.53 (3.37)
Discussing a topic with peers	0	0.05 (0.23)	0.21 (0.92)	0

Notes. Participating and generative talk (mean number of occurrences and standard deviations). Verbally answering simple questions (Answering simple questions); Answering questions that require thinking (Answering thinking questions); Initiating a new idea, topic, experience (Initiating a new idea); Writing questions and/or responses to questions (Writing questions and responses).

4.5. Timing of Vocabulary Activities during Reading Lessons

RQ4. When are teachers delivering vocabulary instruction during their reading lessons? More specifically, what is the probability that vocabulary activities precede and/or follow text reading during the reading lesson?

Lag sequential analysis was used to observe the pattern of when teachers delivered vocabulary activities during the reading lesson. We were interested in further understanding whether vocabulary activities took place before or after reading a text, whether this varied from fall to spring, and whether this varied from 2nd to 3rd grade. In 2nd grade, there was a 0.58 probability that vocabulary activities took place before reading a text in the fall and a 0.60 probability in the spring. However, there was only a 0.20 probability that vocabulary activities followed text reading in the fall and a 0.28 probability in the spring. This pattern was similar in 3rd grade. There was a 0.43 probability that vocabulary activities preceded text reading in the fall and a 0.33 probability in the spring. Yet, there was only a 0.15 probability that vocabulary activities followed text reading in the fall and a 0.15 probability in the spring.

Figure 1 outlines the probability of vocabulary activities preceding (blue) and following (red) text reading in the fall and spring per classroom in 2nd and 3rd grade. We found marked variability between the classrooms and seasons, yet the likelihood that teachers delivered vocabulary activities following text reading was overall low, with 16 2nd-grade teachers at or below 0.30 probability in the fall and 15 teachers in the spring. Similarly, 18 of the 19 3rd grade teachers fell at or below a 0.30 probability in the fall and 17 teachers in the spring. Finally, of the total 19 classrooms, eight 2nd-grade and nine 3rd-grade teachers spent time teaching vocabulary both before and after text reading in the fall and nine 2nd- and 3rd-grade teachers did so in the spring.

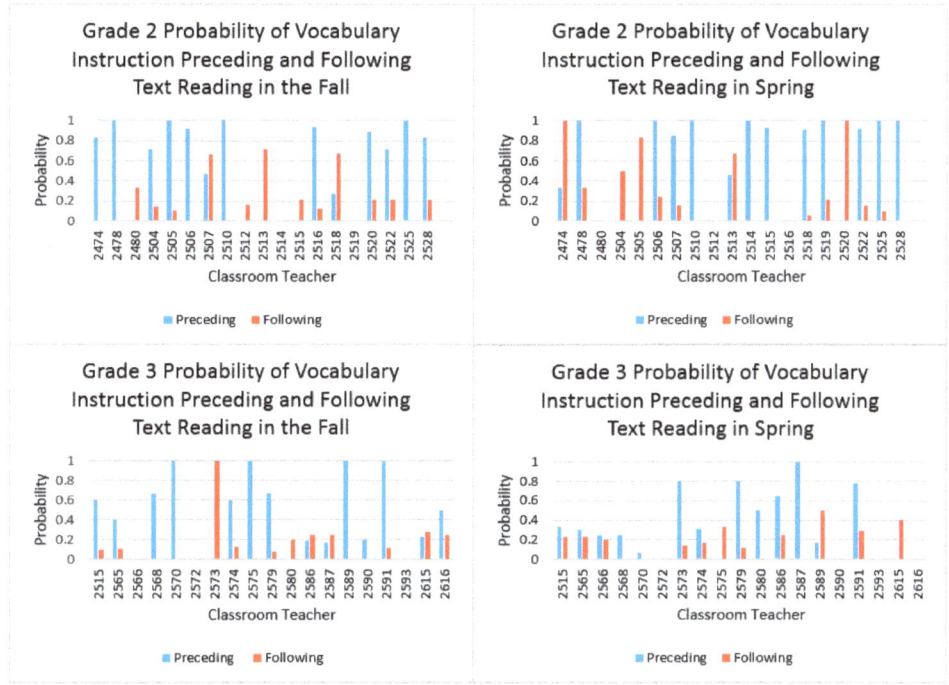

Figure 1. Probability of vocabulary activities preceding and following text reading.

4.6. Additional Exploratory Analyses

After observing means and standard deviations of students' responses, we carried out additional analyses to evaluate whether differences in participating and generative talk existed across the school year. Although not part of our initial hypotheses, it appeared that students responded overall less often in the spring compared to the fall of the school year. We used repeated measures ANOVA to examine mean differences in students' responses between the fall and spring. Findings indicated a significant difference in student participating talk, F (1) 35 = 6.88, *p* = 0.013, between the fall and the spring, with students exhibiting significantly more participating talk in the fall than spring at both grade levels. Differences between students' generative talk from fall to spring were approaching significance, F (1) 35 = 3.80, *p* = 0.059.

5. Discussion

Vocabulary instruction is a critical component of language and literacy lessons in the early school years; it plays a very important role in the development of students' reading comprehension. No wonder experts, such as the RAND Study Group [3], ask whether vocabulary instruction in the elementary years is of sufficient quality to prepare students for the challenges of reading and learning in content areas through school and beyond. In order to answer this question, we need to gather information about the nature and extent of classroom vocabulary activities in these years. To address this need, we examined teachers' vocabulary activities during reading lessons using video observations of early elementary classrooms. We explored the amount of time teachers spent teaching vocabulary activities during their larger literacy block and the timing of teachers' vocabulary activities—that is, how they intertwined vocabulary activities within their reading lessons. We also evaluated teachers' discourse moves and the type and frequency of students' responding. Our study extends the current literature by providing detailed information regarding elementary classrooms' vocabulary activities as well as a foundation for future research to examine how much and what kind of vocabulary instruction may be most beneficial to students as they are learning to read and comprehend text. We outline implications for practice and future directions.

5.1. Teaching Vocabulary Activities during Reading Lessons

In contrast to previous reports of the small amounts of time designated to vocabulary instruction during reading lessons [28], we found that teachers devoted a good portion of their reading lessons to vocabulary activities, especially in the fall of the school year. Third-grade teachers spent an average of 38 min and 2nd-grade teachers spent an average of 31 min teaching vocabulary activities. We observed a decrease in the percentage of time that teachers spent teaching vocabulary activities from the fall to the spring, with 3rd-grade teachers designating 29 min (30%) and 2nd-grade teachers designating 24 min (21%) to vocabulary activities, although we have no basis for interpreting this decrease.

By way of comparison, Watts [15] reported that 10% of reading lesson time was spent on vocabulary; similarly, Wanzek [23] found that 8% of the time was spent on vocabulary. One possible reason for our larger percentages is that the district mandated an uninterrupted block of at least 90 min for literacy lessons in the state of FL, allowing more time for language activities that supplemented text reading. In some cases this involved the use of mandated curriculum and activities required within Reading First schools. Particularly in Reading First schools, teachers were likely to be aware that vocabulary was one of the five required areas of instruction recommended by the National Reading Panel Report [2]. Another explanation for the relatively large amount of time spent on vocabulary may reflect the use of video observations and our observation system. We coded vocabulary activities within classroom observations using a coding system that allowed us to capture both planned and incidental vocabulary activities, such as brief exchanges between teachers and their students around vocabulary words. For example, during a whole group vocabulary activity, a 3rd-grade teacher helped her student make a text-to-self connection when she came across the word "dense" in the text.

T: The trees are very close together?
S1: Yes.
T: So you live by a dense wooded area, don't you?
S1: Yes.
T: So in a dense forest, are there going to be 1 or 2 pine trees or a whole bunch of pine trees?
S1: A whole bunch.

It is likely that we captured more incidental opportunities to talk about word meanings than has been found in most other studies, although Wright and Neuman [16] found that brief explanations of word meanings was a primary means of vocabulary development in kindergarten classes. Because our study is limited by the number of video observations in each classroom and across classrooms, we have only a snapshot of what is happening within reading lessons. That is, there is much variability in how teachers plan or adjust activities during reading lessons. The frequency of in-the-moment explanations of the meaning of a word might come about because teachers want to respond to students' needs [14]. Furthermore, the teachers' goals/objectives of the lesson might not focus on students' familiarity with vocabulary words in a given lesson. It is possible that, by the spring of the school year, teachers in our study focused more on text comprehension and less on the meanings of particular words. To examine such changes, researchers would need to carry out a more comprehensive set of observations across a school year. Still, even with the decrease of time we documented from fall to spring, more time was spent teaching vocabulary activities than has often been reported.

5.2. Teachers' Discourse Moves during Vocabulary Activities

We next took a closer look into what was happening within vocabulary activities. We observed and examined a set of teacher discourse moves, collapsing specific moves into two broad categories. Basic discourse moves include moves, such as asking students short-answer questions and providing them with definitions—moves that have been commonly observed in previous studies of vocabulary instruction [23]. Less common are discourse moves that teachers' use to encourage discussion and elaboration centered on word meanings, such as facilitating sharing of ideas and challenging students to reflect on alternative meanings of a word. Similar to previous studies [22,29], we found that teachers most frequently used basic discourse moves during the vocabulary activities, especially in the fall of the school year. Surprisingly, however, we did not observe significant differences in teacher discourse moves between 2nd and 3rd grade as we had expected.

We found that teachers in both grades made instructional comments and asked short-answer questions relatively more often than all other moves. Similar to the findings of Wright and Neuman [16], we found that the teachers commonly provided brief explanations of words without efforts to support students' understanding beyond the immediate use of the word in a text. For example, during a 2nd-grade reading lesson, the students come across the word "mare" while reading the story, Visit to the County Fair. The student that is reading pronounces the word "mare" as "mayor." The teacher takes a few minutes to explain what "mare" means before having the students continue reading.

T: What's a mare?
S2: It's like a type of horse.
T: A type of horse, and a mare is the type of horse that can have a baby horse. There is another kind of mayor (writes out word "mayor" on a piece of paper) that leads the city, someone that is the leader of a city is called the mayor, spelled like this (she shows the students the word "mayor"). But not mare. This word is mare. A horse. A female horse.

Studies have suggested that the most promising types of teacher-led vocabulary activities for impacting comprehension go beyond having students memorize word meanings. Rather, students become active participants in the word learning process [9,35]. They should have ample opportunities to review and practice using new words and be comfortable using multiple word-learning strategies. The results of our study reveal the relatively infrequent times that teachers introduce discussion or elaboration of word meanings when familiarizing their students with new words. In these early elementary vocabulary activities, teachers might not be using what experts consider to be the most effective means for developing students' vocabulary [27]. However, this study provides only an initial look at how teachers are delivering vocabulary activities. Future research is needed to better understand the impact of varying types of discourse moves, or combinations of moves, on student vocabulary learning and reading achievement more broadly.

5.3. Students' Responses during Vocabulary Activities

Describing Students' Responses in Vocabulary Activities. In addition to teacher discourse moves, we observed and examined a set of student responses to better understand the type and frequency of student engagement during vocabulary activities. We created two broad categories of students' responses, adjusting the coding categories in the original COLT system to suit analysis of students' involvement in vocabulary activities. One is participating talk, which focuses on students' basic or brief responses, such as providing short, simple answers to questions or raising a hand in response to a question. The other is generative talk, which focuses on students' reflections of word meanings and thinking about how words are used in different contexts. This involves cognitive engagement, in which students construct or generate new information, going beyond basic memorization [33]. This sort of active engagement with words has been associated with students' recall of words in vocabulary lessons and with positive effects on reading comprehension [9,17,35]. We found that students most frequently engaged in participating talk overall; we observed very few occurrences of generative talk, especially in 2nd grade.

Differences in Student Responses between 2nd and 3rd Grades. Interestingly, we did not observe significant differences in students' responses in the fall of the school year between 2nd and 3rd grades. However, we did find that students exhibited significantly more participating and generative talk in the spring of 3rd grade. Students exhibited 13 occurrences of participating talk, on average, in the spring of 2nd grade and 28 occurrences in the spring of 3rd grade. They answered non-verbal and short-answer questions as well as chorally responded more often than other responses. Generative talk also increased from an average of two occurrences in the spring of 2nd grade to 13 occurrences in the spring of 3rd grade. Students more commonly initiated new ideas and answered thinking questions; we observed some occurrences of participating in a discussion and reading self-generated text, although not frequently. In the following example, the teacher facilitates a discussion about the word "stage fright," drawing on students' personal experiences to help them understand the meaning of a word.

> S1: I was afraid of the dark when I was little.
> T: (teacher writing). Okay. I overcame, or let's put here, I need to overcome.
> S1: I need to overcome that but it's hard.
> T: I know it is. Me too.
> S2: I like the dark.
> T: When I was little, I used to think there were monsters under my bed, and I had to overcome that fear.
> Ss: (laughing)
> S3: I used to be afraid too. I used to think there was something under my bed too.
> T: Thank you for being brave and willing to share.
> S4: I was afraid when I was reading my book and everyone was staring at me.
> T: I'm going to call that stage fright.
> S4: I have stage fright.
> T: A lot of people have stage fright. Okay, who else is brave enough to share?
> S1: I had to overcome this. I used to be afraid around people I don't know.
> T: You know, that is a good thing. A lot of people are afraid of that. I am too. I can understand that because you don't know what to say.
> S4: I had the same problem. In first grade, I was afraid of singing.
> T: You were afraid of singing in front of a group?
> S3: Same thing happened to me. I was scared to sing. I was in 2nd grade.

We did expect to observe more generative talk in 3rd grade, given the increasing complexities of the texts. Nonetheless, these findings contribute to a limited body of research overall, as previous studies have solely focused on teachers' discourse moves without consideration of students' responses. Although we observed more participating talk overall, it is promising to see the increased amount of participating and generative talk by the end of 3rd grade as well as instances in which students take ownership over their learning, such that they are motivated and interested in learning new words, as observed in the example above.

Differences from Fall to Spring. We observed a significant decrease in students' participating talk from fall to spring in both 2nd and 3rd grade. It is possible that this is a function of less time spent in vocabulary activities and fewer teacher discourse moves in the spring overall, but further research is needed, as we have no basis for understanding this finding. Students' use of generative talk from fall to spring was approaching significance, with students exhibiting more generative talk in 3nd grade. Here, too, with the low frequency of generative talk overall, further research is needed to explore the types of generative talk that students exhibit in classroom vocabulary activities and how they vary across the school year.

5.4. Timing of Vocabulary Activities

The few studies that have examined the timing of vocabulary activities within reading lessons have focused on the need for extended opportunities to learn and use selected words [35,36]. Thus, we were interested in better understanding when teachers taught vocabulary activities during their literacy block (e.g., before or after text reading). We evaluated the likelihood that vocabulary activities preceded and followed text reading in both 2nd and 3rd grade, and we found that there was a relatively strong probability that teachers taught vocabulary activities before reading a text at both grade levels. This finding is not surprising as most comprehensive reading programs encourage teachers to familiarize students with words prior to reading the text. As part of the curriculum, teachers might review specific words, gauge students' understanding of the word meanings, and provide definitions—all before reading a text.

The following example outlines a teacher's efforts to expose her students to a set of vocabulary words prior to reading the text, The Lion and the Mouse. See Appendix B for the complete excerpt. The teacher provides an opportunity for her students to practice using the new words. She first has them cut out and pair vocabulary words and word meanings, and then asks the students to highlight the key words in the definitions. She then turns their attention to the word "aches", providing an example of the word to support comprehension.

> T: Aches. You told me aches means you don't want to do it. Listen, "Oh, my elbow aches after playing tennis. My elbow aches after I played tennis (holding her elbow as if it hurts). She then leans toward S3. So, you are telling me aches means you don't want to do it. Did you hear my sentence about aches?
> S3: (nods her head)
> T1: My elbow hurts because I played tennis (holding her elbow as if it hurts). She then leans toward S1. Oh, but look here (points to the word and definition). You said that aches means to be the best. Looks like we have a mess up here. Let's look here. My elbow hurts. My elbow hurts from playing tennis (points to the correct definition).
> S1: Aches.

Because experts recommend extended opportunities to engage students in understanding unfamiliar words [35], we expected to see teachers carry out vocabulary activities at several times within a reading lesson—before and after text reading, for example. However, most surprising was the low probability that vocabulary activities followed text reading, especially in 3rd-grade classrooms (0.15 probability that vocabulary activities followed text reading). Examining individual plots (Figure 1) from each classroom illustrate that some teachers spend a lot of time on vocabulary in a given lesson while others spend none at all. Such variability is to be expected, as we noted above, and as others have found as well [30]. Again, these data suggest that many factors influence how, when, and what teachers deliver during the literacy block. Even so, by counting times that both before and after activities take place, we can see that there are relatively fewer instances in which teachers follow up initial vocabulary activities after reading. This finding runs counter to the recommendations of experts in vocabulary instruction who argue that students need multiple opportunities to experience unfamiliar words [20,25]. Thus, our findings bring new urgency to answering the question: are students receiving adequate opportunities to develop the vocabulary knowledge they need to read and comprehend text?

5.5. Strengths and Limitations

This descriptive study contributes to the current literature in several ways. We focused on younger children than in previous studies and examined the type and amount of teachers' discourse moves and students' responses during vocabulary activities. The use of video-recorded observations, as well as the ISI and COLT coding systems, allowed for detailed examination of the engagement patterns between teachers and their students during vocabulary activities (both incidental and planned). In addition, we were able evaluate teachers' and students' moves in the fall and spring of 2nd and 3rd grade, providing an overview or a snapshot of vocabulary instruction across the school year. The use of lag sequential analysis to evaluate timing of vocabulary activities is a new contribution to the field, following up on recommendations for repeated exposures and extended learning activities to enhance students' learning of unfamiliar words. Although the descriptive nature of our study in many ways is

Educ. Sci. **2018**, *8*, 198

a strength, it also is a limitation because we were not able to make claims about specific moves that are important for student participation and learning. Nor did we examine how differences in time and talk about vocabulary predicted students' vocabulary gains. Having just two observations for each teacher and 19 teachers at each grade level also affects our ability to make generalizations and draw conclusions about early elementary vocabulary instruction. Thus, replication and extensions of this study are needed, as is research to evaluate how teacher discourse moves and student responses during vocabulary activities relate to one another and to student reading outcomes. Nevertheless, the results of this study are encouraging. Teachers and students were spending more time in vocabulary instruction than previous studies have indicated; while much of the discourse around vocabulary was fairly low level, we did observe instances when students were engaging in generative talk; and most, but not all vocabulary instruction preceded reading text.

Author Contributions: Conceptualization, N.S., J.F.C. and C.M.C.; Formal analysis, N.S.; Methodology, N.S. and J.F.C.; Validation, N.S., J.F.C. and C.M.C.; Writing—original draft, N.S., J.F.C. and C.M.C.; Writing—review & editing, N.S., J.F.C. and C.M.C.

Funding: This research was funded by the U.S. Department of Education, Institute of Education Sciences; grant numbers R305A160399 and R305B070074, and the National Institute of Child Health and Human Development grant number R01HD48539.

Conflicts of Interest: The authors declare no conflict of interest.

Appendix A

Teacher Discourse Moves and Student Responses in Vocabulary Activities

Teachers' Vocabulary Discourse Moves	Description and Examples
Basic Instruction in Word Meanings	
Reading aloud to students	The teacher reads words, lists, or text to the students
Asking students to read aloud	The teacher calls on one or more students to read words or text
Providing explanations/instructional comments	The teacher provides definitions, explanation, or other information about target words
Asking questions that require nonverbal responses	The teacher asks students to signal agreement or disagreement (e.g., raise hand)
Asking short-answer questions	The teacher asks simple questions to evaluate students' knowledge of word
Discussion/Elaboration of Meanings	
Facilitating sharing of ideas	The teacher asks for opinions, points of view, or students' experiences with a word
Asking follow-up questions	The teacher asks questions for clarification or elaboration
Challenging students to reason	The teacher asks questions that require inferencing, drawing conclusions, interpretations, or alternative explanations
Student Responses	**Description and Examples**
Participating Talk	
Answering nonverbal questions	Raising hand in response to teacher question
Verbally answering simple questions	Short-answer questions often requesting meaning of word
Choral responding	Often pronouncing words in a list or repeating a word or phrase as a group
Reading text silently	Often studying use of target word
Choral reading	Reading text as a group
Reading text aloud	Read words or text aloud, as directed or volunteered
Taking notes or writing to dictation	Writing words and meanings or words given by teacher

Generative Talk	
Answering questions that require thinking	Making inference about meaning of a word in context, suggesting alternative meaning
Initiating a new idea, topic, experience	Contributing information about a word or its use
Asking simple, on-topic questions	Raising a question about word meaning or use
Using text to justify a response	Providing evidence of word meaning from text
Writing questions and/or responses to questions	Sometimes completing work sheets or questions about word meaning
Reading self-generated text	After writing definitions/sentences, share with group
Participating in a discussion	Contributing ideas, responding to others' ideas
Discussing a topic with peers	Sharing experiences, making text-to-self connections

Notes. The observation system captures the frequency of each teacher discourse move and student response during vocabulary activities. The discourse moves were combined to comprise the two categories of discourse moves that teachers might use to teacher vocabulary activities; Basic Instruction in Word Meanings and Discussion/Elaboration of Meanings. Student responses were combined to comprise two categories of responding; Participating talk and generative talk.

Appendix B

Vocabulary Activity Preceding Text Reading

Classroom 2474 Fall (from Figure 1**).** Review and practice with vocabulary words. Teacher and a group of students during small group instruction. Students first cut out vocabulary words and word meanings then the teacher starts by having them name the words and pair them with the respective word meanings. The students are doing the same activity but moving through it at different paces. The teacher helps them as they match the words and definitions individually.

T: What is this word?

S1: Clutched.

T: Clutched very good. Now, what did we say clutched meant?

S1: (finds the definition from the cut out word meanings).

T: What is it?

S1: To hold tightly (student reads definition).

T: Clamber (teacher reads next word—student looks for the definition).

S1: To be the best (student finds a definition).

T: I don't think so. Remember, they talked about the bear clambered up the hill.

S1: (chooses a different definition)

T: (the teacher turns to watch how the other students are doing with matching their vocabulary words and definitions. She leans over to help S2) Alright, what's that word?

S2: Clambered.

T: Clambered. So, read all of your definitions to see which one it is.

S2: Clambered is to be the best (student reads definition).

T: Let's see, feels sore or in pain, having a big argument with someone, to be the best, to say something mean, to trip or fall when you can't move easily, to climb with both hands and feet (she points to the definitions).

S2: Climb with both hands and feet.

T: Very good. She turns back to S1 who has now finished matching his words and definitions. Now, let's say the words and read the definitions. Say the word, read your definition. Say the word, read your definition (points to the words and definitions). All the way down, okay? She leans back to S2. What is this word?

S2: Clumsy.

T: Clumsy. The baby cat is clumsy when he tries to walk. She watches S2 and S3 match their words and definitions. Leans toward S3. You are telling me that ache means to be the best?

S3: (shakes head no and goes for a different definition)

S2: (gets teacher's attention) "You don't want to?"

T: The teacher points to the definition "the kitty cat was clumsy when he tried to walk. The kitty cat was clumsy (points to words) She then leans toward S1. Did you do it?

S1: (she nods her head yes)

T: Okay, now what I want you to do (hold up highlighters). Pick a highlighter. Any color you want.

S1: (picks a highlighter)

T: Okay, so what I want you to do . . . (she points to the word) Clutched. What do you think clutched means? When you say clutched, what is the first thing you think of?

S1: To hold.

T: To hold (points to the definition). All you need to do is highlight that. That is your key word (pointing to the key word). So highlight "to hold"

S1: (highlights key words and moves to the next word). Clambered.

T: When you think of clambered, what's the first word that comes to your mind? What's the key word? S1: Both hands and feet (student reads part of definition).

T: Well, what are you going to do with both hands and feet?

S1: Climb? (looks up at the teacher)

T: Yes, climb (nods head). Think about climbing. She then leans toward S2. Aches. You told me aches means you don't want to do it. Listen, "Oh, my elbow aches after playing tennis. My elbow aches after playing tennis (holding her elbow as if it hurts). She then leans toward S3. So, you are telling me aches means you don't want to do it. Did you hear my sentence about aches?

S3: (nods her head yes)

T1: My elbow hurts. She then leans toward S1. Oh, but look here (points to word and definition). You said that aches means to be the best. Looks like we have a mess up here. Let's look here. My elbow hurts. My elbow hurts from playing tennis (points to a different definition)

S1: Aches

The students and teacher continue with the activity. Each student first matches the word and definitions, then they take turns reading each word and definition.

T: Okay, what S1 did (holding up S1s word and definition) is he picked up the word clutch. What helps him remember the word clutch is "to hold" (pointing to highlighted key words). So you are going to highlight your key word that is going to help you remember your vocabulary word. So everyone, start with word clutch. What do you think of when you think of the word clutch? To . . . (she pauses)

S2: Hold.

T: (nods head) Just highlight that.

Ss: (students highlight the words)

T: (she leans toward S1 who has finished highlighting. She points to word and word meaning). What is this word?

S1: Clutch.

T: What does clutch mean?

S1: To hold.

T: (she continues to point to each word)

S1: Clamber. To climb. Clumsy. To trip. (student reads each word and definition)

Educ. Sci. **2018**, *8*, 198

The teacher gives each student a turn read to read the words and definitions after they finish highlighting. She then asks them to open their books so they can read the story.

T: Okay. Let's open our books, we're going to read our story called *The Lion and the Mouse*.

References

1. Cunningham, A.E.; Stanovich, K.E. Early reading acquisition and its relation to reading experience and ability 10 years later. *Dev. Psychol.* **1997**, *33*, 934–945. [CrossRef] [PubMed]
2. National Institute of Child Health and Human Development (NICHD). *Report of the National Reading Panel: Teaching Children to Read*; U.S. Government Printing Office: Washington, DC, USA, 2000.
3. RAND Study Group. *Reading for Understanding: Toward an R&D Program for Reading Comprehension*; RAND: Santa Monica, CA, USA, 2002.
4. Stahl, S.A.; Fairbanks, M.M. The effects of vocabulary instruction: A model-based meta-analysis. *Rev. Educ. Res.* **1986**, *56*, 72–110. [CrossRef]
5. Kieffer, M.J.; Biancarosa, G.; Mancilla-Martinez, J. Role of morphological awareness in the reading comprehension of Spanish-speaking language minority learners: Exploring partial mediation by vocabulary and reading fluency. *Appl. Psycholinguist.* **2013**, *34*, 697–725. [CrossRef]
6. Ricketts, J.; Nation, K.; Bishop, D.V. Vocabulary is important for some but not all reading skills. *Sci. Stud. Read.* **2007**, *11*, 235–257. [CrossRef]
7. Schmitt, N. Size and depth of vocabulary knowledge. *Lang. Learn.* **2014**, *64*, 913–951. [CrossRef]
8. Tannenbaum, K.R.; Torgesen, J.K.; Wagner, R.K. Relationships between word knowledge and reading comprehension in third-grade children. *Sci. Stud. Read.* **2006**, *10*, 381–398. [CrossRef]
9. Wright, T.S.; Cervetti, G.H. A systematic review of research on vocabulary instruction that impacts reading comprehension. *Read. Res. Q.* **2017**, *52*, 203–226. [CrossRef]
10. Hart, B.; Risley, T. *Meaningful Differences in the Everyday Experiences of Young American Children*; Paul H. Brookes: Baltimore, MD, USA, 1995.
11. Dickinson, D.K.; Tabors, P.O. *Beginning Literacy with Language: Young Children Learning at Home and School*; Brookes: Baltimore, MD, USA, 2001.
12. Biemiller, A.; Boote, C. An effective method for building meaning vocabulary in primary grades. *J. Educ. Psychol.* **2006**, *98*, 44–62. [CrossRef]
13. Rupley, W.H.; Nichols, W.D. Vocabulary instruction for the struggling reader. *Read. Writ. Q.* **2005**, *21*, 239–260. [CrossRef]
14. Stahl, S.A. Four problems with teaching word meanings (and what to do to make vocabulary an integral part of instruction. In *Teaching and Learning Vocabulary: Bringing Research to Practice*; Hiebert, E.H., Kamil, M.L., Eds.; Routledge: New York, NY, USA, 2010; pp. 95–114.
15. Watts, S. Vocabulary instruction during reading lessons in six classrooms. *J. Read. Behav.* **1995**, *27*, 399–424. [CrossRef]
16. Wright, T.S.; Neuman, S.B. Paucity and disparity in kindergarten oral vocabulary instruction. *J. Lit. Res.* **2014**, *46*, 330–357. [CrossRef]
17. Hairrell, A.; Rupley, W.H.; Simmons, D. The state of vocabulary research. *Lit. Res. Instr.* **2011**, *50*, 253–271. [CrossRef]
18. Anderson, R.C.; Freebody, P. *Vocabulary Knowledge and Reading*; Reading Education Report #11; Center for the Study of Reading: Campaign-Urbana, IL, USA, 1979.
19. Nagy, W.E.; Scott, J.A. Vocabulary processes. In *Handbook of Reading Research*; Kamil, M.L., Mosenthal, P.B., Pearson, P.D., Barr, R., Eds.; Erlbaum: Mahwah, NJ, USA, 2000; Volume 3, pp. 269–284.
20. Stahl, S.A.; Nagy, W.E. *Teaching Word Meanings*; Erlbaum: Mahwah, NJ, USA, 2006.
21. National Center for Education Statistics. *The Nation's Report Card: A First Look: 2013 Mathematics and Reading (NCES 2014–451)*; NAEP: Washington, DC, USA, 2018.
22. Michener, C.J.; Proctor, C.P.; Silverman, R.D. Features of instructional talk predictive of reading comprehension. *Read. Writ.* **2018**, *31*, 725–756. [CrossRef]
23. Wanzek, J. Building word knowledge: Opportunities for direct vocabulary instruction in general education for students with reading difficulties. *Read. Writ. Q.* **2014**, *30*, 139–164. [CrossRef]

24. Beck, I.L.; McLeown, M.G.; Kucan, L. *Bringing Words to Life: Robust Vocabulary Instruction*, 2nd ed.; Guilford Press: New York, NY, USA, 2013.
25. Graves, M.F. *The Vocabulary Book: Learning and Instruction*; International Reading Association: Newark, DE, USA, 2006.
26. Hiebert, E.H.; Kamil, M.L. *Teaching and Learning Vocabulary: Bringing Research to Practice*; Routledge: New York, NY, USA, 2010.
27. Scott, J.A.; Jamieson-Noel, D.; Asselin, M. Vocabulary instruction throughout the day in twenty-three Canadian upper elementary classrooms. *Elem. Sch. J.* **2003**, *103*, 269–286. [CrossRef]
28. Connor, C.M.; Spencer, M.; Day, S.L.; Giulani, S.; Ingebrand, S.W.; McLean, L.; Morrison, F.J. Capturing the complexity: Content, type, and amount of instruction and quality of the Classroom Learning Environment synergistically predict third graders' vocabulary and reading comprehension outcomes. *J. Educ. Psychol.* **2014**, *106*, 762–778. [CrossRef] [PubMed]
29. Carlisle, J.F.; Kelcey, B.; Berebitsky, D. Teachers' support of teachers' vocabulary learning during literacy instruction in high poverty elementary schools. *Am. Educ. Res. J.* **2013**, *50*, 1360–1391. [CrossRef]
30. Kelcey, B.; Carlisle, J.F. Learning about teachers' literacy instruction from classroom observations. *Read. Res. Q.* **2013**, *48*, 301–317. [CrossRef]
31. Hiebert, E.H.; Mesmer, A.E. Upping the ante of text complexity in the common core state standards: Examining the potential impact on young readers. *Educ. Res.* **2013**, *42*, 44–51. [CrossRef]
32. Nagy, W. Metalinguistic awareness and the vocabulary comprehension connection. In *Vocabulary Acquisition: Implications for Reading Comprehension*; Wagner, R.K., Muse, A.E., Tannenbaum, K.R., Eds.; Guilford Press: New York, NY, USA, 2007; pp. 52–77.
33. Blachowicz, C.; Fisher, P. Teaching vocabulary. In *Handbook of Reading Research*; Kamil, M., Mosenthal, P., Pearson, P.D., Barr, R., Eds.; Erlbaum: Mahwah, NJ, USA, 2000; Volume 3, pp. 503–523.
34. McKeown, M.G.; Beck, I.L.; Omanson, R.C.; Pople, M.T. Some effects of the nature and frequency of vocabulary instruction on the knowledge and use of words. *Read. Res. Q.* **1985**, *20*, 527–535. [CrossRef]
35. Beck, I.L.; McKeown, M.G. Increasing young low-income children's oral vocabulary repertoires through rich and focused instruction. *Elem. Sch. J.* **2007**, *107*, 251–271. [CrossRef]
36. Coyne, M.D.; McCoach, D.B.; Kapp, S. Vocabulary intervention for kindergarten students: Comparing extended instruction to embedded instruction and incidental exposure. *Learn. Disabil. Q.* **2007**, *30*, 74–88. [CrossRef]
37. Connor, C.M.; Morrison, F.J.; Fishman, B.J.; Crowe, E.C.; Al Otaiba, S.; Schatschneider, C. A longitudinal cluster-randomized controlled study on the accumulating effects of individualized literacy instruction on students' reading from first through third grade. *Psychol. Sci.* **2013**, *24*, 1408–1419. [CrossRef] [PubMed]
38. Connor, C.M.; Morrison, F.J.; Fishman, B.; Ponitz, C.C.; Glasney, S.; Underwood, P.; Schatschneider, C. The ISI classroom observation system: Examining the literacy instruction provided to individual students. *Educ. Res.* **2009**, *38*, 85–99. [CrossRef]
39. Connor, C.M.; Kelcey, B.; Sparapani, N.; Petscher, Y.; Siegal, S.; Adams, L.; Hwang, J.; Carlisle, J. Talking in class? Students' and their Classmates' Talking predicts their reading comprehension gains. Manuscript in Preparation.

Article

Peer Effects on Vocabulary Knowledge: A Linear Quantile Mixed-Modeling Approach

Jamie M. Quinn [1,*] [iD], **Jessica Sidler Folsom** [2] [iD] **and Yaacov Petscher** [1] [iD]

1   Florida Center for Reading Research, Florida State University, Tallahassee, FL 32306, USA;
    ypetscher@fcrr.org
2   Iowa Reading Research Center, University of Iowa, Iowa City, IA 52242, USA;
    jessica-folsom@iowareadingresearch.org
*   Correspondence: jquinn@fcrr.org

Received: 31 August 2018; Accepted: 20 October 2018; Published: 23 October 2018

Abstract: Do your peers in the classroom have an effect on your vocabulary learning? The purpose of this study was to determine if group-level peer characteristics and group-level peer achievement account for individual-level differences in vocabulary achievement using a large sample of students in kindergarten through second grade (n = 389,917). We applied a mixed-modeling approach to control for students nested among peers, and used quantile regression to test if group-level peer effects functioned similarly across the range of conditional student ability in vocabulary knowledge. Group-level peer effects were more strongly related to vocabulary achievement for students at the low end of the conditional distribution of vocabulary. The difference in vocabulary achievement between children with and without an individualized education program increased as quantiles of the conditional vocabulary distribution increased. Children with lower relative fall scores had better spring scores when they were in homogenous classrooms (i.e., their peers had similar levels of achievement). The importance of classroom composition and implications for accounting for peer effects are discussed.

Keywords: vocabulary achievement; peer effects; quantile regression; mixed-effects models

---

1. Introduction

The assumption that there are robust peer effects in the classroom is the driving force behind many policy and practical decisions. Discussions around school choice [1,2] and tracking (i.e., ability grouping) [3] are based on the notion that peers influence achievement, which is neither a new nor a novel idea. The first report to address peer or classroom composition effects was the 1966 Coleman Report [4]. The Coleman Report examined the educational opportunities of minority group peers and the relations between student achievement and school type and quality. The report suggested that minority students achieved less and were more affected by school quality than the average Caucasian student [4]. Indeed, classroom compositions matter: schools with a higher average social class or higher skill levels tend to have greater parental support, fewer behavioral and disciplinary problems, and are more likely to retain high quality teachers [5]. In response to the Coleman Report, school composition, and thus classroom composition, were subsequently influenced by reassignment efforts to adjust intellectual, racial, ethnic, and income compositions to more balanced levels [6,7]. Later, in a natural experiment in the early 2000s, whereby a large county in North Carolina reassigned students to schools on the basis of income levels, higher achieving peers were better for a student's achievement after accounting for race, ethnicity, income, and parental education [8]. Even as school systems have reacted to the Coleman Report by attempting to differentially group students, researchers have looked to more rigorous methodologies to better understand if and how peers relate to individual student achievement [1,2,9]. This research, spanning a variety of ideologies, grades, and outcomes, points to a lack of consensus on the nature and size of peer effects on educational achievement.

1.1. What are Peer Effects?

Peer effects are the behavioral, demographic, and achievement level variables that students possess and which can affect their peers' learning within the classroom [10,11]. Such peer effects might include social class or social status in the form of free or reduced lunch classification, family income, or unemployment rates. Additionally, group-level differences in achievement rates might affect peer outcomes, such that depending on if they are placed in classrooms with higher or lower group-level (peer group) achievement, students might experience differential achievement outcomes based on how well or how poorly their peers do academically. Finally, student specific characteristics, such as race, ethnicity, or gender, might have an effect on their peers' achievement levels [8]. The focus of the present study was how the presence of higher achieving peers might have influenced the performance of other peers while controlling for certain demographic characteristics and ignoring the social structure (i.e., the peer relationships) within the classroom.

Establishing that our interest is in the effects of peer achievement, there are a few ways in which the effects of group-level demographic variables and achievement levels on individual-level achievement might manifest in the classroom. One such way could be through interactions with higher-achieving students in small group learning or cooperative activities. If a child does learn from their peers, it would follow that being paired with more highly-skilled peers in small group exercises would have a direct effect on their learning [9]. There might also be indirect effects: if a classroom's achievement levels are particularly high, the teacher might choose to use a higher-quality method than if the classroom's achievement levels are low [10].

Hoxby and Weingarth [8] suggested a few models of peer effects that are relevant to the current study. One such model is the Boutique model, whereby students will have higher achievement when surrounded by similarly-leveled peers. If teachers recognize their students are similarly leveled, they might create and tailor their core content to reflect their students' shared ability levels. A related model is the Focus model, where a student performs better when the classroom is homogenous, even when the student is not part of that homogenous group. The Rainbow model suggests the opposite: heterogeneity in the classroom is best for students, as they must arrive at their own answers in their own ways, and benefit from others' differing perspectives [8].

Two final models might also be relevant: The Bad Apple model and the Shining Light model. Both of these models posit that individual students can have large effects on their peers, by either "spoiling" the classroom through very low performance, or by improving classroom performance through being the "shining light" of high achievement. For students with individual education programs (IEPs) or with a disability status, their presence might influence their peers' achievement, should that student's performance reflect the Bad Apple or Shining Light model of influence. However, students with learning disabilities are more likely to be rejected than comparison children before even examining their achievement scores [12,13].

In the present study, we will explore if and how peer effects manifest through the lens of these models of peer behavior, and how the effects of having a peer with an IEP or disability affects their vocabulary outcomes. Further, we will examine if outcomes for students with an IEP or disability status are affected by their peers' achievements.

1.2. Why Are Peer Achievement Effects Inconsistent?

Wilkinson, Parr, Fung, Hattie, & Townsend [10] posited several reasons that findings on peer effects have been largely inconsistent. First, they suggested that, descriptively, there are compositional and peer effects, but that these effects may be inconsequential to learning above and beyond a child's initial status. Second, they reasoned that the peer effects may be limited to only certain clusters of students, and not manifest as significant findings at the population mean. Third, they proposed that findings are small because reciprocal relations between students, teachers, and schools organization/management is not sufficiently explored. And lastly, they recommended that methodological and analytic differences within previous studies have "fail[ed] to model peer effects in theoretically-appropriate ways" [10] (p. 527).

Measurement and modeling choices continue to affect how peer effects are determined. Using a linear-in-means model, Burke and Sass [14] found small or negligible peer effects on mathematics and reading achievement (improvements in peer achievement increased own achievement by around 1/4 of a percentile). However, using a nonlinear approach by categorizing students in to low-, middle-, and high-type students based on baseline reading achievement, they found that middle- and high-type students significantly benefitted from average improvement in peer achievement in elementary school, but low-type students' achievement was unaffected by peers [14].

1.3. Specific Peer Achievement Effects on Language Outcomes

Presently, we focus on the effects peers may have on vocabulary knowledge, an important component of oral language skills. Previous studies on peer achievement effects have focused on mathematical outcomes or general reading skills [1,8,14] and general language skills in Dutch [15,16]. We chose vocabulary knowledge as our outcome because it is specifically implicated in many educational outcomes. Vocabulary achievement is a particularly strong and direct predictor of reading comprehension skills from first grade through fourth grade [17–19]. Vocabulary knowledge is also a direct and/or indirect predictor of discourse-level listening comprehension [20,21]. The lexical quality hypothesis also supports vocabulary knowledge as a word learning mechanism that leads to faster and more accurate word decoding skills [22,23]. Moreover, vocabulary has been found to be a malleable factor among other peer effect studies with pre-school aged children [24–26]. Within the present study, because oral language is important for skilled reading, and since it may be a malleable factor from an early age, we focused on the effects peers may have on vocabulary learning in the early elementary years (specifically, kindergarten through second grade) to look at the effects of peers on vocabulary achievement both before and after formal reading instruction begins. Understanding how peers influence the vocabulary learning of their classmates can help us to understand if there are optimal ways to structure classrooms to promote vocabulary learning as a facilitator of future skilled reading.

1.4. The Present Study

In an effort to address methodological limitations of the peer effects literature, we presently employed the use of multilevel quantile regression. Hoxby and Weingarth [8] discussed that a linear-in-means model, whereby student outcomes are a linear function of the conditional mean of peers' outcomes (i.e., the peer effect is homogenous), is an insufficient way to model peer effects:

> " ... *we have seen that the data consistently rejects the Linear-in-Means model as a standalone explanation of peer effects. Thus, researchers' common reliance on the Linear-in-Means model guarantees that any effects of peers that operate non-linearly or through moments other than the mean become omitted variables.*" [8] (p. 29).

In quantile regression, the level of importance of a predictor may be different depending on the quantile of the conditional distribution for an outcome variable [27,28]: the model goes beyond simple linear mean effects models to investigate differential relations between predictors and outcomes. Quantile regression, which has been popular in economics for some time, has of late become increasingly popular in the developmental and psychological sciences [29]. Recent advances in quantile regression have introduced the ability to analyze conditional relations in the context of multilevel models, which are relevant to the present study [30–33].

Research Questions

The purpose of this study was to analyze individual effects, peer effects, and the interaction between individuals and peers at various quantiles of the conditional distribution of vocabulary achievement at the end of each of grades K-2. To that end, we answered the following research questions:

1. What are the effects of group-level peer achievement on individual-level vocabulary achievement at each of grades K-2 after controlling for race/ethnicity and free-or-reduced lunch status?
2. Controlling for individual levels of vocabulary achievement in the fall, are there moderating effects of peer characteristics, such as group-level IEP status or disability status, in the classroom on end-of-year individual-level vocabulary outcomes at each of grades K-2?
3. Are there differences in the relations of and interactions between these predictor variables (i.e., fall achievement levels, peer group achievement, and group-level IEP or disability status) across quantiles of the conditional distribution of vocabulary outcomes at each of grades K-2?
4. Are there grade-related differences in how peers' achievement and group-level IEP or disability status affects individual-level performance on end-of-year vocabulary achievement?

2. Materials and Methods

2.1. Data

To address the research questions, the data used in this study were obtained from the Progress Monitoring and Reporting Network (PMRN) database of the archive data core maintained by the Florida Center for Reading Research (FCRR). The archive data core is a historic, centralized data repository that captured student performance in grades K-12 on screening, diagnostic, progress monitoring, and state achievement data pertaining to reading skills. Queried data from the data core for this study stemmed from the 2012/13 school year and reflected students' performance on the Florida Assessments for Instruction in Reading (FAIR). All school districts in Florida ($N = 72$) voluntarily selected to administer the FAIR. In grades K-2, a classroom teacher delivered the FAIR, a battery of early reading and pre-reading skills used for screening and progress monitoring.

2.2. Participants

Participants were a total of 389,917 students in kindergarten ($n = 154{,}220$), first ($n = 122{,}435$), and second grade ($n = 113{,}262$). Students were in 23,233 classes, in 1,869 schools, in 72 school districts. Demographic composition by grade and for the full sample is displayed in Table 1 along with the demographic distributions of all K-12 students in Florida. In general, the sample is representative of the statewide population with the exception of percent of students eligible for free or reduced-price lunch and the percentage of migrant students. The sample used in this study included proportionally more students eligible for free or reduced-price lunch (65.8% versus 57.6%) and proportionally more migrant students (1.5% versus 0.5%).

Table 1. Demographic distribution of participants by grade.

	K	G1	G2	Total	State
n	154,220	122,435	113,262	389,917	
Gender					
% Female	48.6	48.7	49.2	48.8	48.7
% Male	51.4	51.3	50.8	51.2	51.4
Race/Ethnicity					
% Black	22.4	23.4	22.4	22.7	23.0
% Hispanic	29.4	29.3	29.0	29.3	28.6
% Minority other	6.3	6.3	6.6	6.4	6.0
% White	41.8	41.0	42.0	41.6	42.4
% FRL Eligible	64.2	67.5	66.2	65.8	57.6
% with IEP	9.9	13.7	17.2	13.2	13.2
% Migrant	2.1	1.1	1.1	1.5	.5

Note. FRL = Free or reduced lunch; IEP = Individual Education Plan; K= Kindergarten; G1 = First grade; G2 = second grade.

2.3. Measures

2.3.1. Vocabulary

The primary construct of interest was vocabulary achievement, which was measured using the FAIR Vocabulary test. The Vocabulary test is administered in the fall and spring of grades kindergarten through 2 as part of the Broad Diagnostic Inventory of the FAIR. According to the K-2 FAIR Technical Report [34], the Vocabulary test measures a student's breadth and depth of vocabulary and indicates the need for vocabulary instruction. In the test, the student is asked to label objects, actions, or attributes, and is prompted in cases where an answer requires further precision. Words for the test were selected to tap into academic language at the K-2 grade levels. The FAIR Vocabulary test has a reported IRT precision estimate of 0.80, and concurrent correlations of 0.75 to 0.83 with the Expressive Vocabulary Test, 2nd edition [35], and the fall scores explain 24–29% of variance in spring comprehension scores on the SAT-10 [36].

2.3.2. Peer Effects and Relative Status

The peer effect was conceptualized as the relation between classroom peers' initial abilities and end of year vocabulary. Peer effects were calculated in three ways: (1) the average fall vocabulary of the classroom peers (peer group mean), (2) the standard deviation of fall vocabulary of the classroom peers (peer group SD), and (3) the percent of students with IEPs in the classroom (peer group IEP). Additionally, rather than focus on absolute status in the fall, this study sought to determine whether or not peer effects were dependent on students' *relative status* compared to their peers in the fall. To quantify relative status, within each peer group, each student's fall vocabulary score was transformed to a *z*-score, that is, a relative status score of −1 would represent a student performing a standard deviation *below* their peers in the fall, and concordantly, a relative status score of 1 indicates a student performed a standard deviation *above* their peers in the fall.

2.4. Analysis

To address the research questions, peers were first identified using the approach explained below. Afterwards, two sets of related analyses were conducted: conditional means based multilevel models (i.e., conventional hierarchical linear modeling; HLM), and linear quantile mixed models (LQMM). Both analyses were run as two-level models with students (level 1) nested in classrooms (level 2). Because we were interested to determine whether the impact of peers varied within grade and between grades, each set of analyses was run separately for each grade, kindergarten (K), first grade (G1), and second grade (G2). This allowed for a more nuanced analysis of the impact of peers at each grade level, rather than simply including grade as a statistical control. For both the HLM and LQMM, all main effects were allowed to vary randomly. All variables—except for IEP status—were centered such that resulting coefficients could be interpreted as standardized effects.

2.4.1. Identifying Peers

The FAIR was administered three times per year, and data were entered at each assessment point (fall, winter, spring). In addition to the FAIR scores, a district, school, and teacher identifier were included. As not all students remained with the same teacher throughout the year, it was necessary to identify the most likely set of peers for each student in the dataset. For each student, a peer variable was created. The peer variable was the teacher most consistently associated with the student across the 3 assessment points. For example, for a student that had teacher "Ms. Scott" in the fall and teacher "Ms. Jones" in winter and spring, the peer variable would be teacher "Ms. Jones." Similarly, for a student that had teacher "Ms. Scott" in the fall and spring, but teacher "Ms. Jones" in winter, the peer variable would be teacher "Ms. Scott." If there was not a consistent teacher across two or more assessment periods (in 0.8% of cases), the peer variable was the teacher from the first assessment period with data. Approximately 72% of students were in the same peer group at all three assessment periods, 19% of students were with the same peer group at assessment periods 2 and 3, 7% of students were with the same peer group at assessment periods 1 and 2, 1% of students were with the same peer group at assessment periods 1 and 3. The remaining less than 1% of students were not with a consistent peer group for two or more assessment periods; 0.7% were assigned with their peer group from assessment period 1, 0.2% were in assessment period 2, none were in the third assessment period. For the purposes of this study, the peer variable (associated with a unique teacher within a school and district) became the peer group identifier. Thus, students are considered nested within peers (i.e., teachers within schools within districts).

2.4.2. Hierarchical Linear Modeling (HLM)

To identify the most parsimonious model, a standard multilevel building process was conducted at each grade. Four models were tested: (1) an unconditional baseline model, (2) an individual predictors model–relative status and IEP (a dummy variable identifying if a student had an IEP), (3) a peer predictors model–the individual predictors model with the addition of the peer group mean, peer group SD (peer standard deviation), and peer group IEPs (percentage of peers with IEP status), and (4) individual by peer interaction model–the peer effects model with the addition of interactions between relative status and all peer effects and interactions between IEP and all peer effects. Across all grades, the fourth model, the individual by peer interaction model, was the best-fitting model according to deviance index (whereby lower values are deemed better; see online Supplemental Materials for a table with fit indices for each model by grade).

2.4.3. Linear Quantile Mixed Modeling (LQMM)

The final model from the HLM analyses at each grade were then analyzed as a linear quantile mixed model (LQMM) in two phases. LQMMs extend the traditional HLM analyses to a quantile regression framework, allowing the estimation of the independent variables at differing quantiles of the outcome variable. Quantile regression conditions the outcome variable at various points of the distribution, which results in conditional estimates at the specified quantiles without a loss of power [27–29]. Because of the large sample sizes, we tested the LQMMs at 0.05 intervals between the 0.05 and 0.95 quantiles of FAIR Vocabulary in spring. This allowed us to test whether peer effects functioned similarly for a wide range of student vocabulary achievements.

In the first phase, at each grade, each individual predictor was tested separately to determine if, in the absence of other variables or interactions, the predictor functioned differently at each quantile. Additionally, each interaction (with corresponding main effects) was tested separately to determine if, in the absence of other variables or interactions, the interaction or main effects functioned differently at each quantile. In the second phase, at each grade, only the predictors and interactions (with corresponding main effects), that were substantive (i.e., coefficient > 0.1) and/or varied substantively (i.e., the absolute difference in the minimum and maximum coefficient size across quantiles was >0.1) across quantiles were entered into a final model. This final model is used for interpretation.

3. Results

3.1. Descriptive Statistics

Table 2 contains the descriptive statistics for the kindergarten, first grade, and second grade students. On average, children in kindergarten grew 3.35 points in vocabulary between fall and spring. Grade 1 students grew somewhat less, i.e., 2.7 points on average. Grade 2 students grew the most, 3.42 points on average. There was no indication of problematic skewness or kurtosis, though a number of children in all grades were at the floor (0) and ceiling (24) of the FAIR vocabulary measure.

Table 2. Descriptive statistics for vocabulary achievement outcomes.

Variable	n	Mean (SD)	Minimum	Maximum	Skewness	Kurtosis
K Voc (Fall)	179,031	10.09 (4.21)	0	24	−0.187	−0.132
K Voc (Spring)	152,507	13.44 (4.43)	0	24	−0.163	0.001
G1 Voc (Fall)	147,326	10.13 (4.15)	0	24	0.020	−0.114
G1 Voc (Spring)	144,825	12.83 (4.48)	0	24	−0.074	−0.220
G2 Voc (Fall)	143,237	10.59 (3.59)	0	24	0.038	0.641
G2 Voc (Spring)	141,967	14.01 (4.28)	0	24	−0.192	−0.127

K = Kindergarten; G1 = first grade; G2 = Second grade.

3.2. HLM Results

The ICCs of the unconditional models were 0.370, 0.345, and 0.366 for K, G1, and G2 respectively. This suggests that 37%, 35%, and 37% of the variance in spring scores was due to differences between peer groups (i.e., classrooms) at each of grades K-2, respectively, with 63%, 65%, and 63% of the remaining variance in vocabulary due to individual differences among students. The large ICCs indicated that there were meaningful differences among the classrooms in children's spring vocabulary achievement. Therefore, we turned to the three conditional models to explore the individual and peer main effects and the individual by peer interaction effects.

Model fit was ascertained for each of the three conditional models (see online Supplemental Materials for the fit indices of all tested models). According to the deviance index (whereby lower values are deemed better), the final model with all individual by peer interactions had the best fit for all grades. These models explained 55% of variance at the peer level and 54% of variance at the individual level in kindergarten (Appendix A, Table A1), 68% of variance at the peer level and 63% of variance at the individual level in first grade (Appendix A, Table A2), and 54% of variance at the peer level and 44% of variance at the individual level in second grade (Appendix A, Table A3).

Conditional Model Effects

Among the student-level main effects, relative status was strongly associated with spring vocabulary across grades ($0.484 \leq \beta \leq 0.558$; $ps < 0.001$). Students with IEPs had significantly lower spring vocabulary scores across grades ($-0.111 \leq \beta \leq -0.177$; $ps < 0.001$).

Among the peer-level main effects, the peer group mean was positively associated with spring vocabulary across grades ($0.484 \leq \beta \leq 0.558$). The peer group SD (peer group standard deviation), though statistically significant in first and second grade, was not substantively significant in predicting spring vocabulary in any grade ($0.004 \leq \beta \leq 0.021$). Similarly, although the effect of peer group IEP status was statistically significant in first grade, it was not substantively related to spring vocabulary in any grade ($-0.015 \leq \beta \leq -0.002$).

Among the interaction effects, several were statistically significant; however, with the exception of relative status by peer group SD, there were no substantive interactions ($-0.059 \leq \beta \leq 0.070$). The relative status by peer group SD interaction (RSxPSD) was significant across grades ($0.115 \leq \beta \leq 0.126$), suggesting that the relation between peer group SD and spring vocabulary was stronger for individuals with higher relative status.

3.3. LQMM Results

At each grade, each of the individual and interaction effects included in the HLMs, regardless of significance or magnitude, were tested separately in LQMMs to identify substantive effects and/or effects with substantive ranges across the quantiles. Then, effects which were substantive (absolute value greater than 0.1) or varied substantively (absolute value of range greater than 0.1) were included in a single final model for each grade. Across all models, as quantiles increased the intercept steadily increased, which is expected given that the model conditions the regression equation at each quantile, and the scores are normally distributed across a wide range of student skills (the intercept is not discussed further as it is not of primary concern). The main effects and interaction effects from each grade are discussed next.

3.3.1. Kindergarten

The significant effects included in the kindergarten model were the intercept, main effects for relative status, IEP, peer group mean, peer group SD, and the interaction term for relative status by peer group SD (RSxPSD). A quantile process plot of all effects except for intercept is provided in Figure 1. At all quantiles, relative status was the strongest predictor of spring vocabulary ($0.406 \leq \beta \leq 0.589$), but this relation was stronger at lower quantiles than at higher quantiles. The next strongest predictor of spring vocabulary was peer group mean ($0.272 \leq \beta \leq 0.469$). As with relative status, peer group mean was more strongly associated with spring vocabulary at lower quantiles than higher quantiles. The third strongest predictor was IEP status ($-0.251 \leq \beta \leq -0.108$). This effect increased over the quantiles: the difference between individuals with and without an IEP was larger as quantiles increased. The peer group SD, which was included because of the interaction term with relative status (RSxPSD), was statistically but not substantively significant in some quantiles ($-0.030 \leq \beta \leq 0.018$).

The RSxPSD interaction effect decreased from 0.151 to 0.096 as quantiles increased. This interaction is plotted in Figure 2 for classrooms at the low end of the conditional vocabulary distribution (0.25 quantile) and for classrooms high end of the conditional vocabulary distribution (0.75 quantile). For classrooms at the low end of the conditional distribution (top panel), if a child had low relative status (i.e., they were lower than their peers in the fall), that child did better in spring when the classroom was relatively homogenous (i.e., the peer SD was low (PSD)). However, if a child had high relative status (i.e., higher vocabulary than their peers in the fall), that child did *worse* in lower classrooms if the classroom was homogenous (i.e., low PSD), and did *better* if the classroom was relatively heterogeneous (i.e., high PSD). This pattern held for classrooms at the high end of the conditional distribution: children with low relative status did better in classrooms that were relatively homogenous (low PSD), and children with high relative status did better in classrooms that were relatively heterogeneous (high PSD).

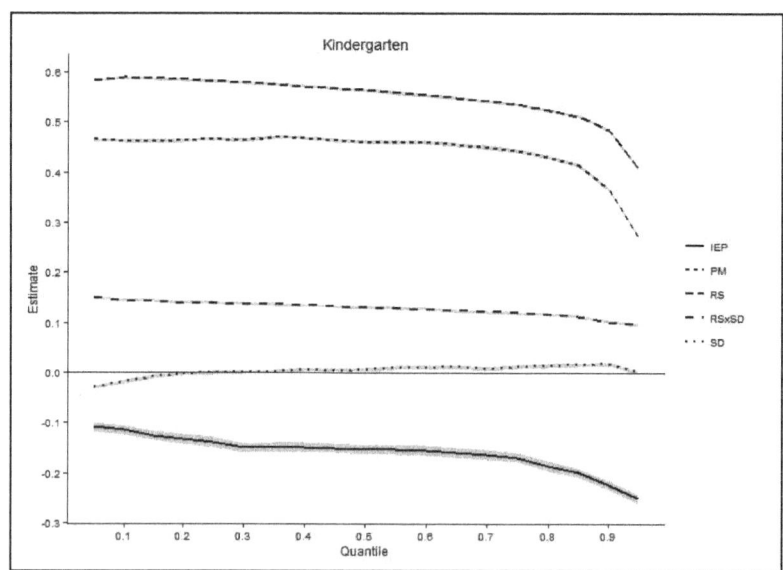

Figure 1. Kindergarten quantile plot with 95% confidence interval bands. PM = peer group mean; SD = peer group SD; RS = relative status; RSxSD = relative status by peer group SD interaction.

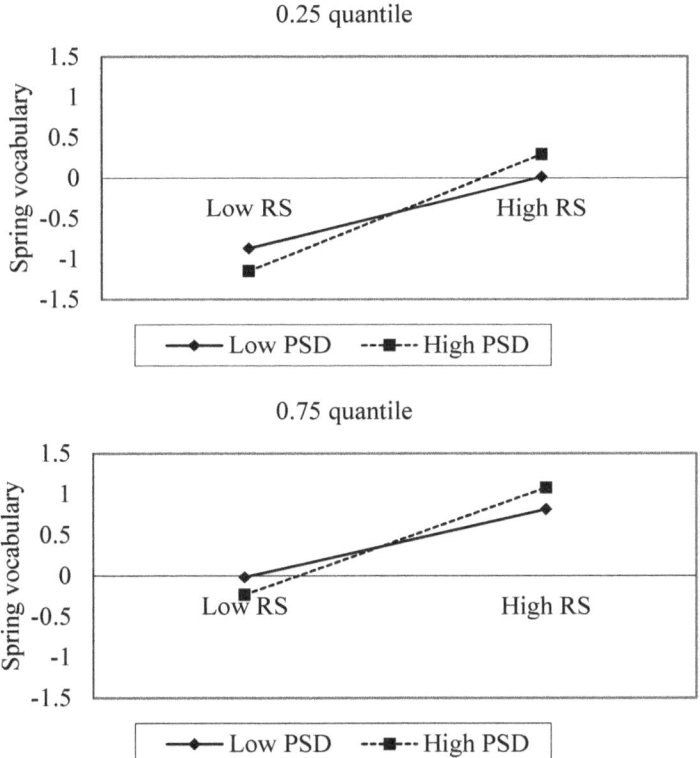

Figure 2. Kindergarten RSxSD interaction at the 0.25 quantile (**top**) and the 0.75 quantile (**bottom**). PSD = peer group standard deviation; RS = relative status.

3.3.2. First Grade

The first grade model included the same predictors as kindergarten with the addition of an IEPxSD interaction. Other than the addition of the IEPxSD interaction, results were similar to kindergarten. A quantile process plot of all effects except for the intercept is provided in Figure 3. Relative status was the strongest predictor of the conditional vocabulary distribution within the 0.05 to 0.95 quantile band ($0.389 \leq \beta \leq 0.593$). The effect of relative status decreased as quantiles increased. The second strongest predictor was PM ($0.309 \leq \beta \leq 0.495$). As with RS, the PM effect decreased as quantiles increased. The third strongest predictor was IEP ($-0.217 \leq \beta \leq -0.075$). As in K, the IEP effect increased as quantiles increased: the difference between individuals with and without IEPS was larger for students in upper quantiles than in lower quantiles. The last main effect tested was peer group SD which, unlike in kindergarten where it was not substantive, was substantive at the higher quantiles ($-0.046 \leq \beta \leq 0.113$), suggesting that peer group SD may be a stronger predictor for students in upper quantiles than lower quantiles.

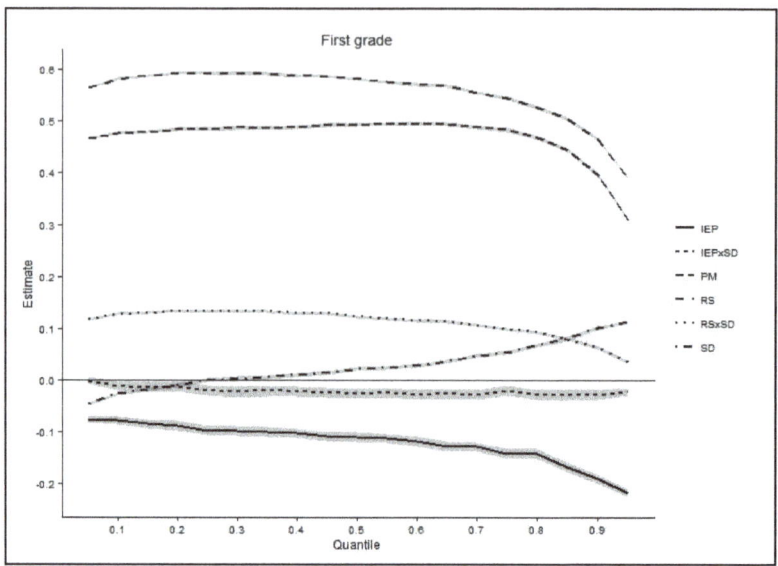

Figure 3. First grade quantile plot with 95% confidence interval bands.

The RSxPSD interaction effect generally decreased from the 0.05 to 0.95 quantile ($0.036 \leq \beta \leq 0.135$). Figure 4 contains the plots of this interaction effect. As with kindergarten, individuals with low relative status did better in classes with low peer SDs, and students with high relative status did better in classes with high peer SDs. However, for children with low relative status in classrooms at the high end of the conditional distribution (0.75 quantile, bottom panel), the classroom homogeneity did not matter (i.e., there was no difference in performance between low PSD and high PSD). For children with high relative status, when peer SD was high, children had better spring vocabulary achievement, regardless of class performance (low or high end of conditional distribution).

The IEPxSD interaction, while statistically significant in some quantiles, was not practically substantive ($-0.028 \leq \beta \leq 0.001$). This interaction is plotted in Figure 5. Regardless of general classroom performance (top or bottom panel), children had higher spring vocabulary scores when they did not themselves have an IEP compared to children who did have an IEP.

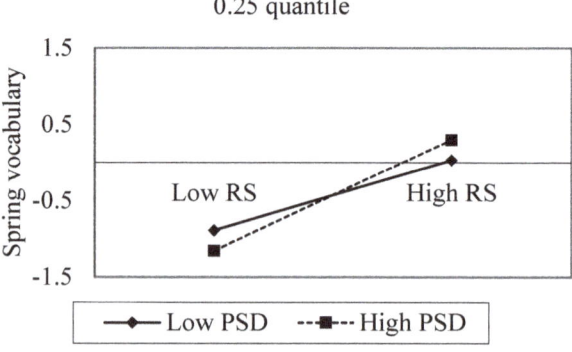

Figure 4. *Cont.*

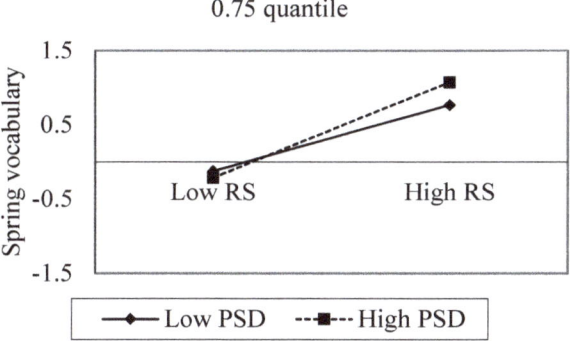

Figure 4. First grade RSxSD interaction at the 0.25 quantile (**top**) and the 0.75 quantile (**bottom**) PSD = peer group standard deviation; RS = student's relative status.

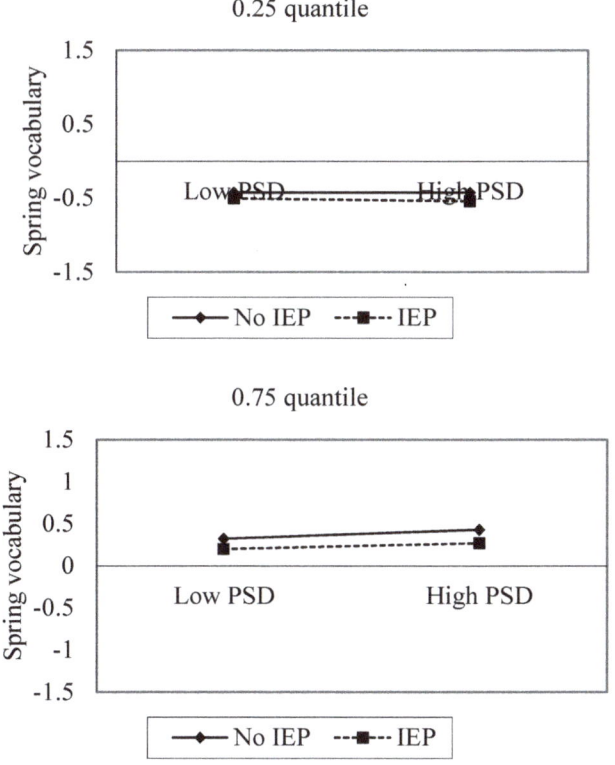

Figure 5. First grade IEPxSD interaction at the 0.25 quantile (**top**) and the 0.75 quantile (**bottom**). PSD = peer group standard deviation.

3.3.3. Second Grade

The second grade model included the same predictors as that of the first grade with the addition of a main effect for peer IEP status and an IEP by relative status interaction. A quantile process plot of all effects except for intercept is provided in Figure 6. Across quantiles, relative status was the strongest predictor of achievement in second grade ($0.296 \leq \beta \leq 0.532$), with the effect decreasing as quantiles increased. The second strongest predictor was peer group mean ($0.281 \leq \beta \leq 0.481$). As with relative status, the peer group mean effect decreased as quantiles increased. However, from the 0.55 through 0.85 quantile, there was no discernable difference (when accounting for confidence intervals) between the magnitude of the relative status and peer group mean effects.

The third strongest predictor was IEP ($-0.235 \leq \beta \leq -0.090$). However, unlike relative status and peer group mean, the absolute value of the IEP effect increased as quantiles increased, i.e., the impact of having an IEP was much higher for higher achieving students. While the main effect for peer group SD was not substantive ($-0.045 \leq \beta \leq 0.057$), it did have a substantive range (0.102). The main effect for peer IEP status was neither substantive in magnitude ($-0.033 \leq \beta \leq 0.001$) nor in range (0.034).

As in K and first grade, the RSxSD interaction effect for second grade generally decreased ($0.144 \leq \beta \leq 0.041$). Students with low relative status had better spring vocabulary scores in classrooms at the low end of the conditional vocabulary distribution when that class was more homogenous (low PSD; Figure 7, top panel), but for students with low relative status in classrooms at the high end of the conditional vocabulary distribution, classroom homogeneity did not matter in predicting their spring vocabulary scores (Figure 7, bottom panel).

The IEP by peer group SD (IEPxPSD), while statistically significant in some quantiles, was not practically substantial. For students who did not have an IEP, they performed better than their counterparts who did have an IEP regardless of classroom homogeneity or conditional classroom performance (See Figure 8).

The IEP by relative status interaction (IEPxRS) plots are presented in Figure 9. The association between relative status and spring vocabulary was more pronounced for individuals with an IEP at the higher quantiles (Figure 9). For students at the lower end of the conditional vocabulary distribution, regardless of relative status, students performed slightly better in spring when they did not have an IEP (Figure 9, top panel). This effect was much more substantial in classrooms at the higher end of the conditional vocabulary distribution (Figure 9, bottom panel): a student with low relative status who did not have an IEP performed nearly a half standard deviation higher in spring vocabulary compared to a similar student with low relative status but who had an IEP. There was a small, but significant difference favoring students who had high relative status but no IEP compared to students with high relative status but who did have an IEP.

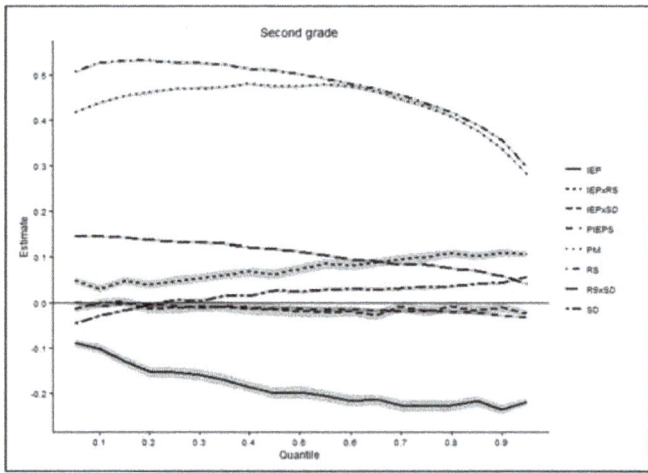

Figure 6. Quantile effects plot for second grade. Note. IEPxRS = IEP by relative status interaction, IEPxSD = IEP by peer SD interaction, PM = peer mean, RS = student's relative status, RSxSD = student's relative status by peer SD interaction, PSD = peer group SD. Intercept is not included. Gray area represents the 95% confidence band.

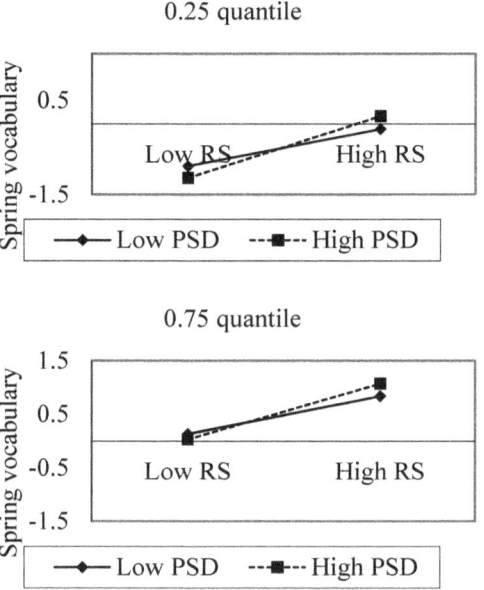

Figure 7. Second grade RSxSD interaction at the 0.25 quantile (**top**) and the 0.75 quantile (**bottom**). PSD = peer group standard deviation.

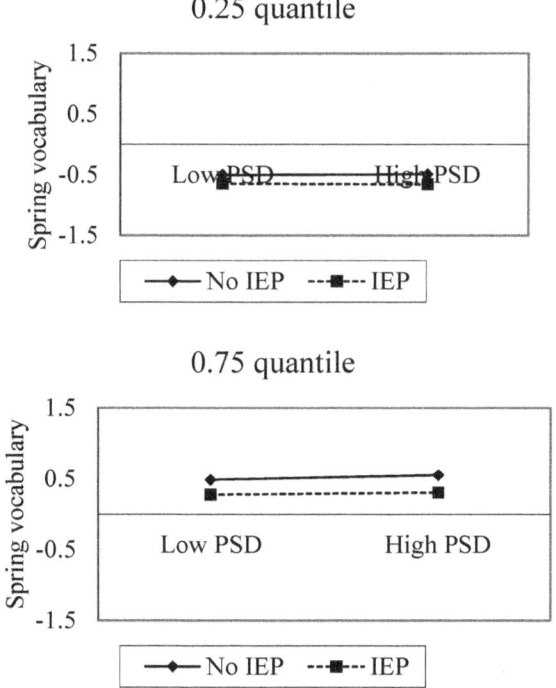

Figure 8. Second grade IEPxPSD interaction at the 0.25 quantile (**top**) and the 0.75 quantile (**bottom**). PSD = peer group SD.

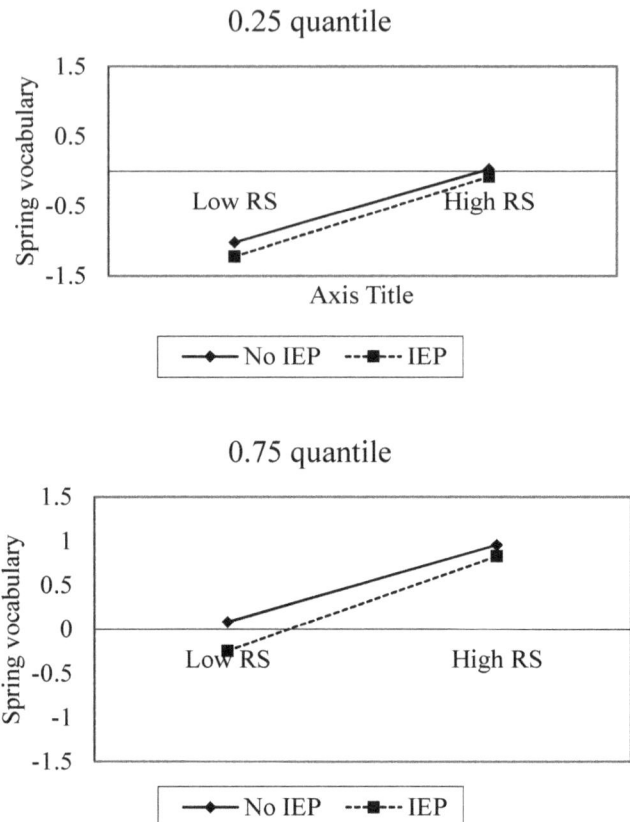

Figure 9. Second grade IEPxRS interaction at the 0.25 quantile (**top**) and the 0.75 quantile (**bottom**). RS = student's relative status.

3.4. Summary

In the present study, we investigated how individual-level vocabulary knowledge was affected by their peers' achievement levels for students in grades K-2. Taken together, there were consistent findings across grades K-2 on the influence of relative status, peer group average achievement, homogeneity of peer achievement in fall vocabulary, and the influence of having students with IEPs in the classroom on spring vocabulary achievement. Across all grades, students' fall vocabulary, relative to their classroom peers, was the strongest predictor of spring vocabulary. However, the predictive nature of relative status was stronger at lower quantiles. Similarly, the effect of the peer average vocabulary was stronger for students at the lower quantiles. An opposite trend was found among IEP status and heterogeneity of the classroom. That is, having an IEP had a stronger effect among students at the higher quantiles, and, students at the higher quantiles were more positively affected by a heterogeneous classroom than by a homogenous classroom. There was a trend where the peer group SD had a stronger effect for students in upper quantiles than lower quantiles. Among students with low relative status in classrooms at the high end of the conditional distribution, classroom homogeneity did not matter. For children with high relative status, when peer SD was high, children had better spring vocabulary achievement, regardless of class performance. Across grades, peer IEP status did not have a substantive effect on individuals' performance.

4. Discussion

4.1. Peer-Level Achievement Effects on Individual-Level Vocabulary Achievement

Students' fall vocabulary status—relative to their peers—had the strongest association with spring vocabulary achievement. This finding corroborates a finding in Dutch-speaking second grade students, whereby student background characteristics and their prior achievement explained about 70% of the variance in their language achievement [15]. Compared to other predictors, relative status had the strongest association to vocabulary achievement across grades, but the magnitude of the association declined across the quantiles of vocabulary achievement.

This study supports the importance of peer achievement. Across grades, it was second only to relative status in predicting spring vocabulary. Interestingly, by second grade, for students between the 0.55 and 0.85 quantile, there was no discernable difference in the relation between spring vocabulary and relative status and the relation between spring vocabulary and peer group mean. Convergent with other studies of peer effects, this study supported a prior hypothesis that the relation between peer group mean and individual-level vocabulary outcomes was stronger for students at lower quantiles than higher quantiles. Regardless, the average vocabulary levels of students' peers in the fall is an important predictor of individual students' spring vocabulary.

Our study examined at-risk children's vocabulary knowledge from schools with high rates of free and reduced lunch status, which can be considered a proxy for low SES. Students from lower SES households tend to have different learning trajectories for their language skills [37], and vocabulary size tends to be the oral language component which is most sensitive to the effects of low SES [38]. In a study of Dutch language learners in grades 4 to 6, language gains for low-SES students improved as the percentage of low-SES peers increased in their classroom; i.e., more homogenous classrooms lead to larger gains [16]. We measured homogeneity as the standard deviation of peers' initial vocabulary achievement. While peer group SD was not a strong predictor in Kindergarten, it increased in magnitude in first and second grade, and it increased across the quantiles. Perhaps the more interesting finding across grades regarding peer group SD was the interaction of peer group SD with relative status. Students' relative status moderated the influence of peer group SD: students with lower relative status did better in classes that were more homogeneous, and students with higher relative status did better in classes that were more heterogeneous. This finding pits models of peer effects against each other: the Boutique model or the Focus model of peer effects supports classroom homogeneity as good for improving achievement levels [8], but our findings suggest that classroom homogeneity might positively impact vocabulary learning only for the children at the lowest end of the vocabulary achievement spectrum.

Disability Status

Although students with disabilities did not perform as well as their peers, the influence of the disability was limited to the individual with the disability. The percentage of students with disabilities in a classroom never had a substantive relation with spring vocabulary. This suggests that while having a disability has substantial implications for the individual, the presence of individuals with disabilities in a classroom is not related to individuals' achievement after accounting for other factors such as relative status and peer achievement. This finding is the opposite of what would be found in a "Bad Apple model" of peer effects [8] (p. 6), whereby the presence of a student with poor outcomes negatively affects the outcomes of other students.

While having a disability did not moderate any effects in Kindergarten, having a disability did interact with the peer group SD effect in first and second grade, and IEP status also interacted with relative status effect in second grade. This interaction was more pronounced in the upper quantiles: in first and second grade, the relation between peer group SD and spring vocabulary was weaker for students with disabilities. In second grade, the relation between relative status and spring vocabulary was stronger for individuals with IEPs.

4.2. Limitations

The present study discovered significant peer effects in the classroom on vocabulary achievement, but the study is not without limitations. We discuss some important limitations of our study below.

4.2.1. School Reassignment and Peer Effects

Voluntary reassignment based on school choice initiatives can greatly affect the estimation of peer effects. Families may self-select into certain schools based on their own family characteristics (e.g., income, job locations, residence) or based on their child's characteristics (e.g., higher performing students may be reassigned to magnet schools or gifted programs). Additionally, homogenous classrooms may be created by families self-selecting into schools with better characteristics (e.g., higher performing classrooms and teachers) or through school assignment of students with similar abilities to the same classrooms, creating homogenous levels of child ability that would not have occurred given natural placement [1]. Given that the majority of schools in this sample are Title I schools, which have a disproportionately high level of students with low achievement, self-selection into these schools is unlikely. However, there are some schools that do choose to be represented in the state archival database that may be higher-achieving or have magnet/gifted programs for high-ability or gifted students.

One noted limitation to this study is that we did not control for students who moved classrooms or did not have a consistent peer group. This decision was made because 72% of students remained with the same peer group across the full year, and less than 1% of students did not have a consistent peer group (i.e., they were with a different teacher at all three assessment points). Thus, while there was a considerable amount of movement between peer groups, the overwhelming majority (over 99%) of students had the same peer group for at least two-thirds of the academic year. Therefore, for these analyses, we did not consider removing or statistically controlling for the less than 1% of individuals that did not have a consistent peer group. Future research may consider investigating student mobility as another potential peer effect.

4.2.2. Theoretical and Empirical Difficulties in Measuring Peer Effects

Studying peer effects is difficult, particularly the nature of measuring and estimating the effects themselves. Selection bias is often an issue: an observer may assume that high achievement is an *effect* of being in a high-achieving group instead of being a *cause* for belonging to it [1]. One way this might manifest is if teachers select students who were high-achieving in the previous school year, thus creating a homogenous classroom of high-achieving students. Our findings suggest, however, that building a homogenous classroom of high achievers may negatively impact those students, particularly with respect to their vocabulary achievement.

Secondly, previous models of peer effects have attempted to disentangle the mean-level differences in achievement through something known as the baseline model. This baseline model assumes that there are linear relations between a student and their peers' achievement levels; thus, a student's score is linearly affected by the average classroom score [1]. This is problematic if one is interested in effects outside of the mean level–such as in our study. We addressed the limitations of the baseline model by employing a multi-level quantile regression approach with random effects. This allowed us to examine the effects at the tails for both low-achieving and high-achieving students without a loss of power through median splits or multi-group modeling. Future studies should consider incorporating quantile regression approaches to condition their regression models at certain quantiles of achievement.

4.2.3. Missing Variables that Might Further Affect Individual-Level Achievement

Within the present study, we were able to include only achievement-related variables and to account for those peer characteristics that were provided by the PMRN database, i.e., gender, race, free-or-reduced lunch status, IEP status, and disability status. As such, we are missing potentially important variables that could influence the effects of peers on individual-level student achievement. First, we have no knowledge of students' parental support or engagement in their schools and classrooms. Previous studies have suggested that students with higher achievement may have more engaged parents [5], but this may be a bidirectional relation, such that more engaged parents may cause higher achievement, and higher achievement may cause parents to be more engaged. Further, we did not account for additional potentially important parent-level characteristics that may explain additional variance in the vocabulary learning of these children.

4.3. Implications and Future Directions

On average, regardless of level of achievement (i.e., where you condition the distribution of vocabulary achievement), the context of the classroom matters. Understanding and accounting for these effects has important implications for educational research, especially with regard to drawing correct conclusions on classroom effectiveness practices [13]. The present findings suggest that peers' average achievement and the homogeneity of peer performance have differential impacts on students' vocabulary knowledge outcomes. Classroom compositions can greatly impact the learning environment [6]; our findings suggest that a student with low relative levels of fall vocabulary knowledge would benefit from being in a class with similarly-leveled students. However, a student with high relative levels of fall vocabulary knowledge would benefit from being placed in a class with peers of ranging levels of vocabulary achievement.

Additionally, across grades and quantiles, there was a negative relation between having a disability and end-of-grade vocabulary achievement, and this relation consistently increased in magnitude. There was a greater difference between students with and without disabilities in the upper quantiles than in the lower quantiles. This suggests that lower-achieving students with and without disabilities are more similar than higher-achieving students with and without disabilities, which has implications for both planning of intervention and remedial services. Among students in lower quantiles, providing services should be dependent on students' relative status to their peers, rather than disability status. However, because the discrepancy between students with and without disabilities increases in the upper quantiles, intervention should still be provided to students with disabilities. Taking the homogeneity of the classroom and the impact of having a disability together, practical implications can be found in structuring the classroom to meet the needs of all students. For example, while having a wide range of abilities may be beneficial for higher achieving students, planning small-group instruction with similarly achieving peers may be a way to meet the needs of lower achieving students.

The present findings leave us with important avenues for future research. First, we did not explore *how* classroom contexts matter, other than peers' performance and characteristics. Other classroom characteristics, such as teacher years of experience [12], curricular decisions [25,26], and class size [12], could have large impacts on student outcomes independent of peer effects. Indeed, a large study of students found that teacher experience and classroom size predicted student outcomes independent of peer achievement [12], but the mechanism of *why* these effects occur is still not known. Experimental studies that randomize students to teachers with similar levels of experience and similar class sizes might yield more insight in to how peer effects manifest when classroom conditions are controlled. However, one must proceed with caution: adjusting peer compositions too wildly can have unintended negative effects, particularly for lower achieving students [39].

5. Conclusions

Classroom contexts matter for students' vocabulary achievement, which is an important predictor of reading comprehension and education outcomes. The results of our study showed that young children's vocabulary achievement is highly dependent on their relative status and the characteristics of their classroom (i.e., peer performance). For students with relatively low fall scores, their spring scores tend to be higher when they are in classrooms with homogenous peers. For students with relatively high fall scores, they often have higher scores in spring when their peers have varying levels of performance. The literature on peer effects would greatly benefit from studies aimed at understanding how and why these peer effects manifest in an effort to improve outcomes for students at the lowest ends of the distribution.

Supplementary Materials: The following are available online at http://www.mdpi.com/2227-7102/8/4/181/s1, Table S1: HLM Fit Indices for Kindergarten, Table S2: HLM Fit Indices for Grade 1, Table S3: HLM Fit Indices for Grade 2.

Author Contributions: Conceptualization, Y.P. & J.S.F.; Data Curation, Y.P.; Formal Analysis: J.S.F. & Y.P.; Methodology, J.S.F. & Y.P.; Visualization, Y.P.; Writing—Original Draft Preparation, J.M.Q. & J.S.F.; Writing—Review & Editing, J.M.Q. & Y.P.

Funding: This research was funded in part by the National Institute of Child Health and Human Development, [P50HD052120], and the Institute of Education Sciences [R305A130131, R305F100005].

Conflicts of Interest: The authors declare no conflict of interest. The funders had no role in the design of the study; in the collection, analyses, or interpretation of data; in the writing of the manuscript, and in the decision to publish the results.

Appendix A

Table A1. HLM Model for Kindergarten.

	β	SE	df	t
Fixed Effects				
Intercept	0.020	0.005	7777	3.832 ***
RS	0.551	0.002	8981	269.188 ***
IEP	−0.138	0.007	7527	−18.587 ***
PM	0.438	0.006	2782	77.042 ***
PSD	0.004	0.005	3425	0.707
PIEPS	−0.002	0.005	1996	−0.320
IEPxRS	0.041	0.006	45,890	6.544 ***
IEPxPM	0.006	0.006	4846	0.924
IEPxPSD	−0.015	0.006	4702	−2.476 *
IEPxPIEPS	−0.016	0.005	2441	−2.846
RSxPM	−0.027	0.002	7573	−13.804 ***
RSxPSD	0.126	0.002	7846	63.711 ***
RSxPIEPS	−0.001	0.002	10,630	−0.296
Random effects				
	Var.	SD	X^2 (df = 6)	
Intercept	0.168	0.410		
RS	0.009	0.097	782.1 ***	
IEP	0.014	0.117	47.0 ***	
pm	0.021	0.146	355.4 ***	
sd	0.006	0.079	34.6 ***	
IEPZ	0.001	0.027	21.8 **	
Residual	0.291	0.539		

*** <0.001; ** <0.01; * <0.05.

Table A2. HLM Model for First Grade.

	β	SE	df	t
Fixed Effects				
Intercept	0.006	0.005	6998	1.375
RS	0.558	0.002	8751	257.864 ***
IEP	−0.111	0.007	7512	−15.248 ***
PM	0.468	0.005	3029	91.278 ***
PSD	0.021	0.005	3473	4.268 ***
PIEPS	−0.015	0.005	1982	−3.244 **

Table A2. *Cont.*

	β	SE	df	t
IEPxRS	0.047	0.006	51,300	7.536 ***
IEPxPM	0.002	0.006	4833	0.379
IEPxPSD	−0.018	0.006	4636	−3.021 **
IEPxPIEPS	0.005	0.006	2716	0.803
RSxPM	−0.051	0.002	7165	−24.841 ***
RSxPSD	0.119	0.002	7308	57.967 ***
RSxPIEPS	0.001	0.002	10,000	0.505

Random effects			
	Var.	SD	X^2 (df = 6)
Intercept	0.112	0.335	
RS	0.008	0.092	558.0 ***
IEP	0.011	0.104	35.7 ***
pm	0.017	0.131	282.4 ***
sd	0.008	0.087	119.8 ***
IEPZ	0.004	0.065	59.7 ***
Residual	0.311	0.558	

*** <0.001; ** <0.01; * <0.05.

Table A3. HLM Model for Second Grade.

	β	SE	df	t
Fixed Effects				
Intercept	0.022	0.006	6718	3.943 ***
RS	0.484	0.002	8138	200.374 ***
IEP	−0.177	0.008	7031	−22.330 ***
PM	0.438	0.006	2504	73.096 ***
PSD	0.013	0.006	2677	2.302 *
PIEPS	−0.008	0.006	1678	−1.422
IEPxRS	0.070	0.007	52,240	10.516 ***
IEPxPM	0.010	0.007	4825	1.503
IEPxPSD	−0.011	0.007	4620	−1.692
IEPxPIEPS	−0.020	0.006	3057	−3.191 **
RSxPM	−0.059	0.002	6522	−26.032 ***
RSxPSD	0.115	0.002	6710	50.200 ***
RSxPIEPS	0.000	0.002	8587	0.131

Random effects			
	Var.	SD	X^2 (df = 6)
Intercept	0.170	0.412	
RS	0.009	0.097	641.3 ***
IEP	0.020	0.143	103.1 ***
pm	0.014	0.119	140.5 ***
sd	0.004	0.066	40.6 ***
IEPZ	0.002	0.044	10.2
Residual	0.357	0.597	

*** <0.001; ** <0.01; * <0.05.

References

1. Hoxby, C. *Peer Effects in the Classroom: Learning from Gender and Race Variation*; Working Paper 7867; National Bureau of Economic Research: Cambridge, MA, USA, 2000; Available online: http://www.nber.org/papers/w7867.pdf (accessed on 22 October 2018).
2. Zimmer, R.W.; Toma, E.F. Peer Effects in Private and Public Schools across Countries. *J. Policy Anal. Manag.* **2000**, *19*, 75–92. [CrossRef]

3. Hattie, J.A.C. Classroom Composition and Peer Effects. *Int. J. Educ. Res.* **2002**, *37*, 449–481. [CrossRef]
4. Coleman, J.S.; Campbell, E.Q.; Hobson, C.J.; McPartland, J.; Mood, A.M.; Weinfeld, F.D.; York, R.L. *Equality of Educational Opportunity*; OE-38001; National Center for Education Statistics: Washington, DC, USA, 1966; p. 746.
5. Willms, J.D. *Monitoring School Performance: A Guide for Educators*; Routledge: Abingdon, UK, 2003.
6. Dar, Y.; Resh, N. Classroom Intellectual Composition and Academic Achievement. *Am. Educ. Res. J.* **1986**, *23*, 357–374. [CrossRef]
7. Leiter, J. Classroom Composition and Achievement Gains. *Sociol. Educ.* **1983**, *56*, 126–132. [CrossRef]
8. Hoxby, C.M.; Weingarth, G. *Taking Race out of the Equation: School Reassignment and the Structure of Peer Effects*; Working Paper 7867; Harvard University: Cambridge, MA, USA, 2003; p. 47.
9. Thrupp, M.; Lauder, H.; Robinson, T. School Composition and Peer Effects. *Int. J. Educ. Res.* **2002**, *37*, 483–504. [CrossRef]
10. Wilkinson, I.A.G.; Parr, J.M.; Fung, I.Y.Y.; Hattie, J.A.C.; Townsend, M.A.R. Discussion: Modeling and Maximizing Peer Effects in School. *Int. J. Educ. Res.* **2002**, *37*, 521–535. [CrossRef]
11. Sacerdote, B. Peer Effects in Education: How Might They Work, How Big Are They and How Much Do We Know Thus Far? In *Handbook of the Economics of Education*; Hanushek, E.A., Machin, S., Woessmann, L., Eds.; Elsevier: Amsterdam, The Netherlands, 2011; Volume 3, pp. 249–277.
12. Bryan, T.H. Peer Popularity of Learning Disabled Children: A Replication. *J. Learn. Disabil.* **1976**, *9*, 307–311. [CrossRef]
13. Vaughn, S.; Elbaum, B.E.; Schumm, J.S. The Effects of Inclusion on the Social Functioning of Students with Learning Disabilities. *J. Learn. Disabil.* **1996**, *29*, 599–608. [CrossRef]
14. Burke, M.A.; Sass, T.R. Classroom Peer Effects and Student Achievement. *J. Labor. Econ.* **2013**, *31*, 51–82. [CrossRef]
15. De Fraine, B.D.; Damme, J.V.; Landeghem, G.V.; Opdenakker, M.-C.; Onghena, P. The Effect of Schools and Classes on Language Achievement. *Br. Educ. Res. J.* **2003**, *29*, 841–859. [CrossRef]
16. Peetsma, T.; van der Veen, I.; Koopman, P.; van Schooten, E. Class Composition Influences on Pupils' Cognitive Development. *Sch. Eff. Sch. Improv.* **2006**, *17*, 275–302. [CrossRef]
17. Foorman, B.R.; Petscher, Y.; Herrera, S. Unique and Common Effects of Decoding and Language Factors in Predicting Reading Comprehension in Grades 1–10. *Learn. Individ. Differ.* **2018**, *63*, 12–23. [CrossRef]
18. Guo, Y.; Tompkins, V.; Justice, L.; Petscher, Y. Classroom Age Composition and Vocabulary Development Among At-Risk Preschoolers. *Early Educ. Dev.* **2014**, *25*, 1016–1034. [CrossRef] [PubMed]
19. Quinn, J.M.; Wagner, R.K.; Petscher, Y.; Lopez, D. Developmental Relations between Vocabulary Knowledge and Reading Comprehension: A Latent Change Score Modeling Study. *Child Dev.* **2015**, *86*, 159–175. [CrossRef] [PubMed]
20. Kim, Y.-S. Language and Cognitive Predictors of Text Comprehension: Evidence from Multivariate Analysis. *Child Dev.* **2015**, *86*, 128–144. [CrossRef] [PubMed]
21. Kim, Y.-S.G. Direct and Mediated Effects of Language and Cognitive Skills on Comprehension of Oral Narrative Texts (Listening Comprehension) for Children. *J. Exp. Child Psychol.* **2016**, *141*, 101–120. [CrossRef] [PubMed]
22. Perfetti, C. Reading Ability: Lexical Quality to Comprehension. *Sci. Stud. Read.* **2007**, *11*, 357–383. [CrossRef]
23. Perfetti, C.; Hart, L. The Lexical Quality Hypothesis. In *Precursors of Functional Literacy*; Verhoeven, L.T., Elbro, C., Reitsma, P., Eds.; John Benjamins Publishing: Amsterdam, The Netherlands, 2002; pp. 189–214. ISBN 978-90-272-1806-3.
24. Henry, G.T.; Rickman, D.K. Do Peers Influence Children's Skill Development in Preschool? *Econ. Educ. Rev.* **2007**, *26*, 100–112. [CrossRef]
25. Justice, L.M.; Logan, J.A.R.; Lin, T.-J.; Kaderavek, J.N. Peer Effects in Early Childhood Education: Testing the Assumptions of Special-Education Inclusion. *Psychol. Sci.* **2014**, *25*, 1722–1729. [CrossRef] [PubMed]
26. Justice, L.M.; Petscher, Y.; Schatschneider, C.; Mashburn, A. Peer Effects in Preschool Classrooms: Is Children's Language Growth Associated with Their Classmates' Skills? *Child Dev.* **2011**, *82*, 1768–1777. [CrossRef] [PubMed]
27. Koenker, R.; Bassett, G. Regression Quantiles. *Econometrica* **1978**, *46*, 33–50. [CrossRef]
28. Petscher, Y. Do Our Means of Inquiry Match Our Intentions? *Front. Psychol.* **2016**, *7*. [CrossRef] [PubMed]

29. Petscher, Y.; Logan, J.A.R. Quantile Regression in the Study of Developmental Sciences. *Child Dev.* **2014**, *85*, 861–881. [CrossRef] [PubMed]

30. Galarza, C.E.; Lachos, V.H. Package 'qrNLMM'; R Package version 1.4. 2015. Available online: https://cran.r-project.org/package=qrNLMM (accessed on 22 October 2018).

31. Galarza, C.E.; Lachos, V.H.; Bandyopadhyay, D. Quantile Regression in Linear Mixed Models: A Stochastic Approximation EM Approach. *Stat. Interface* **2017**, *10*, 471–482. [CrossRef] [PubMed]

32. Geraci, M. Linear Quantile Mixed Models: The Lqmm Package for Laplace Quantile Regression. *J. Stat. Softw.* **2014**, *57*, 1–29. [CrossRef]

33. Geraci, M.; Bottai, M. Linear Quantile Mixed Models. *Stat. Comput.* **2014**, *24*, 461–479. [CrossRef]

34. Florida Department of Education. *Florida Assessments for Instruction in Reading Kindergarten—Grade 2 Technical Manual*; Florida Department of Education: Tallahassee, FL, USA, 2009.

35. Williams, K. *Expressive Vocabulary Test*, 2nd ed.; Pearson: San Antonio, TX, USA, 2007.

36. Harcourt Brace Educational Measurement. *Stanford Achievement Test*, 10th ed.; Harcourt Assessment: San Antonio, TX, USA, 2003.

37. Hoff, E. Interpreting the Early Language Trajectories of Children from Low-SES and Language Minority Homes: Implications for Closing Achievement Gaps. *Dev. Psychol.* **2013**, *49*, 4–14. [CrossRef] [PubMed]

38. Hart, B.; Risley, T.R. *Meaningful Differences in the Everyday Experience of Young American Children*; Meaningful Differences in the Everyday Experience of Young American Children; Paul H Brookes Publishing: Baltimore, MD, USA, 1995.

39. Carrell, S.E.; Sacerdote, B.I.; West, J.E. *From Natural Variation to Optimal Policy? The Lucas Critique Meets Peer Effects*; Working Paper 16865; National Bureau of Economic Research: Cambridge, MA, USA, 2011; Available online: http://www.nber.org/papers/w16865 (accessed on 22 October 2018).

Article

Concept Raps versus Concept Maps: A Culturally Responsive Approach to STEM Vocabulary Development

Jamaal Young [1,*][iD], Jemimah Young [1], Marti Cason [1], Nickolaus Ortiz [2], Marquita Foster [1] and Christina Hamilton [3]

1   Department of Teacher Education & Administration, University of North Texas, Dallas, TX 75201, USA;
    Jemimah.young@unt.edu (J.Y.); marti.cason@unt.edu (M.C.); Foster@unt.edu (M.F.)
2   Department of Teaching, Learning, and Culture, Texas A&M University, College Station, TX 77843, USA;
    Nickortiz@tamu.edu
3   Department of Curriculum and Instruction, Texas A&M Central Texas, Killeen, TX 76549, USA;
    hamilton.c@tamuct.edu
*   Correspondence: Jamaal.young@unt.edu; Tel.: +1-(940)-220-4050

Received: 2 May 2018; Accepted: 27 June 2018; Published: 31 July 2018

Abstract: This article argues that the development of rap song lyrics or lyrical concept mapping can be a viable pedagogical alternative to the development of concept maps as a means to reinforce STEM vocabulary. Hip-hop pedagogy is a culturally responsive pedagogy that leverages the funds of knowledge acquired from hip-hop culture. Unfortunately, many students with strong hip-hop cultural identities may lack equally strong mathematics identities. Given the success of hip-hop pedagogies within the science content area, we posit that hip-hop pedagogies are appropriate in other STEM content areas such as mathematics. Concept mapping is an instructional tool that has been empirically validated as an effective means to develop strong conceptualizations of mathematics content. While hip-hop pedagogy is well established in the science content area, it remains underdeveloped within mathematics education. We argue that the lyrical structure of a rap song is fundamentally similar to the structure of a concept map. This article provides a framework to support lyrical concept mapping as a culturally responsive instructional tool that can be used as an alternative to traditional concept mapping. Special attention is placed on the use of hip-hop pedagogy to affirm and empower dually marginalized students.

Keywords: hip-hop pedagogy; concept maps; vocabulary development; STEM

1. Introduction

Vocabulary development is essential to conceptual understanding and sustained disciplinary knowledge in Science, Technology, Engineering and Mathematics (STEM). "Vocabulary is at the surface level of language usage; thus, students need to develop mathematical and scientific vocabulary to be able to explicitly communicate their mathematical and scientific reasoning with others" [1] (p. 69). Therefore, a lack of vocabulary mastery can pose a significant challenge for student achievement in STEM. For instance, data suggest that underachievement in STEM content areas is often the result of acute challenges related to a lack of fluency and understanding of fundamental STEM vocabulary [2,3]. Increasing the number of culturally and linguistically diverse STEM professionals remains a challenge for educators, businesses and our nation.

Many underrepresented populations of learners have tremendous STEM potential that remains untapped due to the cultural discontinuity that can exist between the student and traditional pedagogical approaches to STEM content or instruction. Culturally informed practices, such as hip-hop pedagogy, are proffered as a means to overcome the instructional challenges of these and other cultural discontinuities in the mathematics classroom. We argue that the lyrical structure of a rap song is fundamentally similar to the structure of a well-defined concept map. Therefore, this article provides a framework to support lyrical concept mapping as a culturally informed instructional tool that can be used as an alternative to traditional concept mapping. Special attention will be placed on the use of lyrical concept maps to address challenges related to vocabulary development in mathematics.

The National Council of Mathematics Teachers (NCTM) has placed a renewed interest in the development of effective mechanisms to increase access and equity within all mathematics classrooms. As such, the Access and Equity Principle explicitly encourages teachers to become more responsive to students' backgrounds, experiences, cultural perspectives, traditions and knowledge when designing and implementing a mathematics program and assessing its effectiveness [4] (p. 1). Likewise, NCTM has consistently advocated for an increased focus on mathematics disciplinary vocabulary development. For example, "communication is an essential part of mathematics," therefore, students need opportunities to use writing to express mathematical ideas [5] (p. 60). Hence, merging culturally informed tasks that incorporate writing skills represents a plausible pedagogical practice that can yield meaningful changes in student engagement and achievement in mathematics.

Hip-hop includes four pillars: rapping, deejaying, breakdancing and graffiti art [6,7]. Dimitriadis, Cole and Costello indicate that hip-hop culture is the medium that informs how youth construct their identities and social networks [6]; this embodies a notion of a fifth, often less noted pillar of hip-hop that is referred to as Knowledge of Self [7]. Hip-hop pedagogy leverages student cultural funds of knowledge to foster a deeper understanding of complex ideas and information by drawing connections to the cultural norms of the growing international hip-hop society. Hip-hop pedagogy is hence considered to represent a natural extension, adaption or remix to the established culturally responsive pedagogical practices [8,9]. Authentic implementation of culturally relevant or culturally specific pedagogies and their applications in Science, Technology, Engineering and Mathematics (STEM) classrooms remain relatively absent from professional practice. However, intersections exist between hip-hop identity and mathematics identity, which can potentially carve out an academic space for creativity, social justice, and strength-based instructional practices that reflect authentic cases of culturally sustaining pedagogies within the mathematics content area. The authors provide a more thorough discussion of hip-hop pedagogy and its foundations in hip-hop more generally within the body of this paper.

Many critics of culturally informed pedagogies cite that many of the proposed approaches lack practicality. The translation of culturally responsive teaching from theory to practice is difficult for the majority of classroom teachers. This perspective is substantiated by self-efficacy data that suggest that both in-service and pre-service teachers lack the culturally responsive teaching self-efficacy (CRTSE) to execute culturally responsive practices in their classrooms [10,11]. Appropriately, it is important to build connections between practices that are familiar or well established within the discipline. Concept mapping represents a pedagogical practice that has documented success across multiple STEM content areas and is relatively commonplace in most teacher education and professional development activities. The substantial uptake and acceptance of concept mapping provides an ideal pedagogical strategy to bridge connections between traditional STEM teaching approaches and hip-hop pedagogies.

Hip-hop pedagogy is one means to increase access and equity in the mathematics classroom by leveraging hip-hop identities to foster mathematics identities. For the purpose of this discussion, we argue that many mathematically disenfranchised youth are rich in hip-hop cultural capital that can be harnessed as a transformational instructional tool. However, this transformation requires more pedagogically specific "high expectations and strong support for all students" [12] (p. 8). The guiding principles for school mathematics state "[a]n excellent mathematics program requires that all students have access to a high-quality mathematics curriculum, effective teaching and learning, high expectations, and support and resources needed to maximize their learning potential" [13] (p. 5). This suggests that to be considered excellent, a mathematics program must meet the instructional needs of all students by providing the support and resources necessary to build their mathematics capacity.

2. Purpose

The purpose of this article is to provide an explicit pathway between hip-hop pedagogy and formal mathematics instruction. Concept mapping is an established instructional tool that has been empirically validated as an effective means of developing strong conceptualizations of mathematics content. Consider the wealth of research supporting the benefits of concept mapping as an instructional support for relational understanding, and then, consider if you could repackage this tool to make it not only accessible to, but a strength of traditionally underserved youth. We propose that a rap is simply a "lyrical concept map" within which a central concept is connected by verses and summarized by the hook.

Here we posit that lyrical concept maps or concept rapping can serve as a conduit between traditional pedagogical approaches to STEM disciplinary vocabulary development and emergent approaches such as hip-hop pedagogy. While hip-hop pedagogy is well established in the science content area, it remains underdeveloped in other STEM domains such as mathematics. Given the success of hip-hop pedagogies within the science content area, we suggest that hip-hop pedagogies are appropriate across Science, Technology, Engineering and Mathematics (STEM) content areas. In the discussion that follows, we explicate the importance of vocabulary development as a means to support achievement in STEM content areas. Then we argue that hip-hop lyrics are fundamentally similar to traditional concept maps. To facilitate this argument, we review the literature on concept mapping within the context of STEM. Then we examine the current effects of hip-hop pedagogy on STEM content learning. Lastly, we compare and contrast the structure of concept maps and the structure of rap songs to clarify the inherent connections between them to build a case for the consideration of lyrical concept maps as instructional tools within STEM education.

3. Vocabulary Development and STEM Achievement

Achievement in STEM content areas remains a challenge for many minoritized populations of learners. These achievement disparities jeopardize the nation's scientific, technology and engineering capacity. Thus, the shortage of women and other traditionally underrepresented populations is a well-known challenge [14]. According to data from the National Center for Education Statistics, low-income and minoritized youth lack foundational skills in STEM content [15]. One of these often-overlooked foundational skills is a strong grasp of STEM discipline-specific vocabulary. A strong disciplinary vocabulary is recognized as a key component of achievement and retention in STEM-related content areas. According to the NCTM Principles and Standards for School Mathematics, students should be encouraged and supported as "they communicate to learn mathematics, and they learn to communicate mathematically." [5] (p. 60). To edify this notion, intensive research conducted by Knuth and Peressini suggest students engaging in mathematical language increases their mathematical understanding [16]. Little is known regarding teachers' or even students' development of STEM-specific language across the individual content areas [17] (p. 188). For instance, very few measures exist to solely measure vocabulary understanding in mathematics and other STEM content areas [18]. However, there is mounting evidence that concept maps are effective tools for developing deep conceptual understanding in STEM content areas [19–21]. Concept maps also align with general recommendations for mathematics vocabulary development, which urges teachers to use varied approaches that utilize multiple representations [22].

Concept maps facilitate disciplinary literacy development, which is key to sustained achievement in STEM content areas. A disciplinary literacy approach emphasizes the knowledge and skills possessed by practitioners as the knowledge is used in the field [23]. Concept maps represent an established vocabulary development tool utilized by STEM educators. Within most STEM content areas, and mathematics specifically, conceptual understanding is key to the discipline. Thus, students must understand more than the definition of a triangle, but rather, all of the geometric and measurement properties associated with all triangles. Hence, when a mathematician describes a triangle the definition goes beyond the obvious characteristics and focuses on the properties that can be used to identity all triangles, and well as the unique categories or different types of triangles. Concept maps are the perfect tools to summarize, organize and represent this information in a meaningful way. In the next section, we review the literature on concept mapping in STEM and highlight the recent connections to mathematics content learning.4. Concept Mapping in STEM: Mathematics Connections.

Graphical representations of concepts and data have a long history in the educational literature. For example, flow charts, pie charts, and other visual data displays date back to the early 1970s [24]. Concepts maps represent one of several visual display tools that can be used to present connections between concepts and ideas. Other mapping processes include mind mapping and argument mapping. Concept maps are described as graphical representations for organizing and representing knowledge. According to Davies, concept maps are relational devices that use a hierarchical "tree" structure with super-ordinate and subordinate parts (primary, secondary and tertiary ideas) [25]. Concept mapping as an instructional tool helps students to visualize the structure of knowledge. The concept map was originally developed as a means of representing frameworks for the interrelationships between concepts. However, the concept map can be utilized as an assessment tool to facilitate the meaningful assessment learning [26]. Today, concepts maps are used across multiple content areas and have shown positive effects on student learning outcomes.

The literature on the use and effects of concepts in STEM content areas is vast. Concept maps are consistently recognized for their ability to help students develop a greater conceptual understanding of content compared to more traditional methods such as reading textbooks, listening to lectures, or taking notes [27]. This is often attributed to the notion that pictures or diagrams are more comprehensible than words, and often provide a clearer illustration of complex topics [28]. The effects of content mapping on student information retention are also attributed to map development process. Accordingly, concept maps have been used to assess changes in student conceptual understanding. In their seminal study, Wallace and Mintzes observed that students' concept maps were substantially different in complexity and structure of the knowledge base from the pre-test to the post-test [29]. This led the researchers to conclude that concept mapping is a valid tool to document students' changes in conceptual understanding. The effects of concept maps on student learning outcomes have been documented in several meta-analyses and research syntheses [30,31]. The results of these literature syntheses consistently conclude that concept maps are more effective than traditional interventions such as note-taking or direct instruction.

Concept mapping is an established pedagogical practice within the STEM content areas. Concept maps are recognized as effective instructional tools for the development of relational understanding in the mathematics classroom [32]. Concept maps are effective tools for previewing or reviewing a topic, formal or informal assessment, facilitating classroom discourse, and providing visual representations of mathematical connections [33]. Therefore, concept maps are utilized in many mathematics classrooms to develop student conceptual understanding. One key to a strong conceptual understanding of mathematics is a rich and fluid mathematics vocabulary.

4. Hip-Hip Pedagogy in the STEM Classroom: Mathematizing Hip-Hop

As alluded to in the introduction, hip-hop pedagogy translates naturally into the STEM classroom through a culturally relevant pedagogical lens that seeks to infuse the elements of hip-hop culture into teaching, learning and assessment. Beyond the five pillars of hip-hop, other elements of the culture include fashion, street language, spoken word poetry, beat boxing, entrepreneurialism and activism. Creative expression is central to forming the beliefs and customs within hip-hop culture. Hip-hop culture, that which precedes the pedagogy, was born in the Bronx in the mid-1970s and is now a global phenomenon that has spread to all corners of the world [34]. Hicks Harper noted the complexity and shifts that happen in hip-hop as youth culture changes, yet it is the global power and consistent elements of hip-hop that continue to influence the attitudes and choices of students Emdin and Lee and Ortiz contend that hip-hop serves as an outlet for youth, who have been disregarded and devalued, to share with others who have similar experiences [35–37]. Hip-hop identity is commonly perceived as an anti-school identity, and addressing this issue will require a shift in focus to hip-hop culture as valuable for education.

The necessity of hip-hop pedagogy is evident when one considers the origins of mathematics education and the mathematics teaching that has been normalized in U.S. schools. Traditional pedagogy often fails to account for students as contributors, and rarely considers their interests in the lesson design. Learner interest matters in the classroom, as it promotes engagement, motivation and "stick-with-it-ness." The disconnect is particularly detrimental to marginalized Black and Brown students whose interests have often been characterized as unsuitable for the formal educational setting; thus, the subtractive, intolerant nature of traditional instruction ignores their intellectual potential. Whereas, hip-hop pedagogy is unabashedly progressive, deliberate in its outreach to its targeted audience, marrying the students' culture/interests, in this case, with mathematics in a most Deweyian fashion. Hip-hop pedagogy affords students the ability to use their interests and activities from the outside, bridging the gap between school and society and blurring the lines between traditional schoolhouse curricula and schooling that occurs outside of the school [38,39]. This juxtaposition offers insight into exactly how hip-hop pedagogy can impact the experiences that children with hip-hop identities have with mathematics. Additionally, hip-hop pedagogy represents a unique application of culturally responsive and relevant teaching. This is important because it adds further credence to the utility of hip-hop pedagogy. Gay defined culturally responsive teaching as understanding students' prior experiences and learning styles, as well as using cultural knowledge to ensure that learning is appropriate to culturally diverse learners [40]. While, Ladson-Billings defines culturally relevant pedagogy as pedagogy of opposition not unlike critical pedagogy, but specifically committed to collective, not merely individual, empowerment [41]. Hip-hop pedagogies utilize these elements to support the teaching and learning of traditionally marginalized youth.

A strong component to attending to these funds of knowledge is the development of a strong mathematics identity in students who are traditionally underserved in mathematics classrooms. According to Martin, "mathematics identity refers to the dispositions and deeply held beliefs that individuals develop, within their overall self-concept, about their ability to participate and perform effectively in mathematical contexts and to use mathematics to change the conditions of their lives" [42] (p. 206). Hip-Hop identity formation frames the lens through which a multitude of ethnically and socially diverse youth and young adults view the world and themselves. Adjapong recommends that STEM educators participate in co-generative dialogues, or co-gens, as cyphers. He believes that in order to implement hip-hop pedagogy effectively, these educators should engage in co-gens with their students because this forum serves several purposes: collective decision-making, differentiation, equity, and feedback on the implementation of hip-hop pedagogical approaches like content raps [43].

5. Concept Maps vs. Concept Raps

Concept maps are built by placing terms, which represent the concepts to be mapped, in structures called nodes. The nodes, which are linked together into propositions, show how students connect or link concepts. The propositions are represented by arrows to connect individual concepts. An arrow indicates the directionality of the link. The conceptualization of the materials by the students is indicated by the directionality and the connecting proposition [44]. The proposition thus illustrates the contextual relationship of the concepts to each other. Concept maps and rap songs share four elements in common. Both include: the main idea or major point for consideration; a series of connections to the main idea; explicit explanations/elaborations on the relational structure of the main idea; and a formal organizational structure that users recognize.

The main idea in a concept map is the concept, while the song title is typically recognized as the main idea in a rap song. Connections to the main idea are made through linking words in concept maps and the hook in a rap song. The next common element is explanations/elaborations that come in the form of semantic units in concept maps and as verses in rap songs. Table 1 presented below provides a detailed comparison of the similarities between concept maps and rap songs on the four common elements identified.

Table 1. Description of common elements present in concept maps and rap songs.

Elements	Concept Maps	Description	Rap Songs	Description
Main Idea	Concept	Central idea or key notion	Song title	Song content or purpose (intro/outro)
Connections	Linking Words	The relationship between the two nodes of concept map	Hook	Relationship between song title and verses (8 bars in length repeated)
Explanation or Elaborations	Semantic Units	Meaningful statements made up of two or more concepts connected with linking words	Verse	Rapping segment of hip-hop song that clarifies and provides context (16 bars)
Organization	Hierarchical Structure	The most general and inclusive concepts are positioned at the top of a concept map, following by subordinate ideas	Alternating Pattern	Intro Hook 1st verse hook 2nd verse hook 3rd verse outro (Can vary across songs)

The challenge for some STEM educators in regard to embracing content raps will lie in their willingness to realize their miseducation, even their own biases, and reject research about vocabulary development and economically marginalized children of color. This position is important, as 80% of teachers in the United States are White, middle-class individuals with limited experience of culturally and linguistically diverse students. Moreover, according to the National Science Foundation, STEM is a field dominated by White men. In 1995, researchers Hart and Risley released their book *Meaningful Differences in the Everyday Experience of Young American Children,* which contained their well-known study on the 30 million-word gap between the vocabularies of three-year-olds in "welfare" and working-class families as compared to their White counterparts in professional families. The study was not published until 1992, but their findings reached wider and more influential audience after the publication in their book and have shaped educational policies, pedagogical practices, and parenting initiatives to this very day. Initial reactions to the word gap sparked positive changes such as federal investments in early childhood intervention programs like Head Start. However, despite the fact that this study's findings have not been replicated in the last twenty-six years and current researchers have discovered that the gap is closer to 3 million, the long-term, long-lasting result has been deficit thinking about the ability of Black and Brown children to handle complicated subject matter due to subpar vocabulary development.

There is no doubt that there is a link between vocabulary and comprehension and thereby achievement. What some failed to do is understand that learners of color actually possess word wealth, which is experienced by children who grow up in homes where a different dialect or language is spoken versus the dominant Standard English of school [45]. It is not that these children are not prepared for traditional education. Just the opposite. Traditional education is not prepared for them. That is why STEM educators' appreciation for content raps is advised. They must initially expect a cultural mismatch between students of color lexicon and the academic vocabulary in STEM content areas. However, vocabulary development and growth will depend largely on the teachers' ability to support the role that formal and informal substitutions, analogies, synonyms, multiple meaning words, and inference play in bridging the connection between personal and academic words in the classroom. Dando cautions educators to see hip-hop as more than a motivator to engage students, but rather to use hip-hop, such as with content raps, to generate new ways of thinking.

6. Discussion

As Emdin addressed in his book, some practitioners are resistant to using hip-hop as a pedagogical tool [46]. One misconception is that teachers have to be masters of the art to utilize it effectively. However, this directly contradicts the need to use this alternative form of pedagogy, for which the intent is to privilege the knowledge that students bring into mathematics classrooms. In seeing that the expert role no longer belongs exclusively to the teacher, students begin to view the classroom as a place in which they are valued and seen as competent. Still, others view hip-hop pedagogy as a waste of time and disparage its utility, yet no strategy that motivates greater populations of children to achieve in mathematics should be regarded as a waste of time or effort. Here are some of the common challenges to the use of hip-hop pedagogy in mathematics classrooms. First, many teachers may struggle to garner administrator support for implementing hip-hop pedagogy. Principals are charged with ensuring that instructional materials are research-based, age-appropriate, and free of bias. If the principal cannot appreciate the value of hip-hop in the classroom, the teacher will find it very difficult to obtain its approval.

Secondly, novice implementers may misinterpret the utility of the practices and cause student confusion. This is not a challenge that is unique to hip-hop pedagogy, but it can be more pronounced if the teacher does not have to be an expert, but he or she must have a clear and sound understanding of hip-hop pedagogy to use it effectively. Much like all classroom interventions, teachers will have to overcome time constraints when considering hip-hop pedagogy. Most teachers are guided by scope and sequence or pacing calendar and are given a certain amount of days to cover a specific skill or concept.

Depending on the time allocated to a particular standard, teachers may be forced to choose between hip-hop pedagogy and traditional methods. Differentiation can also be challenging when teachers first consider hip-hop pedagogy. The teacher may struggle to find ways to use hip-hop pedagogy with all learners, especially those at risk with moderate-to-severe delays in basic mathematical literacy and computation skills. Finally, the excessive use or misuse of hip-hop pedagogy can create major challenges for the student that does not engage in hip-hop culture. As hip-hop pedagogy becomes the new shiny toy in education, educators must be cautioned against using it haphazardly, trying to make it fit where it does not, or overusing it to the point that it dulls students' interest and attention in the way some forms of technology have.

7. Conclusions

Meeting the needs of current and future STEM learners remains a challenge for educators and researchers. Appropriately, many argue that developing effective STEM education is one of the most significant challenges facing educators [47]. Here we have urged educators and researchers to consider diversifying their pedagogical approaches to reach a more diverse population of STEM learners. Specifically, we have argued for hip-hop pedagogy and culture to be employed to engage underrepresented students in mathematics and other STEM content areas. This shift, however, requires a focus on hip-hop in mathematics curricula that requires educators to recognize that both mathematics and hip-hop have shared elements. For example, mathematicians search for patterns to solve problems and create models. For example, hip-hop artists create patterns in their music to generate new and unique sounds, while mathematicians utilized numerical patterns to solve complex problems. Finding authentic ways to spark student interest in mathematics requires educators to stay current with youth culture and recognize hip-hop pedagogy as a viable instructional resource. Here we present one pedagogical connection; however, hip-hop pedagogy should not be limited to this one example. We hope that teachers and teacher educators will embrace hip-hop pedagogy as a culturally responsive instructional tool for the hip-hop generation and beyond.

Author Contributions: Conceptualization, J.Y. and M.C.; Writing—Original Draft Preparation, J.Y. and N.O.; Writing—Review & Editing, M.F., C.H., and J.Y.

Conflicts of Interest: The authors declare no conflict of interest.

References

1. Bilgin, A.; Boedeker, P.; Capraro, R.M.; Capraro, M.M. The effects of STEM PBL on students' mathematical and scientific vocabulary knowledge. *Online Submiss.* **2015**, *2*, 69–75.
2. Collier, S.; Burston, B.; Rhodes, A. Teaching STEM as a second language: Utilizing SLA to develop equitable learning for all students. *J. Multicult. Educ.* **2016**, *10*, 257–273. [CrossRef]
3. Bowie, A.L. The relationship between middle school students' mathematical vocabulary and their achievement in mathematics. *Nat. Teach. Educ. J.* **2016**, *9*, 65–69.
4. National Council of Teachers of Mathematics. *Principles to Action: Ensuring Success for All*; NCTM: Reston, VC, USA, 2014.
5. National Council of Teachers of Mathematics. *Principles and Standards for School Mathematics*; NCTM: Reston, VA, USA, 2000.
6. Dimitriadis, G.; Cole, E.; Costello, A. The social field(s) of arts education today: Living vulnerability in neo-liberal times. *Discourse Stud. Cult. Politics Educ.* **2009**, *30*, 361–379. [CrossRef]
7. Emdin, C.; Lee, O. Hip-Hop, the 'Obama Effect,' and Urban Science Education. *Teach. Coll. Rec.* **2012**, *114*, 1–24.
8. Love, B.L. What is hip-hop-based education doing in nice fields such as early childhood and elementary education? *Urban Educ.* **2015**, *50*, 106–131. [CrossRef]
9. Milner, H.R. A Black male teacher's culturally responsive practices. *J. Negro Educ.* **2016**, *85*, 417–432. [CrossRef]

10. Siwatu, K.O. Preservice teachers' culturally responsive teaching self-efficacy and outcome expectancy beliefs. *Teach. Teach. Educ.* **2017**, *23*, 1086–1101. [CrossRef]

11. Siwatu, K.O. Preservice teachers' sense of preparedness and self-efficacy to teach in America's urban and suburban schools: Does context matter? *Teach. Teach. Educ.* **2011**, *27*, 357–365. [CrossRef]

12. Cason, M.; Young, J.; Foster, M.; Ortiz, N. Is mathematics identity development possible with hip-hop pedagogy? *Intersect. Points* **2017**, *42*, 7–9.

13. National Council of Teachers of Mathematics. Access and Equity in Mathematics Education. 2014. Available online: http://www.nctm.org/uploadedFiles/Standards_and_Positions/Position_Statements/Access_and_Equity.pdf (accessed on 19 July 2019).

14. National Academy of Sciences. *Expanding Underrepresented Minority Participation: America's Science and Technology Talent at the Crossroads*; National Academy of Engineering, Institute of Medicine, & National Research Council; National Academies Press: Washington, DC, USA, 2010.

15. National Center for Education Statistics. *The Nation's Report Card: Mathematics 2011*; Department of Education, Institute of Education Sciences: Washington, DC, USA, 2011.

16. Knuth, E.; Peressini, D. Unpacking the nature of discourse in mathematics classrooms. *Math. Teach. Middle Sch.* **2001**, *6*, 320–325.

17. Barroso, L.R.; Bicer, A.; Capraro, M.M.; Capraro, R.M.; Foran, A.L.; Grant, M.R.; Lincoln, Y.S.; Nite, S.B.; Oner, A.T.; Rice, D. Run! Spot. Run! Vocabulary development and the evolution of STEM disciplinary language for secondary teachers. *ZDM* **2017**, *49*, 187–201. [CrossRef]

18. Powell, S.R.; Nelson, G. An Investigation of the Mathematics-Vocabulary Knowledge of First-Grade Students. *Elem. Sch. J.* **2017**, *117*, 664–686. [CrossRef]

19. Turns, J.; Cynthia, J.A.; Robin, A. Concept maps for engineering education: A cognitively motivated tool supporting varied assessment functions. *IEEE Trans. Educ.* **2000**, *43*, 164–173. [CrossRef]

20. Owens, L.; Chad, H.; Helen, M. STEM Faculty Perceptions of Concept Map Assessments. In *Transforming Insitutions: 21st Century Undergraduate STEM Education*; Purdue University press: West Lafayette, IN, USA, 2015.

21. Raman, R.; Mithun, H.; Prema, N. Blending Concept Maps with Online Labs for STEM Learning. In *Advances in Intelligent Informatics*; Springer: Cham, Switzerland, 2015; pp. 133–141.

22. Bruun, F.; Diaz, J.M.; Dykes, V.J. The language of mathematics. *Teach. Child. Math.* **2015**, *21*, 530–536. [CrossRef]

23. Shanahan, T.; Shanahan, C. What is disciplinary literacy and why does it matter? *Top. Lang. Disord.* **2012**, *32*, 7–18. [CrossRef]

24. Nassi, I.; Shneiderman, B. Flowchart techniques for structured programming. *SIGPLAN Not.* **1973**, *8*, 12–26. [CrossRef]

25. Davies, M. Concept mapping, mind mapping and argument mapping: What are the differences and do they matter? *High. Educ.* **2010**, *62*, 279–301. [CrossRef]

26. Novak, J.D. Concept mapping: A useful tool for science education. *J. Res. Sci. Teach.* **1990**, *27*, 937–949. [CrossRef]

27. Novak, J.D. *Learning, Creating, and Using Knowledge: Concept Maps as Facilitative Tools in Schools and Corporations*; Routledge: New York, NY, USA, 2010.

28. Schwendimann, B.A. Concept maps as versatile tools to integrate complex ideas: From kindergarten to higher and professional education. *Knowl. Manag. E-Learn.* **2015**, *7*, 73–99.

29. Wallace, J.D.; Mintzes, J.J. The concept map as a research tool: Exploring conceptual change in biology. *J. Res. Sci. Teach.* **1990**, *27*, 1033–1052. [CrossRef]

30. Dexter, D.D.; Hughes, C.A. Graphic organizers and students with learning disabilities: A meta-analysis. *Learn. Disabil. Q.* **2011**, *34*, 51–72. [CrossRef]

31. Nesbit, J.C.; Adesope, O.O. Learning with concept and knowledge maps: A meta-analysis. *Rev. Educ. Res.* **2006**, *76*, 413–448. [CrossRef]

32. Afamasaga-Fuata'I, K. *Concept Mapping in Mathematics: Research into Practice*; Springer: New York, NY, USA, 2009.

33. Bartels, B.H. Promoting mathematics connections with concept mapping. *Math. Teach. Middle Sch.* **1995**, *1*, 542–549.

34. Chang, J. *Can't Stop Won't Stop: A History of the Hip Hop Generation*; St. Martin's: New York, NY, USA, 2005.

35. Osumare, H. Beat Streets in the Global Hood: Connective Marginalities of the Hip Hop Globe. *J. Am. Comp. C* **2001**, *24*, 171–181.

36. Ortiz, N.A.; Capraro, R.; Capraro, M.M. Does it really matter? Exploring cultural relevance within a majority White classroom. *J. Negro Educ.* in press.

37. Emdin, C. Affiliation and Alienation Hip-Hop 2012, Rap, and Urban Science Education. *J. Curric. Stud.* **2010**, *42*, 1–25. [CrossRef]

38. Slattery, P. A postmodern vision of time and learning: A response to the National Education Commission Report Prisoners of Time. *Harv. Educ. Rev.* **1995**, *65*, 612–634. [CrossRef]

39. Tillman, D.A. Learning from the College Dropout: Depictions of Numeracy and Mathematics within Hip Hop Music. *J. Math. Educ.* **2016**, *9*, 53–71.

40. Gay, G. *Culturally Responsive Teaching: Theory 1992, Research, and Practice*; Teachers College Press: New York, NY, USA, 2000.

41. Ladson-Billings, G. Culturally relevant teaching: The key to making multicultural education work. In *Research and Multicultural Education: From the Margins to the Mainstream*; The Falmer Press: Bristol, UK, 1992; pp. 106–121.

42. Martin, D.M. Mathematics Learning and Participation as Racialized Forms of Experience: African American Parents Speak on the Struggle for Mathematics Literacy. *Math. Think. Learn.* **2006**, *8*, 197–229. [CrossRef]

43. Adjapong, E.S. Bridging Theory and Practice: Using Hip-Hop Pedagogy as a Culturally Relevant. Approach in the Urban Science Classroom. Ph.D. Thesis, Columbia University, New York, NY, USA, 2017. Available online: https://academiccommons.columbia.edu/catalog/ac:kd51c59zxp (accessed on 19 July 2019).

44. Awofala, A.O.A. Effect of concept mapping strategy on students' achievement in Junior Secondary School Mathematics. *Int. J. Math. Trends Technol.* **2011**, *2*, 11–16.

45. Kamenetz, A. Let's Stop Talking about the 30 Million Word Gap. Available online: https://www.npr.org/sections/ed/2018/06/01/615188051/lets-stop-talking-about-the-30-million-word-gap (accessed on 1 June 2018).

46. Emdin, C. *For White Folks Who Teach in the Hood … and the Rest of Y'all Too: Reality Pedagogy and Urban Education*; Beacon Press: Boston, MA, USA, 2016.

47. Han, S.; Capraro, R.; Capraro, M.M. How science, technology, engineering, and mathematics (STEM) project-based learning (PBL) affects high, middle, and low achievers differently: The impact of student factors on achievement. *Int. J. Sci. Math. Educ.* **2015**, *13*, 1089–1113. [CrossRef]

Concept Paper

The Vocabulary-Comprehension Relationship across the Disciplines: Implications for Instruction

Janis Harmon [1],* and Karen Wood [2]

[1] Department of Interdisciplinary Learning and Teaching, College of Education and Human Development, University of Texas, San Antonio, TX 78249, USA

[2] Department of Reading and Elementary Education, University of North Carolina, Charlotte, NC 28223, USA; kdwood@uncc.edu

* Correspondence: janis.harmon@utsa.edu

Received: 10 June 2018; Accepted: 12 July 2018; Published: 17 July 2018

Abstract: The main purpose of vocabulary instruction is to enhance and support reading comprehension. This goal spans across the grade levels and different disciplines and is supported by a plethora of research. In recent years, a great deal of needed attention has been finally given to academic vocabulary and disciplinary literacy. To contribute to this body of knowledge, we believe it is critical to examine how the complex relationship between vocabulary and comprehension may be addressed in secondary content area classrooms, given the unique nature of the academic vocabulary students encounter daily in school. This conceptual paper contains the following: (1) definition of academic vocabulary; (2) description of what is known about the vocabulary–comprehension relationship; (3) conceptualization of the intersection of academic vocabulary and the vocabulary–comprehension relationship; and (4) instructional implications emerging from this intersection. Perhaps this conceptualization may provide disciplinary practitioners more insight to help them make decisions regarding vocabulary instruction.

Keywords: academic vocabulary; disciplinary literacy; comprehension

In recent years, a great deal of needed attention has been given to the literacy demands of different content areas (i.e., science, history, mathematics, literature) and how these demands are unique to each subject area. Moving away from a focus on generic strategies promoted under the umbrella of content area literacy, we are now drawing attention to disciplinary literacy with an emphasis on discipline-specific practices employed by the experts in each field of study [1–3]. Disciplinary literacy, in contrast to content area literacy, looks closely at what Fang and Coatoam call "disciplinary habits of mind" [4] (p. 628) in regard to the unique ways, in which experts in different subject areas use to communicate through reading, writing, viewing, visually representing, speaking, and reasoning. As a result, there is increasing evidence that infusing literacy practices tailored to particular disciplines can enhance students' academic achievement [5].

While both content area literacy and disciplinary literacy practices are useful to promote learning in various subject-matter areas [6], one important component in each view is vocabulary. We know that the main purpose of vocabulary instruction is to enhance and support reading comprehension. This goal spans across the grade levels and different disciplines and has been supported by a plethora of research across the decades. In regard to different disciplines, there are two major categories of vocabulary—the specific academic vocabularies associated with particular disciplines as well as general vocabularies shared by the disciplines. To contribute to the understandings of the body of knowledge about vocabulary and comprehension, we believe it is critical to examine how the complex relationship between vocabulary and comprehension may be addressed in secondary content area classrooms, given the unique nature of the academic vocabulary students encounter daily in school. An examination of the intersection of the academic vocabulary in the disciplines and the vocabulary–comprehension relationship may provide disciplinary practitioners more insight to inform decision-making regarding vocabulary instruction. We begin by providing an overview of the meaning of academic vocabulary and an explanation of the relationship between vocabulary and comprehension. We then examine the intersection of academic vocabulary and the vocabulary–comprehension relationship and the instructional implications for enhancing learning.

1. Academic Vocabulary

Vocabulary growth occurs in both oral and written contexts. Oral contexts appear to support vocabulary more easily, given the natural opportunity for multiple uses and repetition of words as well as the presence of concrete referents [7]. In the case of written contexts, vocabulary acquisition involves engagement in more sophisticated language, especially as students move into the upper grades. In middle schools and high schools, the focus is primarily on reading texts across different subject-matter areas, each of which has its own distinctive language patterns. Nagy and Townsend define this academic language as the "specialized language, both oral and written, of academic settings that facilitate communication and thinking about disciplinary content" [8] (p. 92). In the words of Zwiers, the academic language in each discipline is "the set of words, grammar, and organizational strategies used to describe complex ideas, higher-order thinking processes, and abstract concepts" [9] (p. 20). The complex and multi-dimensional nature of each discipline requires that students learn about the language of each area in order to gain conceptual knowledge in these fields.

Academic vocabulary is a critical component embedded in the language of all disciplines and places challenging demands on all learners. This vocabulary is critically important for disciplinary learning and thinking. Descriptions about academic vocabulary focus on two distinctive categories of words—technical, content-specific terms and general academic vocabulary. As noted by Baumann and Graves [10], scholars label these content-specific terms in different ways, including *technical vocabulary* and *domain-specific words*. Regardless of the label, these are terms representing concepts in particular disciplines, such as fossil fuels, greenhouse effect, and atmosphere when learning about global warming.

General academic vocabulary, on the other hand, are generalized terms that appear across different content areas with their meanings sometimes changing depending upon the context. Examples of general academic vocabulary include *analyze*, *market*, *legend*, and *grade*. McKeown and her colleagues aptly note the importance of general academic vocabulary, especially for second-language learners by stating that "[high frequency general words] provide the foundation upon which the knowledge of rarer words must build. Developing knowledge of academic vocabulary—mid-frequency, high dispersion words preferentially appearing in academic written texts—is particularly important for K-12 vocabulary development and for advanced language learners" [11] (pp. 55–56).

2. Vocabulary–Comprehension Relationship

For many decades, we have accumulated well-documented evidence that vocabulary size is a strong predictor of a student's ability to comprehend text [12,13]. This strong correlation between vocabulary and comprehension leads to an obvious conclusion that if teachers teach word meanings, students will comprehend better. However, the relationship between vocabulary and comprehension is not that straightforward and is highly complex involving a host of other variables. To explain this relationship, Anderson and Freebody [12] considered three standpoints that they labeled as the instrumental hypothesis, the knowledge hypothesis, and the aptitude hypothesis. Since then, researchers in the field have augmented these explanations to include others, such as the access hypothesis [14], the metalinguistic hypothesis [15], and the reciprocal hypothesis [16]. These explanations do not contradict each other, but rather illustrate the interplay of multiple variables involved in the vocabulary–comprehension relationship [17]. We provide an explanation of each standpoint or hypothesis.

Instrumental hypothesis. This common sense explanation suggests that learning word meanings influences comprehension, thus leaning more toward a causal connection between vocabulary and comprehension [12]. Stahl [18] points out two implications embedded in this standpoint. First, if knowledge of words can directly enhance comprehension, texts with more challenging words will be more difficult to understand. Another implication is that directly teaching word meanings will improve comprehension. However, Stahl [18] cautions that not all vocabulary instructional methods will influence comprehension. While knowing word meanings is necessary for comprehension to occur, it is not a sufficient explanation by itself to explain the relationship between vocabulary and comprehension [15].

Knowledge hypothesis. Moving away from the direct, causal relationship implied by the instrumental hypothesis, the knowledge hypothesis takes into account the influence of a mediating variable—that of background knowledge. This explanation of the relationship between vocabulary and comprehension illustrates that word meanings are not learned in isolation; rather, they are developed while learning about a new topic. Such contexts allow students to see how words are semantically related to other words [19]. Furthermore, as Nagy states, " . . . it is not [the idea of] knowing the meaning of words that causes readers to understand what they read; rather, knowing the meanings of words is an indication of the readers' knowledge of a topic or concept. It is this knowledge that help readers comprehend" [15] (p. 31). Thus, word knowledge is one aspect of topic knowledge needed for comprehension to occur, and learning about a topic provides the opportunity to increase word knowledge [15,18].

Aptitude hypothesis. Similar to the knowledge hypothesis, the aptitude hypothesis also considers a third variable to explain the relationship between vocabulary and comprehension. In this case, verbal ability plays an important role, since students with a high verbal aptitude tend to know more words, and are better able to learn new words, and comprehend what they read [12,17]. Both Sternberg and Powell [20] and Stahl and Nagy [17] expand the aptitude hypothesis in different ways. Sternberg and Powell [20] interpret this hypothesis to include a reader's ability to make inferences. In this way, inferential ability, as a subset of the aptitude hypothesis, has a critical impact on comprehension, especially when readers must infer the meanings of unfamiliar words encountered in texts. Using a different perspective about the aptitude hypothesis, Stahl and Nagy [17] consider metalinguistic aspects of word learning that can impact comprehension. They argue that readers use their knowledge of language as they construct an understanding of what is being read, that is, they use what they know about morphology (e.g., affixes, roots), syntax, figurative language, polysemy (i.e., multiple meanings of some words), and other language cueing systems, all of which relate to the aptitude hypothesis.

Reciprocal hypothesis. Beck, McKeown, and Omanson question " . . . . are people good comprehenders because they know a lot of words, or do people know a lot of words because they are good comprehenders and in the course of comprehending text, learn a lot of words, or is there some combination of directionality?" [21] (pp. 147–148). To address this question, Stanovich [16] suggests that there is a reciprocal relationship between vocabulary and comprehension, where vocabulary is increased through reading and comprehending and comprehension is enhanced by knowledge of more words. In the words of Stahl and Nagy, "having a bigger vocabulary makes you a better reader, being a better reader makes it possible for you to read more, and reading more gives you a bigger vocabulary" [17] (p. 13).

Access hypothesis. To explain the complex relationship between vocabulary and reading comprehension, Mezynski [14] suggests another dimension called the access hypothesis. Based upon the theoretical work of LaBerge and Samuels [22] concerning automaticity in reading, the access hypothesis indicates that the quick and easy retrieval of word meanings is necessary for comprehension to occur. Thus, readers must know the various aspects of word meanings (e.g., correct nuances of meanings) well enough for easy access and use while reading.

Each of these explanations helps to illustrate the complexity of the relationship between vocabulary and comprehension in general and do not contradict each other. Furthermore, they offer a way to examine the relationship between academic vocabulary and reading comprehension in different disciplines.

3. Intersection of Academic Vocabulary and the Vocabulary–Comprehension Relationship

Teacher beliefs about teaching in general, and specifically about vocabulary learning and instruction, are important across all grade levels and disciplines [23]. One study by Konopak and Williams [19] examines teacher beliefs about vocabulary teaching and learning from the perspective of the relationship between vocabulary and comprehension. Enlightened by this work, we attempt to conceptualize the intersection between the academic vocabulary across subject-matter areas specifically and the vocabulary–comprehension relationship as represented by the aforementioned hypotheses. Perhaps this perspective may provide insights into what vocabulary practices in content area classrooms may enhance reading comprehension. We address each hypothesis or standpoint in light of both technical, content-specific vocabulary and general academic vocabulary.

Instrumental hypothesis. This hypothesis supports the direct teaching of both technical vocabulary and general academic vocabulary. Explicit instruction that provides definitions of words, both technical and general, is an initiating, introductory event that is necessary but not totally sufficient to ensure that students internalize word meanings. Variability in the kinds of content-specific words is one factor that must be considered. Some words lend themselves well to explicit instruction with definitions. For example, a simple definition for words, such as *triangle* and *perimeter* in mathematics, may suffice. Direct instruction for some general academic terms may also work for such words and phrases as *find the least* amount and *record your answer*. However, other content-specific words need more detailed and integrated instruction for students to internalize these ideas. For example, in keeping with mathematics examples, the more complex concepts of both *slope* and *functions* require more detailed and extensive instruction than the use of simple explanations using definitions. Furthermore, particular general academic words also require more in-depth instruction with words and phrases, such as *analyze the data, demonstrate your understanding*, and *relationship to*.

Knowledge hypothesis. Conceptual knowledge speaks explicitly to the teaching and learning of disciplinary vocabulary. In the case of content-specific academic vocabulary, building word knowledge is closely related to building conceptual knowledge. As Vacca and his colleagues point out, "Words are labels for concepts. A single concept, however, represents much more than the meaning of a single word. It may take thousands of words to explain a concept" [24] (p. 243). Moving away from the definitional level, a focus on conceptual knowledge acquisition requires that students engage in meaningful, purposeful experiences, both firsthand and vicariously, in order to learn [24].

Conceptual knowledge, in this case of subject-matter knowledge, is part of a reader's prior knowledge. Two types of prior knowledge are important for literacy learning in the disciplines—topic knowledge and domain knowledge, both of which involve academic vocabulary [25–27]. Topic knowledge focuses on the depth of knowledge a student may have about a topic, that is, what background knowledge and experiences the student has acquired about a topic or a concept. If a student has a strong knowledge base about the topic of *diabetes*, for example, this student will also have the depth of knowledge about the words and terms that are used in talking and writing about this topic (how well the words are known), words and ideas, such as *glucose level, insulin*, and *proper diet*. Domain knowledge, on the other hand, represents the breadth of knowledge that readers have about a particular discipline, including not only the breadth of knowledge about vocabulary (the size of word knowledge), but also the language and thinking associated with a given field of study. In other words, domain knowledge can be considered to be general knowledge experts have in a particular field of study [25]. In the *diabetes* example, domain knowledge would include knowledge about *metabolism*, how *glucose* is used as the main source of energy for the body, health problems caused by a great deal of glucose in the blood (e.g., *neuropathy, hypertension, ketones*), and the use of *hemoglobin* testing for measuring control of diabetes. Specifically in regard to vocabulary knowledge, both topic and domain knowledge illustrate Schmitt's statement that "all aspects of vocabulary knowledge are interrelated" [28] (p. 942).

In addition to the role of vocabulary in conceptual knowledge, it is important to consider academic vocabulary in light of both linguistic and lexical knowledge. From a disciplinary perspective, linguistic knowledge is knowledge of the language used in particular subject-matter areas and knowledge of language differences across disciplines. Linguistic knowledge is the basis, from which students understand how authors frame the ways in which concepts are explained and described in disciplinary texts. This includes such features as syntactic knowledge, nominalization, multiple meanings of similar words, collocational knowledge, and morphological structures [11]. Table 1 provides explanations and examples for some of these particular features in regard to content specific vocabulary and general academic vocabulary.

Table 1. Features of linguistic knowledge in academic language.

Features	Examples of Content-Specific Vocabulary	Examples of General Academic Vocabulary
Nominalization The practice of changing a verb or adjective into a noun form	*Multiply multiplication* *Legislate legislation* *Extinct extinction*	*Demonstrate demonstration* *Complete completion* *Approximate approximation*
Multiple meanings of similar words The same words having different meanings depending upon the contexts in which they are used	Fish *scales* Balance *scales* Worship in a *temple* *Temple* on the side of a face *Major* in the army *Major* project	*Count* the numbers *Count* a nobleman *List* the battles *List*—tilting to one side *Place*—a particular area *Place*—arranging or putting something down Fresh *produce* at the grocery store *Produce* a chart for your data
Collocational knowledge Grouping of words that typically are used together	*Chain reaction* *Chemical reaction* *Blood pressure* *Atmospheric pressure* *Tectonic plate* *Fifth power of six* *Square root of nine* *Reciprocal of a number* *Multiplicative inverse* *Greenhouse effect* *Supply and demand*	*Pay tribute to* *Major catastrophe* *Present with* *Important for* *Draw a conclusion* *Solve the problem* *Is produced by*
Morphological structures Patterns of words that share the same meaning and belong to the same word family	*Linear line* *Multiplicative multiply* *Number numerical* *Genes genetics* *Colony colonial*	*Benefit* *Beneficial* *Compare* *Comparative* *Represent* *Representative* *Minimum* *minimal*

Aptitude hypothesis. The relationship between vocabulary and comprehension in different disciplines is also influenced by verbal ability. As students read the informational texts that are unique to each content area, they need to be skillful in inferring particular meanings of technical vocabulary as well as the different uses of general academic vocabulary in each discipline of study. For both sets of words, metalinguistic knowledge enables readers to reflect upon and manipulate the special vocabulary and language found in each discipline [15]. Given that all the disciplines have unique and significantly different language patterns and terminology [4], it is even more imperative that students acquire the metalinguistic knowledge needed for each field.

Reciprocal hypothesis. The reciprocal relationship between vocabulary and comprehension holds true for reading and understanding in the content areas. When students read more in science, history, and the other disciplines, they are exposed to more of the technical terms as well as the general academic terms used in conveying meaning. The more they read, the more both vocabularies grow and become internalized. The richer their vocabularies become, the better they are able to comprehend different texts and more challenging texts.

Access hypothesis. As in any field of study, the need to internalize word meanings to the point of automatic retrieval is important for comprehension to occur. Again, the richness or depth of word knowledge, as well as the breadth or size of word knowledge about a given topic, aids in the accessibility of word meanings. This accessibility is needed for both content-specific words and general academic vocabulary. Students need multiple opportunities to engage in meaningful, topic-centered contexts and situations, in which both types of disciplinary vocabulary are internalized. Based upon the International Literacy Association's use of the term "literacy" [29], these encounters can include opportunities for students to read, write, speak, listen, view, and visually represent their understandings about specific topics across all disciplines—opportunities that cannot occur without vocabulary and language.

It is important to keep in mind that vocabulary learning is complex and multifaceted. Hence, all of these hypotheses have value and play different roles in helping students attain the necessary vocabulary to be successful in understanding academic texts.

4. Instructional Implications

The vocabulary–comprehension hypotheses previously described form the basis of effective vocabulary instructional practices across different disciplines. Structured lesson frameworks typically include teacher preparation, initial explanations, applications, and reinforcement [30]. The support for both content-specific terms and general academic vocabulary can be integrated simultaneously in these instructional formats. Furthermore, each aspect of the lesson draws from what we know about the vocabulary–comprehension connection in disciplinary learning. However, it is important to be mindful that the hypotheses used to explain the vocabulary–comprehension connection can be recursive and overlapping in each segment of a structured lesson.

Teacher preparation. A critical part of any vocabulary lesson is the careful selection of words and phrases that need close attention to support reading. To support comprehension, these words and phrases need to be those that are important for conceptual learning (i.e., technical words) and those that build upon the reader's linguistic knowledge (i.e., general academic vocabulary). Ultimately, the assessment of a student's background knowledge about the terms and phrases is needed for making informed decisions about word selection. The use of the Knowledge Rating Scale [31] for such purposes should include not only the content-specific words but also general academic words and phrases to ensure that all aspects of vocabulary and language are taken into consideration. The *knowledge hypothesis* supports these efforts to attend to the background knowledge of students.

Initial explanation. The work of Beck and her associates [32] provides important guidelines for introducing new terminology to students. They advocate for the introductions of new words and phrases to include both a context and a "student-friendly" definition that students can understand. This initial step embraces the *instrumental hypothesis* with a focus on establishing the basic meanings of the terms within a context and not in isolation. The context would especially provide students with a sense of how general academic terms and phrases are used within the language of the text. Again, the variability of both content-specific vocabulary and general academic vocabulary as previously described (i.e., the degree of abstractness of concepts) must be considered in order to provide an explanation that students will understand. From an *instrumental* standpoint, these initial explanations can be multimodal to include verbal, visual, and virtual tools. The non-linguistic approach of using pictures, drawings, charts, graphs and other visual representations has much support in the professional literature for assisting students of all ability levels including English language learners with newly introduced vocabulary [33,34]. In addition, digital tools are readily available to help reinforce the student's friendly explanations, such as visuwords.com which shows a graph of related terms and www.visualthesaurus.com which provides an interactive map complete with definitions and pronunciations.

These introductory tasks also reflect the *knowledge hypothesis*, especially in light of the specific contexts used to build conceptual knowledge. Students must have a working knowledge of the particular contexts used to explain the targeted words and phrases in order to make understandable connections to increase word learning.

Application. Once students have a general understanding of the word meanings, the next instructional step is to have students engage in multiple, meaningful encounters of the words through readings, class discussions, and related activities, in which the conceptually loaded terms and the general academic vocabulary are used. These tasks enable students to make connections of the word usage to a variety of different contexts and situations. However, to be able to connect to the situations, students must have appropriate background knowledge and experiences. Again, the *knowledge hypothesis* becomes the basis for these learning opportunities. These experiences are even more apparent and necessary across different disciplines. Furthermore, the fact that students need multiple encounters with these varied contexts is supported by the *access hypothesis* to ensure that the word meanings are internalized deeply, so that students are able to transfer newly acquired learning to other disciplinary-related encounters with the words and phrases. One means for ensuring significant and multiple encounters with words is to pre-teach the key academic vocabulary before reading, ask students to focus on the key words during reading (making notes, drawings, charts) and then revisit the words after the reading [35]. Additional follow-up can take the form of small-group writing activities using the words in the context of the content studied [36].

Reinforcement. As previously mentioned, multiple encounters with newly acquired word meanings not only help students develop breadth and depth of word meanings (*knowledge hypothesis*), but also reinforce the integration of this new knowledge. Continual revisiting of previously learned word meanings, both content-specific words and general academic vocabulary, is a critical component in the instructional framework. Students need a great deal of exposure to both vocabularies to enable them to use this dynamic knowledge base to learn more unfamiliar words and phrases. The purpose of reinforcement is not only based upon the *instrumental, knowledge,* and *access hypotheses,* but also on the *aptitude* and *reciprocal hypotheses.* In other words, the more students use newly acquired word meanings in their disciplinary readings, the more they will be exposed to and learn new word meanings, thus building an even greater knowledge from which learning can be continued. This reciprocal nature of word learning occurs through opportunities for students to engage in explanations, explorations, elaborations, and evaluations of various topics and concepts across the disciplines.

5. Conclusions

The hypotheses presented in this article suggest important implications for vocabulary instruction [17]. With these theoretical positions as a basis, the potential exists to change the face of vocabulary instruction from merely mentioning, telling, and assigning rote memorization and "look it up in the dictionary" tasks to more meaningful, contextual approaches. To this end, we feel that the single term "vocabulary", which suggests teaching words in isolation be replaced with the broader, multi-dimensional term "vocabulary literacy," which involves making the vocabulary/comprehension connection using all aspects of literacy: reading, writing, listening, speaking, viewing, and visually representing [30]. With this perspective undergirding our teaching of both content-specific and general academic vocabulary terms, students process word meanings more deeply as they actively engage in multi-modal activities designed to promote strategic learning and long-term conceptual understanding.

Funding: This research received no external funding.

Conflicts of Interest: The author declares no conflict of interest.

References

1. Conley, M.W. Improving adolescent comprehension. In *Handbook of Research on Reading Comprehension*, 2nd ed.; Israel, S.E., Ed.; Guilford Press: New York, NY, USA, 2017; pp. 406–427, ISBN 978-1-4625-2888-2.

2. Moje, E.B. Foregrounding the disciplines in secondary literacy teaching and learning: A call for change. *J. Adolesc. Adult Lit.* **2008**, *52*, 96–107. [CrossRef]

3. Shanahan, C.; Shanahan, T.; Misischia, C. Analysis of expert readers in three disciplines: History, mathematics, and chemistry. *J. Lit. Res.* **2011**, *43*, 393–429. [CrossRef]

4. Fang, Z.; Coatoam, S. Disciplinary literacy: What you want to know about it. *J. Adolesc. Adult Lit.* **2013**, *56*, 627–632. [CrossRef]

5. Hynd-Shanahan, C. What does it take? The challenge of disciplinary literacy. *J. Adolesc. Adult Lit.* **2013**, *57*, 93–98. [CrossRef]

6. Dunkerly-Bean, J.; Bean, T.W. Missing the *savoir* for the *connaissance*: Disciplinary and content area literacy as regimes of truth. *J. Lit. Res.* **2016**, *48*, 448–475. [CrossRef]

7. Blachowicz, C.; Fisher, P.; Ogle, D.; Watts-Taffe, S. *Teaching Academic Vocabulary K-8: Effective Practices Across the Curriculum*; Guilford Press: New York, NY, USA, 2013; ISBN 978-1-4625-1029-0.

8. Nagy, W.E.; Townsend, D. Words as tools: Learning Academic Vocabulary as Language Acquisition. *Read. Res. Q.* **2012**, *47*, 91–108. [CrossRef]

9. Zwiers, J. *Building Academic Language: Essential Practices for Content Classrooms*; Jossey-Bass: San Francisco, CA, USA, 2008; ISBN 978-0-7879-8761-9.

10. Baumann, J.F.; Graves, M.F. What is academic vocabulary? *J. Adolesc. Adult Lit.* **2010**, *54*, 4–12. [CrossRef]

11. McKeown, M.G.; Deane, P.D.; Scott, J.A.; Krovetz, R.; Lawless, R.R. *Vocabulary Assessment: Buliding Rich Word-Learning Experiences*; Guilford Press: New York, NY, USA, 2017; ISBN 978-1-4625-3079-3.

12. Anderson, R.C.; Freebody, P. Vocabulary knowledge. In *Comprehension and Teaching: Research Reviews*; Guthrie, J., Ed.; International Reading Association: Newark, DE, USA, 1981; pp. 77–117, ISBN 0-87207-943-0.

13. Davis, F.B. Fundamental factors of comprehension in reading. *Psychometrika* **1944**, *9*, 185–195. [CrossRef]

14. Mezynski, K. Issues concerning the acquisition of knowledge: Effects of vocabulary training on reading comprehension. *Rev. Educ. Res.* **1983**, *53*, 253–279. [CrossRef]

15. Nagy, W.E. Why vocabulary instruction needs to be long-term and comprehensive. In *Teaching and Learning Vocabulary: Bringing Research to Practice*; Hiebert, E.H., Kamil, M.L., Eds.; Erbaum: Mahwah, NJ, USA, 2005; pp. 27–44, ISBN 0-8058-5286-7.

16. Stanovich, K. Matthew effects in reading: Some consequences of individual differences in the acquisition of literacy. *Read. Res. Q.* **1986**, *21*, 360–407. [CrossRef]

17. Stahl, S.; Nagy, W.E. *Teaching Word Meanings*; Lawrence Erlbaum Associates: Mahwah, NJ, USA, 2006; ISBN 0-8058-4364-7.

18. Stahl, S. *Vocabulary Development*; Brookline Books: Cambridge, MA, USA, 1999; ISBN 1-57129-072-9.

19. Konopak, B.C.; Williams, N.L. Elementary teachers' beliefs and decisions about vocabulary learning and instruction. In *43rd Yearbook of the National Reading Conference*; Kinzer, C.K., Leu, D.J., Eds.; National Reading Conference, Inc.: Chicago, IL, USA, 1994; pp. 485–495, ISSN 0547-8375.

20. Sternberg, R.; Powell, J.S. Comprehending verbal comprehension. *Am. Psychol.* **1983**, *38*, 878–893. [CrossRef]

21. Beck, I.L.; McKeown, M.G.; Omanson, R.C. The effects and uses of diverse vocabulary instructional techniques. In *The Nature of Vocabulary Acquisition*; McKeown, M.G., Curtis, M.E., Eds.; Lawrence Erlbaum Associates, Inc.: Hillsdale NJ, USA, 1987; pp. 147–163, ISBN 0-89859-548-7.

22. LaBerge, D.; Samuels, S.J. Toward a theory of automatic information processing in reading. *Cogn. Psychol.* **1974**, *6*, 293–323. [CrossRef]

23. Fang, Z. A review of research on teacher beliefs and practices. *Educ. Res.* **1996**, *38*, 47–65. [CrossRef]

24. Vacca, R.T.; Vacca, J.L.; Mraz, M. *Content Area Reading: Literacy and Learning Across the Curriculum*, 11th ed.; Pearson: Boston, MA, USA, 2014; ISBN 13: 978-0-13-306678-4.

25. Alexander, P.A.; Kulikowich, J.M.; Schulze, S.K. The influence of topic knowledge, domain knowledge, and interest on the comprehension of scientific exposition. *Learn. Individ. Differ.* **1994**, *6*, 379–397. [CrossRef]

26. Buehl, D. *Developing Readers in the Academic Disciplines*; International Reading Association: Newark, DE, USA, 2011; ISBN 13: 978-0872078451.

27. Jetton, T.L.; Alexander, P.A. Domains, teaching, and literacy. In *Adolescent Literacy Research and Practice*; Jetton, T.L., Dole, J.A., Eds.; Guilford Press: New York, NY, USA, 2004; pp. 15–39. ISBN 1-59385-021-2.

28. Schmitt, N. Size and depth of vocabulary knowledge: What the research shows. *Lang. Learn.* **2014**, *64*, 913–951. [CrossRef]

29. International Literacy Association. *Standards for the Preparation of Literacy Professionals 2017*; International Literacy Association: Newark, NJ, USA, 2017; ISBN 978-0-87207-379-1.

30. Karen, W.; Wood, K.D.; Harmon, J.; Taylor, D.B. Guidelines for integrating comprehension-based word study in content classrooms. *Middle Sch. J.* **2011**, *42*, 57–64.

31. Blachowicz, C.; Fisher, P. *Teaching Vocabulary in All Classrooms*, 3rd ed.; Pearson Education: Upper Saddle River, NJ, USA, 2006; ISBN 0-13-119803-3.

32. Beck, I.L.; McKeown, M.G.; Kucan, L. *Bringing Words to Life: Robust Vocabulary Instruction*, 2nd ed.; Guilford Press: New York, NY, USA, 2013; ISBN 978-1-4625-0816-7.

33. Marzano, R.J. The art and science of teaching/Six steps to better vocabulary instruction. *Educ. Leadersh.* **2009**, *67*, 83–84.

34. Wood, K.D.; Tinajero, J. Using pictures to teach content to second language learners. *Middle Sch. J.* **2002**, *33*, 47–51. [CrossRef]

35. Wood, K.D.; Soares, L.M. *How to Integrate Vocabulary, Comprehension and Writing across the Disciplines: Questions from the Classroom*; Association of Middle Level Educators: Westerville, OH, USA, 2015.

36. Wood, K.D.; Taylor, D.B.; Stover, K. *Smuggling Writing: Getting Students to Write Everyday in Every Content Area, Grades 3–12*; Corwin: Thousand Oaks, CA, USA, 2016.

Article

Academic Vocabulary and Reading Fluency: Unlikely Bedfellows in the Quest for Textual Meaning

David D. Paige *[ORCID] and Grant S. Smith

Annsley Frazier Thornton School of Education, Bellarmine University, Louisville, KY 40205, USA; gssmith@bellarmine.edu
* Correspondence: dpaige@bellarmine.edu; Tel.: +1-502-272-8153

Received: 6 August 2018; Accepted: 25 September 2018; Published: 5 October 2018

Abstract: Academic vocabulary is the specialized language used to communicate within academic settings. The Coxhead (2000) taxonomy is one such list that identifies 570 headwords representing academic vocabulary. Researchers have hypothesized that students possessing greater fluent reading skills are more likely to benefit from exposure to vocabulary due to greater amounts of time spent reading (Nagy and Stahl, 2007; Stanovich, 1986). In this study of 138 sixth- and seventh-grade students, we assess academic vocabulary, indicators of fluent reading, and silent reading comprehension to gain insight into relationships between the three. Our results found that reading rate mediates the relationship between academic vocabulary and reading comprehension, accounting for nearly one-third of the explained variance. Using simple slope analysis, we identified a threshold suggesting the point where reading rate exerts a neutral effect on reading comprehension beyond which vocabulary learning is no longer hindered.

Keywords: academic vocabulary; comprehension; reading fluency; middle grades

1. Introduction

The most recent reading results from the National Assessment of Educational Progress reports that some 36% of eighth-grade students scored at or above the proficient level, an increase from 34% in 2015 [1]. While the improvement is welcomed, the fact is that nearly two-thirds of students achieve at a less-than-proficient level. When these scores are analyzed by ethnicity, the results reveal that 45% of White students score at or above proficiency compared to 18% and 23% of Black and Hispanic students, respectively. In fact, an inspection of below- basic scores reveals that 18% of White students scoring at this lowest level compared to 40% of Black and 33% of Hispanic students. Many reading processes contribute to ultimate reading achievement, one of which is the understanding of words [2]. Research has linked word understanding to improvement in text comprehension both within and across grade levels [3–6]. Oulette and Beers [6] described in sixth-grade students the transition from decoding to dependency on breadth and depth of word understanding as critical to continued reading growth. A close corollary to general vocabulary during this period is growth in the understanding of academic vocabulary, a subset of words pertaining to academic discourse [7]. This study considers the role of academic vocabulary and the extent to which reading fluency may affect its contribution to reading comprehension in sixth- and seventh-grade students.

2. Background

2.1. Theoretical Framework

A defining feature of an educated individual is the ability to create understanding of what they read. Ideally, the reader extracts meaning at the textbase level where a literal or "just the facts" interpretation is made of the text. The second level, the situational model level, is where the text is integrated with the reader's existing schema [8,9]. It is this level where the reader considers the text in conjunction with what they already know, or believe they know about the topic. To arrive at understanding, it is important the reader successfully develops a meaning-based representation of the text at the situational level [8,10]. To create these representations, the construction–integration (CI) model demonstrates that effective comprehension is supported by both top-down and bottom-up processes that function on an interactive basis [8]. The effective decoding of words and fluent reading of text reflects the automatic reading processes that allow critical working memory and attentional resources to be directed to the creation of a situational model [11,12]. The verbal efficiency theory claims that through rapid word identification processes the reader is able to retrieve both the phonology and word meaning that contributes to comprehension [13]. While word retrieval speed is critical in this process and has support in the research base, what is likely as important is the ability of the reader to arrive at the appropriate context-based meaning of the words [14]. This leads to the notion that the nuances found within word meanings are intricately tied to reading fluency and comprehension. This study explores the importance of academic word knowledge and its relationship with reading fluency indicators, and the ultimate contribution of both to silent reading comprehension.

2.2. Vocabulary Learning

Anderson and Freebody proposed that the extent to which a reader knows word meanings directly detracts or enhances comprehension [15]. Cunningham and Stanovich argued that it is the volume of reading that becomes the primary contributor to differences in vocabulary knowledge between readers [16]. Stanovich's reciprocal model of vocabulary hypothesizes that a virtuous cycle occurs where the reader's vocabulary knowledge facilitates engagement with texts, which results in greater word knowledge, which in turn encourages more reading [17]. Stated differently, word knowledge begets word knowledge, to which Perfetti would add enhances text comprehension [14]. This virtuous, reciprocal cycle of reading and learning words was viewed by Stahl and Nagy as the most likely scenario accounting for vocabulary growth in readers, where those who read more expand their breadth and depth of word knowledge [18]. Of interest then is the operational structure of the word learning cycle and how the cycle may vary between readers of different abilities. To further understand this cycle, Perfetti and Stafura made two points about effective readers [19]. First, they are more skilled at understanding words and integrating them into a mental model of a text than are those who are less effective [20–22]. Secondly, when encountering a new word, skilled readers are more effective at acquiring orthographic and semantic information about the word [23–25]. A fundamental characteristic defining a skilled reader is the extent to which they read with fluency [2]. This suggests that vocabulary learning may differ based on the degree to which a student possesses the indicators associated with fluent reading.

The lexical quality hypothesis claims that a reader's ability to rapidly retrieve a words' phonology (its sound constituent) and its associated meaning is a potentially limiting factor to comprehension [26]. The theory provides an explanation for word learning by recognizing that lexical entries are tri-part, meaning they consist of an orthographic, phonological, and semantic component. The quality of each of these three components in terms of reliability, coherence, and consistency reflects the overall lexical quality of the word. It may not be assumed that the quality of each part of a lexical entry is equal as a reader may be able to connect the orthography to the phonology of a word, but may have little to no corresponding semantic association [27]. For any given reader, the inventory of high-quality word representations can be placed on a continuum ranging from few to many. Skilled readers are those whose high-quality word representations tend toward the high end of the continuum, while the inventory of less-skilled readers aggregates towards the lower end. Although both skilled and less-skilled readers have many words for which they have low-quality representations, the former group is in a much better position to improve their understanding of a new word, and hence improve its lexical quality. For example, a skilled reader may have little trouble quickly applying their orthographic and phonological knowledge to unlock an unknown word from print. At the same time a less-skilled reader may be more likely to struggle in their attempt to pronounce the word due to less-than-adequate decoding skill. The skilled reader is thus in a better position to improve the quality of an impoverished word representation by leveraging their deeper knowledge of spelling, pronunciation, or meaning in an effort to extract new information about the word. The less-skilled reader has a shallower inventory of these foundational skills from which to draw making it more difficult to engage in new learning of impoverished words. Hence, effective word learning for less-skilled readers often requires explicit instruction and frequent encounters with the word.

2.3. Decoding Processes and Vocabulary

The simple view of reading hypothesizes that decoding and linguistic comprehension plus the interaction of the two results in reading comprehension [28]. Two accounts of the role of vocabulary in decoding have been proposed. One view proposes that breadth rather than depth in vocabulary growth promotes decoding growth and development. As young readers add words to their lexicon they become increasingly sensitive to sublexical details in those words including their phonemes [29–31]. This view privileges vocabulary breadth as the mechanism that drives decoding development. The second view is derived from the triangle model that hypothesizes an interaction between decoding, vocabulary, and semantics suggesting that depth of vocabulary knowledge is related to decoding proficiency [32]. To unravel these relationships, Ouellette studied decoding, vocabulary, word recognition, and comprehension processes in fourth-grade students [33]. The author found that breadth of receptive vocabulary alone predicted decoding while expressive vocabulary predicted visual word recognition (non-decodable words). Through its association with expressive vocabulary, vocabulary depth predicted both visual word recognition and comprehension above and beyond the measures of vocabulary breadth. Ouellette surmised that the relationship between decoding and oral vocabulary is a function of the size of one's receptive vocabulary. This supports the notion by Levelt, Roelofs, and Meyer [34] that a reader's ability to encode phonological information about a word may at least partly explain the relationship between oral vocabulary and reading comprehension reported by other authors [35–37]. In sum, these results suggest a perspective where an initial emphasis on decoding is followed by a focus on building automatic sight-word reading skills that leads to fluent reading and an increase in vocabulary breadth.

Decoding processes are reflected in the degree to which a student can fluently read connected text, which along with comprehension is a necessary condition for effective reading [28]. We adopt a definition of fluent reading that includes the indicators of reading rate (word automaticity), word identification accuracy, and prosody [38,39]. Word automaticity is the ability to quickly recall the phonological representation of a printed word without the need to apply decoding strategies [12]. In addition to speed, the reader must also accurately recall the letter–sound correspondences resulting in the correct pronunciation of the word. For students struggling with reading, accurate word identification has been found to be problematic at the elementary, middle, and secondary levels [40–42]. However, other researchers have found that word accuracy is not a significant issue for readers [43–45]. Despite differences in findings automatic and accurate recall of words is necessary to becoming a fluent reader and for maintaining the attentional resources critical to comprehension [11]. Reading is often measured by a metric where the number of words read (rate) minus reading miscues (word mispronunciations, omissions, and insertions) is calculated to reflect the number of correctly read words-per-minute. We call this metric accumaticity and distinguish it from the term reading fluency as the latter also includes expressive reading or prosody [46]. Numerous studies over the past several decades have found that one or more of the indicators of fluent reading accounts for significant variance in reading across multiple grade levels [38,47]. Although prosody has often been ignored, it has been found to contribute unique variance to silent reading comprehension across elementary, middle, and secondary grades beyond that accounted for by automaticity and word identification accuracy [42,48–53]. Prosody is important because as in speech, it provides a kind of cognitive architecture that aids the reader in comprehension [54–57]. Accumaticity has been found to explain from 25% to 50% or more of the variance in reading comprehension [38,42,47,52]. while prosody has been shown to contribute an additional 3 to 7% of variance to reading comprehension [42,48,52,58–60].

2.4. Academic Vocabulary

Hiebert and Lubliner decomposed academic words into those that are general and those that are content specific [61]. Academic vocabulary is a component of academic language and is critical to successful achievement in school [62–65]. Nagy and Townsend explained that "Academic language is the specialized language, both oral and written, of academic settings that facilitates communication and thinking about disciplinary content" [66] (p. 92). This definition situates academic language as a subset of general vocabulary and includes words such as paradigm, allocate, and preliminary that are used in both oral and written language across academic settings. Such words convey abstract ideas outside the realm of informal, casual conversation and reflect the nuanced meanings that are used across disciplines. Academic settings refer to educational institutions which includes the associated print and digital literature that discusses disciplinary concepts. In Beck, McKeown, and Kucan's word tiers, academic vocabulary is situated in Tier 2 as words used across disciplines while Tier 3 refers to discipline-specific words [67]. To further differentiate academic vocabulary from more general and pedestrian language, Biber outlined characteristics of academic words stating they are often derived from Latin and Greek vocabulary, consist of nouns, adjectives, and prepositions that are morphologically complex, are often used as grammatical metaphors, are abstract, and are informationally dense [68]. Latin and Greek words were introduced into English by the educated classes in the eleventh century. For example, where the vernacular was deer, the new term became venison, pig became pork, to eat became to dine, be was now exist, right was correct, tooth became dental, and by hand was referred to as manual. Additional words were introduced for which no previous corollary existed and include words such as accommodate, arbitrary, and analyze [7].

Nagy and Townsend pointed out that students from less educated backgrounds will not learn academic words without explicit instruction of their meanings and repeated encounters of their use [66]. In a seminal study Coxhead proposed a list of 570 of the most common academic word families. Research has since shown that the study of these words can significantly improve a student's word knowledge [7,69–71]. At the same time such lists have been criticized, particularly when they have been used as lists to be taught prescriptively to students [72]. Despite these criticisms academic words have been found to contribute significant, unique variance to academic achievement. The correlation between general vocabulary and reading comprehension is generally in the 0.70 to 0.95 range [73,74]. Townsend, Filippini, Collins, and Biancarosa found that after controlling for general vocabulary, academic vocabulary accounted for 2% to 7% of additional variance in math, social studies, ELA (English Language Arts), and science achievement [75].

2.5. Study Rationale

The importance of word knowledge to comprehension has been long established in the literature base. Our review of the literature discussed evidence suggesting the importance of academic vocabulary to academic achievement across disciplines. It is also established that students who struggle with reading require significantly more exposure to words, particularly academic words, to incorporate them into their lexical inventory. However, there remains little evidence of the extent to which academic vocabulary is acquired by middle school students, and as a corollary there are few validated instruments to assess academic vocabulary. Stanovich, Stahl, and others have suggested that fluent readers are more likely to acquire deeper word knowledge because they spend more time engaged with text and thus have an increased exposure to words [17,74]. We assume that the same fluent reading process responsible for general vocabulary acquisition is at work in learning academic vocabulary. While there are limitations to a strict focus on academic vocabulary per se, a deeper understanding can provide insight into its role and influence on comprehension, and whether those with fluent reading skills are likely to possess larger academic vocabularies that contribute to comprehension.

The goal of this study then is to describe the extent to which reading fluency and academic vocabulary contribute to reading comprehension in sixth- and seventh-grade students. The research questions guiding this study are as follows:

- RQ1: What is the attainment level of students on measures of academic vocabulary, reading fluency, and comprehension?
- RQ2: Do differences exist in students between grades on the measured variables?
- RQ3: To what extent is silent reading comprehension predicted by academic vocabulary and reading fluency indicators?
- RQ4: Does reading fluency mediate the relationship between academic vocabulary and reading comprehension?

We hypothesized that students with adequate indicators of reading fluency possess greater academic vocabulary knowledge and reading comprehension.

3. Methods

3.1. Participants

This study was conducted in a large, urban school district in the southeast U.S. containing 24 middle schools. From these schools, ten agreed to participate in the present study. Of the students attending these schools 49% are white, 37% African-American, 9% Hispanic/Latino, and 5% are of other ethnicities. Sixty-two percent of these students receive free- or reduced-priced lunch. From the 10 middle schools, 29 ELA teachers who taught sixth- and/or seventh-grade volunteered to participate in the study. A total of 320 students were randomly sampled from the class rosters of participating teachers with half drawn from sixth-grade and the other from seventh. Of these students, the final analytic sample is $n = 138$.

3.2. Assessments

Students were assessed over the course of 10 days in the early fall on measures of academic vocabulary, reading fluency (reading rate, word identification accuracy, and prosody), and reading comprehension. Vocabulary and reading fluency assessments were administered by researchers trained in their administration while a standardized, computer-based reading comprehension assessment was administered by the district.

3.3. Test of Academic Word Knowledge (TAWK)

The TAWK is a 50-item test of academic word knowledge created by the researchers. Word level test items were drawn from the Academic Word List (AWL) created by Coxhead [7]. The 570 headwords in the AWL are divided into 10 sub-lists containing 60 words each with list 10 containing 30 words. The frequency of occurrence in academic texts of the words in each sub-list diminishes in frequency as one moves from sub-list 1 to 2 to 3, and so on. To develop items for the TAWK an equal number of words were randomly drawn from each sub-list resulting in 110 items. For each of these items three words were selected with the one most closely associated with the target word being the correct answer. Over the course of five administrations of the 110 items to middle school students, a total of 50 emerged that demonstrated acceptable discrimination (good ≥ 0.40, reasonable > 0.30 and ≤ 0.39, fair > 0.20 and ≤ 0.29, and poor ≤ 0.20) and difficulty characteristics (easy > 0.60, moderate ≥ 0.30 and < 0.60, and hard > 0.33). Nunnally and Bernstein suggested that the difficulty of the test items should be mixed and that when a test is not designed to make placement decisions for individual students a reliability coefficient of $r = 0.80$ is adequate [76]. The final 50-item version of the TAWK was administered to 278 middle school students across 15 schools and resulted in a

Cronbach's alpha of internal consistency = 0.85. The TAWK is group-administered on a whole-class basis where students are instructed to circle from options A, B, and C the word that most nearly means the same as the target word. Results for internal consistency yielded a Cronbach's alpha equal to 0.85. Split-half reliability using the Spearman–Brown and Gutman coefficients both equaled 0.940. Indices of normality exhibited a normal distribution as evidenced by a mean of 24.7(8.31), median equal to 24.0, and a mode equal to 24.0.

3.4. Reading Accumaticity Indicators

To assess accumaticity students read a primarily narrative passage selected to be grade-level appropriate. Curriculum-based measures have been established as both valid and reliable measures of reading competency [77–80]. For each grade, a passage was selected based on narrativity and appropriate textual complexity. Sixth-grade students read a passage with a complexity level between 950 L and 1000 L while the seventh-grade passage measured between 1050 L and 1100 L. Both complexity levels are within the text complexity grade bands recommended by the Common Core [81]. Narrativity was measured using Coh–Metrix with the sixth- and seventh-grade passages measuring at 58% and 61%, respectively, where 100% would indicate a completely narrative text and 0% one that is totally informational [82]. All students read aloud the narrative passage for one minute while a researcher recorded the total number of words read and the number of reading miscues that included mispronunciations, word omissions, and insertion of words not in the text. To compute accumaticity, miscues were subtracted from the total words read for one minute which resulted in the number of words read correctly. Test–retest reliability of the measures used in this study resulted in Pearson's $r = 0.962$.

3.5. Reading Prosody

To assess reading prosody a recording was made of each student reading the one-minute passage and then saved for later analysis. The Multi-Dimensional Fluency Rubric (MDFS) was used to assess the quality of each student's reading [83]. When using the MDFS the rater evaluates four domains of reading quality that include pacing, smoothness, expression, and phrasing. Each of these domains is assigned a rating from a low of 1, indicating very poor quality, to a maximum score of 4 indicating excellent reading. The four ratings are then summed resulting in a composite score ranging from 4–16. Our interpretation of the composite is that a score ≥ 12 indicates appropriate fluency, 9–11 indicates fluency that is developing, and ≤ 8 suggests poorly developed fluency. It is important to remember that reading fluency is assessed on a per-reading basis and that fluent reading with a particular passage does not guarantee that a student reads every passage with equal fluency.

The MDFS has been found to be a valid and reliable tool for assessing reading fluency with two particularly rigorous studies reporting reliability coefficients well above the accepted norm of 0.80 [84–86]. Moser, Sudweeks, Morrison, and Wilcox studied two raters who scored 144 readings of 36 fourth-grade students [87]. Each student read two narrative and two informational passages. The authors implemented a research design using a generalizability study (G-study) which found that variability attributed to readers ranged from 79.2% to 83.3% for narrative text, and 70.7% and 81.8% for informational text. The authors then used a decision study (D-study) that found reliability coefficients ranging from 0.94 to 0.97 for narrative text and 0.92 to 0.98 for informational text suggesting high rater reliability. Smith and Paige conducted a study involving 354 narrative readings by 177 first- to third-grade students [88]. Each student had read one text each in the fall and spring of their respective grade with all readings recorded for later analysis. Four teachers with no experience in formal reading instruction received five hours of training in the use of the MDFS after which the raters independently evaluated each reading. Generalizability coefficients were analyzed by grade resulting in statistics equal to 0.92, 0.93, and 0.93 for first- to third-grade, respectively. Decision study results revealed generalizability coefficients for any single rater evaluating one reading equal to 0.77, 0.77, and 0.78 for first- to third-grade, respectively. When single raters evaluated two readings reliabilities increased to

0.87 across all grades. These two studies provide strong evidence of the reliability of the MDFS as a tool to assess oral reading fluency and prosody. Test–retest reliability of rating in the present study is 0.948 ($n = 274$).

3.6. Scholastic Reading Inventory

Students were assessed for reading comprehension in the fall and spring by school personnel using the Scholastic Reading Inventory (SRI), a computer-adaptive, individually administered assessment. During the assessment students independently and silently read a series of passages and then answered a multiple choice inferential question. Students typically spent about 25 min taking the SRI. Test results are in student-level Lexile levels that provide the highest level of text-complexity for which the student reads with 75% comprehension [89]. The test authors provide the results of multiple studies showing concurrent validity with other standardized tests ranging from 0.88 to 0.93. Test–retest reliability is reported as 0.87 to 0.89. In the present study correlations between the fall and spring administrations of the SRI are Pearson's $r = 0.85$ ($n = 185$).

4. Results

Our first research question sought to describe student attainment on the measured variables, while the second asks if differences exist between sixth- and seventh-grade readers. Table 1 shows the means and standard deviations of the variables under study while Table 2 displays the bivariate correlations. Numerical differences in mean scores appear to exist between grades for comprehension, vocabulary, and prosody with seventh-grade scoring higher. However, in the case of reading rate and word identification accuracy the sixth-grade means exceed those of seventh-grade. Accumaticity, the difference between reading rate and miscues adjusted for time, was calculated at 134.43 (33.99) words-correct-per-minute for sixth-grade and 125.22 (38.92) for seventh-grade. This places sixth-grade accumaticity at approximately the 55th percentile and sixth-graders just below the 50th percentile on oral reading norms from Hasbrouck and Tindal [90].

Table 1. Means and standard deviations of the measured variables by grade.

Variable	Sixth-Grade ($n = 83$)	Seventh-Grade ($n = 55$)	All Students ($n = 138$)
Comprehension	851.52(206.57)	942.49(196.14)	887.78(206.64)
Academic Vocabulary	23.30(7.99)	26.16(8.42)	24.44(8.25)
Reading Rate	136.93(33.48)	131.36(29.97)	134.71(32.13)
Word Identification Accuracy	134.43(33.99)	126.89(34.46)	130.33(38.26)
Prosody	10.64(2.18)	10.05(1.67)	10.41(2.01)

Table 2. Bivariate Correlations among the Measured Variables.

Variable	Comprehension	Academic Vocabulary	Reading Rate	Word Accuracy	Prosody
Comprehension	1				
Academic Vocabulary	0.485	1			
Reading Rate	0.566	0.337	1		
Word Accuracy	0.544	0.321	0.958	1	
Prosody	0.489	0.380	0.755	0.738	1

Note: All correlations significant at $p < 0.01$ (two-tailed); N = 138; Word accuracy = word identification accuracy.

Moderate to large correlations were statistically significant between all mean variables with the strongest occurring among comprehension, reading rate, word identification accuracy, and prosody. On the measure of academic vocabulary mean scores show sixth- and seventh-grade attainment to be at the 52nd and 53rd percentiles, respectively.

Our second question asked if students differed by grade on the measured variables. We conducted an analysis of variance (ANOVA) using grade as the between-subject factor while applying a Bonferroni adjustment to account for inflated Type I error. Results revealed a statistically significant difference in favor of seventh-grade for reading comprehension (F (1,136) = 6.68, MSE = 174048.02, p = 0.011, d = 0.45) while vocabulary approached significance (F (1,136) = 4.07, MSE = 327256.98, p = 0.046) with seventh-grade scoring higher. No other variables approached statistical significance.

The third research question asks the extent to which silent reading comprehension is predicted by academic vocabulary and the indicators of fluent reading. We proceeded by regressing silent reading comprehension onto academic vocabulary, reading rate, word identification accuracy, and reading prosody. Results (Table 3) revealed academic vocabulary and reading rate to be significant predictors of comprehension while a test of the interaction of the two was non-significant. Regression results show that academic vocabulary explained 22.9% of the variance in comprehension (F (1,136) = 41.78, MSE = 367806.71, p < 0.001) while reading rate explained 18.0% of the variance (F (1,135) = 42.43, MSE = 327256.98, p < 0.001). The two variables accounted for 40.9% of the variance in silent reading comprehension.

Our fourth research question asked if reading fluency mediates the relationship between academic vocabulary and comprehension. Results from question three revealed that of the three fluency indicators only reading rate was a significant predictor of comprehension. Scatterplot analysis (Figure 1) shows a nonlinear relationship for comprehension and reading rate where the influence of rate decreases as comprehension increases. Figure 2 shows that as rate increases vocabulary also increases, while Figure 3 shows that as vocabulary increases so does comprehension. In sum, these graphs suggest the possibility that rate may function as a mediator between academic vocabulary and reading comprehension.

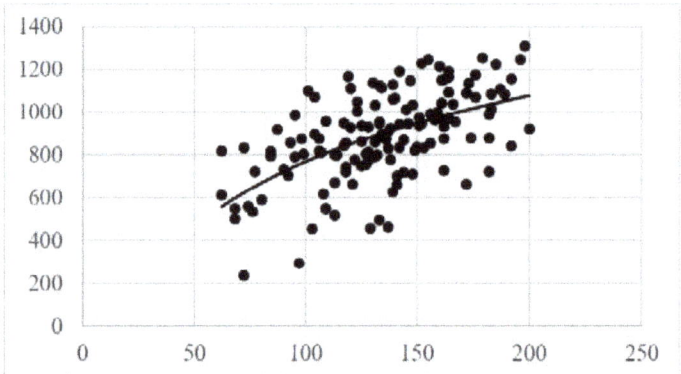

Figure 1. Graph of the Relationship between Comprehension and Rate.

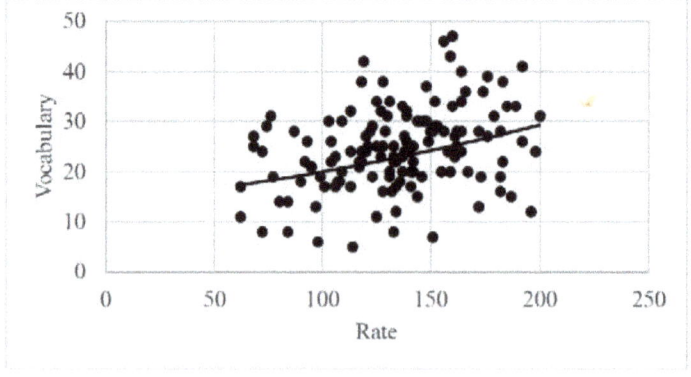

Figure 2. Graph of the Relationship between Vocabulary and Rate.

Table 3. Hierarchical Regression Results for Measures Predicting Silent Reading Comprehension.

Variable	All Students (n = 138)							Low-Rate Students (n = 58; Rate < 127)							High-Rate Students (n = 80; Rate ≥ 127)						
	B	Std. Error	SEβ	β	R^2	ΔR^2	t	B	Std. Error	SEβ	β	R^2	ΔR^2	t	B	Std. Error	SEβ	β	R^2	ΔR^2	t
Constant	591.14	55.72	48.42				12.21 ***	517.08	79.19	68.61				7.39 ***	729.73	61.78	60.81				11.52 ***
TAWK	12.14	2.16	1.88	0.485	0.229		6.46 ***	11.78	3.37	2.90	0.477	0.214		4.07 ***	9.09	2.26	2.23	0.418	0.165		4.06 ***
Constant	291.30	67.40	62.58				4.66 ***	221.23	128.49	124.45				1.78	376.26	150.79	145.85				2.58 *
TAWK	8.30	1.91	1.75	0.332	0.229		4.76 ***	10.41	3.18	2.78	0.422	0.214		3.75 ***	6.96	2.35	2.30	0.320	0.165		3.03 **
Rate	2.92	0.47	0.45	0.454	0.409	0.18	6.51 ***	3.12	0.33	1.12	0.314	0.299	0.085	2.79 ***	2.61	1.01	0.99	0.280	0.224	0.059	2.65 *

* $p < 0.05$, ** $p < 0.01$, *** $p < 0.001$; TAWK, Test of Academic Word Knowledge (academic vocabulary).

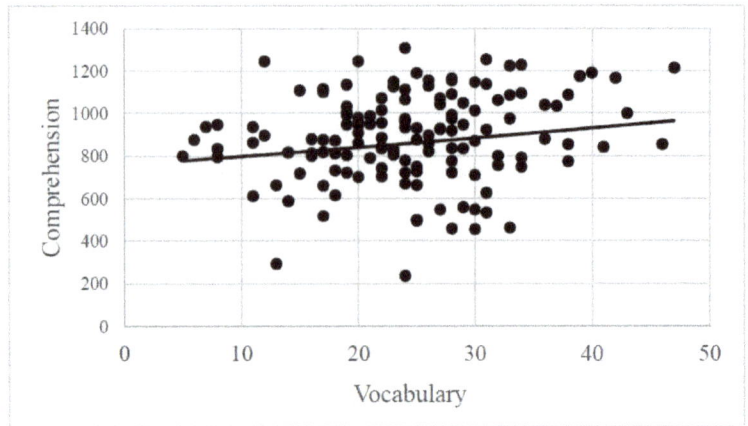

Figure 3. Graph of Relationship between Comprehension and Vocabulary.

The path model defining the relationships between vocabulary, rate, and comprehension is shown in Figure 4.

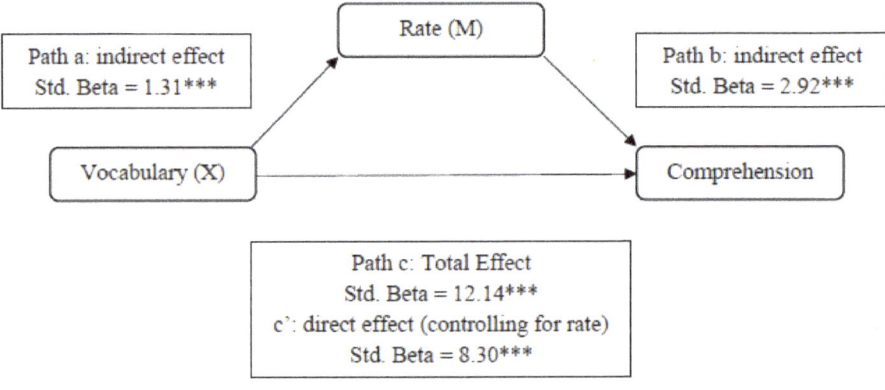

Figure 4. Pathway of Mediation Analysis.

Following recommendations by Baron and Kenny for determining if a variable acts as a mediator, we began by regressing the criterion variable comprehension onto academic vocabulary to determine the total effect [91]. We next regressed reading rate, the suspected mediation variable, onto academic vocabulary to determine a portion of the indirect effect. Finally, comprehension was regressed onto both reading rate and academic vocabulary. The final multiple regression (Table 4) gives estimates of the direct effect of academic vocabulary on comprehension while controlling for reading rate, as well as estimating the other component of the indirect effect, reading rate, on comprehension. The standardized beta coefficients associated with each of these conditions are all statically significant ($p < 0.001$). Consistent with Baron and Kenny's partial mediation designation is the finding that the effect of academic vocabulary on comprehension is reduced but not eliminated when reading rate is added to the model, decreasing the effect from 12.14 to 8.30 and making the effect of reading rate equal to 3.84.

Table 4. Regression Results for the Mediation of Rate on Vocabulary and Comprehension.

Model/Path	Estimate	SE	95% CI (Lower)	95% CI (Upper)
Vocabulary—Reading Rate (a)	1.31 ***	0.314	0.691	1.934
$R^2_{M.X}$	0.114			
Reading Rate—Comprehension (b)	2.92 ***	0.449	2.034	3.809
$R^2_{Y.M}$				
Vocabulary—Comprehension (c)	12.14 ***	1.878	8.423	15.850
$R^2_{Y.X.}$	0.235			
Vocabulary—Comprehension (c′)	8.30 ***	1.746	4.849	11.756
$R^2_{Y.M.X}$	0.418			
Indirect Effect of Rate in $_{Y.M.X}$	3.84 ***	1.139	1.839	6.278

Note: Estimates for model/path effects are standardized coefficients (betas); $R^2_{M.X}$ is the proportion of variance in reading rate (*M*) explained by academic vocabulary (*X*); $R^2_{Y.M}$ is the proportion of variance in comprehension (*Y*) explained by reading rate (*M*). $R^2_{Y.X}$ is the proportion of variance in comprehension (*Y*) explained by academic vocabulary (*X*). $R^2_{Y.MX}$ is the proportion of variance in comprehension (*Y*) explained by academic vocabulary (*X*) when controlling for rate (*M*). Number of bootstrap samples = 1000. CI; confidence interval. *** $p < 0.001$.

Weaknesses in the method of the Baron and Kenny model identified by Preacher and Hayes and Preacher and Kelly concerns beta estimation, particularly in the case of small sample sizes. To address these concerns, these authors recommended bootstrapping, a resampling approach that increases the stability of parameter estimates [92,93]. In line with this recommendation, we conducted 1000 bootstrap samples to increase the stability of our parameter estimates. Because our bootstrapping results at the 95% confidence interval in Table 4 do not include 0, it may be concluded that all effects are significant considering a null hypothesis of $b = 0$. The results of both the Baron and Kenny approach and the more robust bootstrap estimation method indicate that reading rate has a significant mediating effect on the relationship between academic vocabulary and silent reading comprehension.

Using the finding that reading rate acts as a mediator we sought to determine the point at which it had a neutral effect on reading comprehension. In other words, how much reading rate is enough to avoid degradation in comprehension? Using simple slope analysis recommended by Preacher, Curran, and Bauer we proceeded through a series of iterations where we assigned a conditional value or cut-point based on reading rate in order to split the analytic sample into low- and high-rate groups [94]. For each reading rate data point (e.g., 119, 120, 121, etc.), we regressed comprehension onto rate to estimate the standardized beta coefficients for each of the two groups. Results in Table 5 show that at a rate of 127 words-per-minute, the beta coefficients are nearly equal, suggesting the influence of rate is now neutral for the low- and high-rate groups. Using this finding, we then split the analytic sample into low- and high-rate readers using the cut-point of 127 words per minute. We then conducted an analysis of variance (ANOVA) test to determine the differences in academic vocabulary, comprehension, and reading rate between low- and high-rate readers. Table 6 reveals statistically significant differences for comprehension ($F_{(1,137)} = 33.70$, $p < 0.001$, $d = 0.700$), academic vocabulary ($F_{(1,137)} = 6.85$, $p = 0.01$, $d = 0.32$), and reading rate ($F_{(1,1,137)} = 242.15$, $p < 0.001$, $d = 1.88$). For the low- and high-rate reading groups we then regressed comprehension onto academic vocabulary and reading rate. Results in Figure 5 and Table 3 for the low-rate group show that academic vocabulary explained 21.4% of the variance in reading comprehension ($F_{(1,56)} = 16.52$, $p < 0.000$) while 8.5% was explained by rate ($F_{(1.55)} = 7.76$, $p = 0.007$). Beta coefficients were $b = 0.422$ and 0.314 for academic vocabulary and reading rate respectively. For the high-rate group academic vocabulary explained 16.5% of the variance ($F_{(1,78)} = 16.56$, $p < 0.001$) while rate explained an additional 5.9% of variance ($F_{(1,77)} = 7.00$, $p = 0.01$). When the coefficients for the two models are compared, the impact of vocabulary on the low rate reading group is 32% greater than the impact on the high rate group.

Table 5. Effect of Reading Rate on Comprehension by Reading Group.

Rate Cut-Point	Group Low Rate (b)	High Rate (b)	ΔRate
114	0.287ns	0.418 ***	ns
117	0.293ns	0.412 ***	ns
118	0.336 *	0.414 ***	0.78
119	0.329 *	0.390 ***	0.61
120	0.374 **	0.417 ***	0.43
121	0.398 **	0.428 ***	0.30
122	0.398 **	0.428 ***	0.30
123	0.392 **	0.420 ***	0.28
125	0.437 **	0.445 **	0.08
127	0.429 **	0.427 ***	0.02
128	0.416 **	0.409 ***	0.07
129	0.417 **	0.395 ***	0.22
130	0.363 **	0.369 **	0.06
131	0.388 **	0.392 ***	0.04
133	0.387 **	0.377 **	0.10
134	0.364 **	0.356 **	0.08
136	0.395 **	0.368 **	0.27
137	0.398 **	0.363 **	0.35

Note: b, coefficient beta; Rate, words read per minute; * $p < 0.05$, ** $p < 0.01$, *** $p < 0.001$. Data not available for cut-points 115, 116, 124, 126, 132, and 135.

Table 6. Means and Standard Deviations for Reading Rate, Academic Vocabulary, and Comprehension by Low- and High-Rate Readers.

Group	Comprehension	Academic Vocabulary	Reading Rate
Low-Rate ($n = 58$, 42%)	780.02(196.32)	22.33(7.96)	104.62(19.75)
High-Rate ($n = 80$, 58%)	965.90(177.59)	25.98(8.17)	156.53(19.04)

Note: Differences between low- and high-rate groups for comprehension and reading rate are statistically significant at $p < 0.001$. Differences between low- and high-rate groups for academic vocabulary are significant at $p = 0.01$.

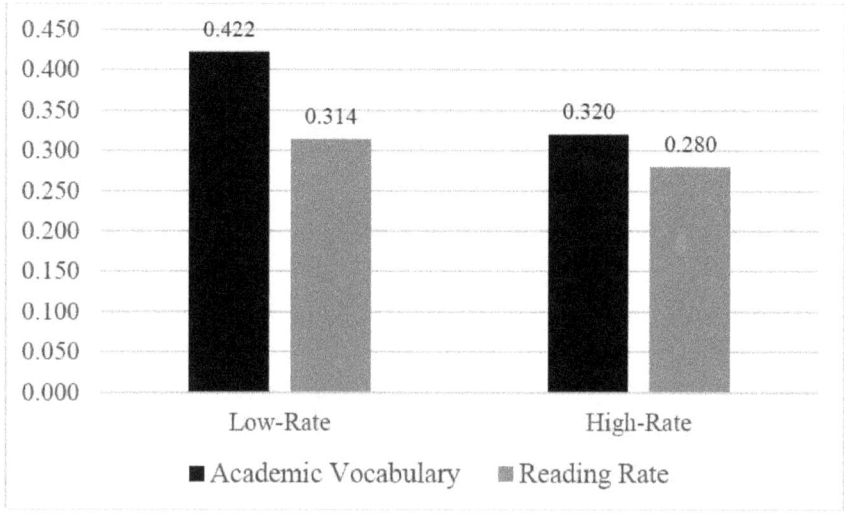

Figure 5. Beta Coefficients (b) for Academic Vocabulary and Reading Rate Predicting Comprehension by Group.

5. Discussion

In this study we investigated the relationships among academic vocabulary, indicators of reading fluency, and reading comprehension. Our results found that mean accumaticity was at or above the 50th percentile for students in both grades while as a group readers generally exhibited less than adequate reading prosody. Our results also showed that sixth-grade students out-performed those in seventh-grade on all reading fluency measures, although the results were not statistically significant. We found statistically significant differences between grades in reading comprehension with seventh-grade outscoring those in sixth, while on the measure of academic vocabulary we found no statistically significant difference between the two grades, although results approached significance.

Our multivariate regression results found that of the three indicators of reading fluency, only reading rate was a significant predictor of comprehension, a finding consistent with other researchers [95]. Accompanying reading rate as a significant predictor of reading comprehension was academic vocabulary. While reading rate predicted 18% of the variance in comprehension, academic vocabulary predicted an additional 22.9% for a total of 40.9% of explained variance. We remind the reader that we measured silent reading comprehension with a standardized instrument, the results of which are often less robust than are researcher-constructed instruments. Although we did not include a measure of general vocabulary in the study, these results provide evidence for the role of academic vocabulary and reading rate as co-predictors of reading comprehension. In previous studies we have found reading prosody to be a significant predictor of reading comprehension so we were mildly surprised that in this sample of students it predicted no unique variance. A possibility for this result may rest in the constrained range of scores. We consider a score of 12 (out of a range of 12) on the MDFS to reflect appropriate prosody. In this sample, a 12 reflected attainment at the 75th percentile, nearly a full standard deviation above the sample mean of 10.4(2.00). We suspect that the suppression of scores in the upper range may have restricted the utility of prosody as a statistically significant predictor of reading comprehension.

Given research showing that fluent readers spend more time engaged with text which exposes them to more words than their less-fluent peers, we tested hypotheses from Stanovich and Stahl and Nagy that the former group would possess larger academic vocabularies that positively influence their reading comprehension. We began by testing a model showing that reading rate does indeed function as a mediator between academic vocabulary and reading comprehension. Our findings demonstrated that reading rate reduces the direct effect of academic vocabulary on comprehension by nearly one-third (32%). We interpret this result to mean that languid reading rates negatively influence growth in academic vocabulary that may ultimately reduce reading comprehension. Digging deeper into this finding we found through a simple slope analysis that a reading rate equal to 127 words-per-minute was the distinguishing point between low- and high-rate readers where the effect on comprehension became neutralized. In other words, 127 words-per-minute was the "bar" that when attained, appeared to negate the effect of reading rate on comprehension. To be clear, we do not recommend that our finding of 127 words-per-minute be interpreted as an absolute minimum standard for reading rate as it is restricted to the sample set in the present study. At the same time, we do believe it to be a *plausible estimate* that distinguishes the influence of reading rate on comprehension. Our estimate of 127 also happens to be the approximate accumaticity level that is equal to the 50th percentile for sixth- and seventh-grade readers as indicated by the Hasbrouck and Tindal reading norms [90]. We do not assume that these norms reflect a national sample, however, because of the large number of readers represented within each cell (approximately 15,000–17,000 readers), they do provide opportunity for an interesting insight. If our estimated cut-point of 127 words-per-minute for the present sample of students were to be applied to the sixth- and seventh-grade Hasbrouck and Tindal fall sample, then approximately half of students in the sample read at a less-than-adequate reading rate to fully benefit from exposure to academic vocabulary and its effect on comprehension. Regardless, poor reading rate represents an *opportunity cost* for low-rate readers as they learn less of the critical vocabulary necessary to achieve at levels commensurate with their peers possessing adequate reading rates. Our results suggest that improved reading rate offers the opportunity for improved vocabulary learning and comprehension.

It is important to remember the hypotheses put forth by Stanovich as well as Nagy and Stahl [17,18]. The authors suggest that readers with adequate fluency are more likely to engage in reading and as a result, experience greater vocabulary growth. Because an individual's attentional capacity is a zero-sum resource, there is a finite amount that when reading, is typically divided between decoding and comprehension. If resources are over-taxed because of poor decoding, there is little attention left to direct to comprehension. On the other hand, efficient decoding leaves most of the reader's attention capacity for making sense of the text. We say *typically* to allow for cases of fluent readers who expend little attention on decoding but do not focus their attention on creating meaning when they read. The point here is that it cannot be taken for granted that all readers who become rate-proficient will be inclined to engage in a sufficient amount of reading of the right texts to experience growth in academic vocabulary. Nonetheless, getting over the reading rate "bar" appears from our results, to be an important accomplishment that potentially sets the student up for further vocabulary growth due to improved engagement in reading.

There are several limitations to this study. The reader should keep in mind that this is a descriptive study and does not make use of random assignment to control for confounds necessary to draw causal conclusions of the results. We did not gather a measure for receptive vocabulary to determine the extent to which academic vocabulary provides additional, unique variance explaining differences in comprehension which would likely reduce or perhaps eliminate the percentage of explained variance found in this study. Our analytic sample is limited to students attending 10 middle schools across a large urban district and is not generalizable to a larger population or to other geographic areas. We also advise that our results may be problematic if applied to populations that differ in socio-economic status and academic achievement.

Future research into this area can explore the extent to which students possess academic vocabulary and how this subset of vocabulary affects academic achievement. While it would be expected that correlations between general and academic vocabulary would be large, this has yet to be strongly established. As many subskills in education are distributed along socioeconomic strata, it is expected that academic vocabulary would be no different, however, this too has little empirical evidence. There is also a need to determine at what point across grade levels academic vocabulary becomes a significant predictor of reading comprehension. Academic vocabulary is also a constrained set of words that can be purposely learned. As such, we do not know if there is a point in the educational continuum when academic vocabulary loses its predictive power on comprehension. Finally, the effect of academic vocabulary on state achievement assessments is unknown.

Author Contributions: Conceptualization, D.D.P.; Data curation, G.S.S.; Formal analysis, G.S.S.; Writing—original draft, D.D.P.; Writing—review & editing, D.D.P.

Funding: This research received no external funding.

Conflicts of Interest: The authors declare no conflict of interest.

References

1. NAEP Reading: National Average Scores. Available online: https://www.nationsreportcard.gov/reading_2017/#nation/scores?grade=8 (accessed on 26 September 2018).
2. National Institute of Child Health and Development. National Reading Panel. Teaching Children to Read: An Evidence-Based Assessment of the Scientific Research Literature on Reading and Its Implications for Reading Instruction. Available online: https://www.nichd.nih.gov/sites/default/files/publications/pubs/nrp/Documents/report.pdf (accessed on 26 September 2018).
3. Beck, I.L.; Perfetti, C.A.; McKeown, M.G. Effects of long-term vocabulary instruction on lexical access and reading comprehension. *J. Educ. Psychol.* **1982**, *74*, 506–521. [CrossRef]

4.   Kameenui, E.J.; Carmine, D.; Freschi, R. Effects of text construction and instructional procedures for teaching word meanings on comprehension and recall. *RRQ* **1982**, *17*, 367–388. [CrossRef]

5.   McKeown, M.G.; Beck, I.L.; Omanson, R.C.; Perfetti, C.A. The effects of long-term vocabulary instruction on reading comprehension: A replication. *J. Read. Behav.* **1983**, *15*, 3–18. [CrossRef]

6.   Ouellette, G.; Beers, A. A not-so-simple view of reading: How oral vocabulary and visual-word recognition complicate the story. *Read. Writ.* **2010**, *23*, 189–208. [CrossRef]

7.   Coxhead, A. A new academic word list. *TESOL Q.* **2000**, *34*, 213–238. [CrossRef]

8.   Kintsch, W. *Comprehension: A Paradigm for Cognition*; Cambridge University Press: Cambridge, UK, 1998.

9.   Paris, S.G.; Hamilton, E.E. The development of children's reading comprehension. In *Handbook of Research on Reading Comprehension*; Israel, S.E., Duffy, G.G., Eds.; Routledge: New York, NY, USA, 2009; pp. 32–53.

10.   Gernsbacher, M.A. *Language Comprehension as Structure Building*; Erlbaum: Hillsdale, NJ, USA, 1990.

11.   LaBerge, D.; Samuels, S.J. Toward a theory of automatic information processing in reading. *Cogn. Psychol.* **1974**, *6*, 293–323. [CrossRef]

12.   Logan, G.D. Toward an instance theory of automatization. *Psychol. Rev.* **1988**, *95*, 492–527. [CrossRef]

13.   Perfetti, C.A. *Reading Ability*; Oxford University Press: New York, NY, USA, 1985.

14.   Perfetti, C.A. Reading ability: Lexical quality to comprehension. *Sci. Stud. Read.* **2007**, *11*, 357–383. [CrossRef]

15.   Anderson, R.C.; Freebody, P. Vocabulary knowledge. In *Comprehension and Teaching: Research Reviews*; Guthrie, J.T., Ed.; International Reading Association: Newark, DE, USA, 1981; pp. 77–117.

16.   Cunningham, A.E.; Stanovich, K.E. What reading does for the mind. *Am. Educ.* **1998**, *22*, 8–15.

17.   Stanovich, K.E. Matthew effects in reading: Some consequences of individual differences in the acquisition of literacy. *RRQ* **1986**, *21*, 360–407. [CrossRef]

18.   Stahl, S.A.; Nagy, W.E. *Teaching Word Meanings*; Erlbaum: Mahwah, NJ, USA, 2006.

19.   Perfetti, C.A.; Stafura, J. Word knowledge in a theory of reading comprehension. *Sci. Stud. Read.* **2014**, *18*, 22–37. [CrossRef]

20.   Perfetti, C.; Yang, C.L.; Schmalhofer, F. Comprehension skill and word-to-text integration processes. *Appl. Cogn. Psychol.* **2008**, *22*, 303–318. [CrossRef]

21.   Yang, C.L.; Perfetti, C.A.; Schmalhofer, F. Less skilled comprehenders ERPs show sluggish word-to-text integration processes. *WL&L* **2005**, *8*, 157–181.

22.   Yang, C.L.; Perfetti, C.A.; Schmalhofer, F. Event-related potential indicators of text integration across sentence boundaries. *J. Exp. Psychol. Learn. Mem. Cogn.* **2007**, *33*, 55–89. [CrossRef] [PubMed]

23.   Bolger, D.J.; Balass, M.; Landen, E.; Perfetti, C.A. Context variation and definitions in learning the meanings of words: An instance-based learning approach. *Discourse Process.* **2008**, *45*, 122–159. [CrossRef]

24.   Perfetti, C.A.; Wlotko, E.W.; Hart, L.A. Word learning and individual differences in word learning reflected in event-related potentials. *J. Exp. Psychol. Learn. Mem. Cogn.* **2005**, *31*, 1281. [CrossRef] [PubMed]

25.   Van Daalen-Kapteijns, M.M.; Elshout-Mohr, M. The acquisition of word meanings as a cognitive learning process. *J. Verbal Learn. Verbal Behav.* **1981**, *20*, 386–399. [CrossRef]

26.   Perfetti, C.A.; Hart, L. The lexical quality hypothesis. In *Precursors of Functional Literacy*; Vehoeven, L., Elbro, C., Reitsma, P., Eds.; John Benjamins: Amsterdam, The Netherlands, 2002; pp. 189–213.

27.   Lahey, M. *Language Disorders and Language Development*; Macmillan: Needham, MA, USA, 1988.

28.   Hoover, W.A.; Gough, P.B. A simple view of reading. *Read. Writ.* **1990**, *2*, 127–160. [CrossRef]

29.   Goswami, U. Early phonological development and the acquisition of literacy. In *Handbook of Early Literacy Research*; Neuman, S.B., Dickinson, D.K., Eds.; Guilford Press: New York, NY, USA, 2001; pp. 111–125.

30.   Metsala, J.L. Young children's phonological awareness and nonword repetition as a function of vocabulary development. *J. Educ. Psychol.* **1999**, *91*, 3–19. [CrossRef]

31.   Walley, A.C.; Metsala, J.L.; Garlock, V.M. Spoken vocabulary growth: Its role in the development of phonological awareness and early reading ability. *Read. Writ.* **2003**, *16*, 5–20. [CrossRef]

32.   Seidenberg, M.S.; McClelland, J.L. A distributed developmental model of word recognition and naming. *Psychol. Rev.* **1989**, *96*, 523–568. [CrossRef] [PubMed]

33.   Ouellette, G.P. What's meaning got to do with it: The role of vocabulary in word reading and reading comprehension. *J. Educ. Psychol.* **2006**, *98*, 554–566. [CrossRef]

34.   Levelt, W.J.M.; Roelofs, A.; Meyer, A.S. A theory of lexical access in speech production. *BBS* **1999**, *22*, 1–75.

35. Dickinson, D.K.; McCabe, A.; Anastasopoulos, L.; Feinberg, E.S.; Poe, M.D. The comprehensive language approach to early literacy: The interrelationships among vocabulary, phonological sensitivity, and print knowledge among preschool-aged children. *J. Educ. Psychol.* **2003**, *95*, 465–481. [CrossRef]

36. Scarborough, H.S. Connecting early language and literacy to later reading (dis)abilities: Evidence, theory, and practice. In *Handbook of Early Literacy Research*; Neuman, S.B., Dickinson, D.K., Eds.; Guilford Press: New York, NY, USA, 2001; pp. 97–110.

37. Sénéchal, M.; Ouellette, G.; Rodney, D. The misunderstood giant: On the predictive role of early vocabulary to future reading. In *Handbook of Early Literacy Research*; Neuman, S.B., Dickinson, D.K., Eds.; Guilford Press: New York, NY, USA 2006; pp. 173–182.

38. Rasinski, T.V.; Reutzel, C.R.; Chard, D.; Linan-Thompson, S. Reading fluency. In *Handbook of Reading Research*; Kamil, M.L., Pearson, P.D., Moje, E.B., Afflerbach, P.P., Eds.; Routledge: New York, NY, USA, 2011; pp. 286–319.

39. Samuels, S.J. The DIBELS tests: Is speed of barking at print what we mean by reading fluency? *RRQ* **2007**, *42*, 563–566.

40. Hock, M.F.; Brasseur, I.F.; Deshler, D.D.; Catts, H.W.; Marquis, J.G.; Mark, C.A.; Stibling, J.W. What is the reading component skill profile of struggling adolescent readers in urban schools? *LDQ* **2009**, *32*, 21–38.

41. Paige, D.D.; Smith, G.S.; Rasinski, T.V.; Rupley, W.H.; Magpuri-Lavell, T.; Nichols, W.D. A PATH analytic model linking foundational skills to grade 3 reading achievement. *J. Educ. Res.* **2018**. [CrossRef]

42. Paige, D.D.; Rasinski, T.; Magpuri-Lavell, T.; Smith, G. Interpreting the relationships among prosody, automaticity, accuracy, and silent reading comprehension in secondary students. *J. Lit. Res.* **2014**, *46*, 123–156. [CrossRef]

43. Jenkins, J.R.; Fuchs, L.S.; van den Broek, P.; Espin, C.; Deno, S.L. Accuracy and fluency in list and context reading of skilled and RD groups: Absolute and relative performance levels. *LDRP* **2003**, *18*, 237–245. [CrossRef]

44. Pinnell, G.S.; Pikulski, J.J.; Wixson, K.K.; Campbell, J.R.; Gough, P.B.; Beatty, A.S. Listening to Children Read Aloud: Data from Naep's Integrated Reading Performance Record (IRPR) at Grade 4. Available online: https://eric.ed.gov/?id=ED378550 (accessed on 26 September 2018).

45. Wise, B.W.; Ring, J.; Olson, R.K. Training phonological awareness with and without explicit attention to articulation. *J. Exp. Child Psychol.* **1999**, *72*, 271–304. [CrossRef] [PubMed]

46. Paige, D.D.; Rupley, W.H.; Smith, G.S.; Rasinski, T.V.; Nichols, W.; Magpuri-Lavell, T. Is prosodic reading a strategy for comprehension? *J. Educ. Res. Online* **2017**, *9*, 245–275.

47. Kuhn, M.R.; Stahl, S.A. Fluency: A Review of Developmental and Remedial Practices. Available online: http://psycnet.apa.org/buy/2003-01605-001 (accessed on 26 September 2018).

48. Benjamin, R.G.; Schwanenflugel, P.J. Text complexity and oral reading prosody in young children. *RRQ* **2010**, *45*, 388–404. [CrossRef]

49. Daane, M.C.; Campbell, J.R.; Grigg, W.S.; Goodman, M.J.; Oranje, A. Fourth-Grade Students Reading Aloud: NAEP 2002 Special Study of Oral Reading. Available online: https://nces.ed.gov/pubsearch/pubsinfo.asp?pubid=2006469 (accessed on 26 September 2018).

50. Klauda, S.L.; Guthrie, J.T. Relationships of three components of reading fluency to reading comprehension. *J. Educ. Psychol.* **2008**, *100*, 310–321. [CrossRef]

51. Paige, D.D.; Rasinski, T.V.; Magpuri-Lavell, T. If fluent, expressive reading important for high school readers? *JAAL* **2012**, *56*, 67–76. [CrossRef]

52. Rasinski, T.V.; Rikli, A.; Johnston, S. Reading fluency: More than automaticity? More than a concern for the primary grades? *Lit. Res. Instr.* **2009**, *48*, 350–361. [CrossRef]

53. Valencia, S.W.; Smith, A.; Reece, A.M.; Li, M.; Wixon, K.K.; Newman, H. Oral reading fluency assessment: Issues of content, construct, criterion, and consequent validity. *RRQ* **2010**, *45*, 270–291. [CrossRef]

54. Beckman, M.E. The parsing of prosody. *Lang. Cogn. Process.* **1996**, *11*, 17–67. [CrossRef]

55. Cutler, A.; Dahan, D.; van Donselaar, W. Prosody in the comprehension of spoken language: A literature review. *Lang. Speech* **1997**, *40*, 141–201. [CrossRef] [PubMed]

56. Peppé, S.; McCann, J. Assessing intonation and prosody in children with atypical language development: The PEPS-C test and the revised version. *Clin. Linguist. Phon.* **2003**, *17*, 345–354. [CrossRef] [PubMed]

57. Sanderman, A.A.; Collier, R. Prosodic phrasing and comprehension. *Lang. Speech* **1997**, *40*, 391–409. [CrossRef]

58. Schwanenflugel, P.J.; Benjamin, R.G. Lexical prosody as an aspect of reading fluency. *Read. Writ.* **2017**, *30*, 143–162. [CrossRef]

59. Veenendaal, N.J.; Groen, M.A.; Verhoeven, L. The role of speech prosody and text reading prosody in children's reading comprehension. *Br. J. Educ. Psychol.* **2014**, *84*, 521–536. [CrossRef] [PubMed]

60. Veenendaal, N.J.; Groen, M.A.; Verhoeven, L. What oral reading fluency can reveal about reading comprehension. *J. Res. Read.* **2015**, *38*, 213–225. [CrossRef]

61. Hiebert, E.H.; Lubliner, S. The nature, learning, and instruction of general academic vocabulary. In *What Research Has to Say about Vocabulary Instruction*; Farstrup, A.E., Samuels, S.J., Eds.; International Reading Association: Newark, DE, USA, 2008; pp. 106–129.

62. Corson, D. The learning and use of academic English words. *Lang. Learn.* **1997**, *47*, 671–718. [CrossRef]

63. Cunningham, J.W.; Moore, D.W. The contribution of understanding academic vocabulary to answering comprehension questions. *J. Read. Behav.* **1993**, *25*, 171–180. [CrossRef]

64. Nation, I.S.P.; Kyongho, H. Where would general service vocabulary stop and special purposes vocabulary begin? *System* **1995**, *23*, 35–41. [CrossRef]

65. Scarcella, R.C. Accelerating Academic English: A Focus on English Language Learners. Available online: https://www.librarything.com/work/3402943 (accessed on 29 September 2018).

66. Nagy, W.; Townsend, D. Words as tools: Learning academic vocabulary as language acquisition. *RRQ* **2012**, *47*, 91–108. [CrossRef]

67. Beck, I.L.; McKeown, M.G.; Kucan, L. *Bringing Words to Life*; The Guilford Press: New York, NY, USA, 2002.

68. Biber, D. *University Language: A Corpus-Based Study of Spoken and Written Registers*; John Benjamins: Philadelphia, PA, USA, 2006.

69. Lesaux, N.K.; Kieffer, M.J.; Faller, S.E.; Kelley, J.G. The effectiveness and ease of implementation of an academic vocabulary intervention for linguistically diverse students in urban middle schools. *RRQ* **2010**, *45*, 196–228. [CrossRef]

70. Snow, C.E.; Lawrence, J.; White, C. Generating knowledge of academic language among urban middle school students. *SREE* **2009**, *2*, 325–344. [CrossRef]

71. Townsend, D.; Collins, P. Academic vocabulary and middle school English learners: An intervention study. *Read. Writ.* **2009**, *22*, 993–1019. [CrossRef]

72. Hancioğlu, N.; Neufeld, S.; Eldridge, J. Through the looking glass and into the land of lexico-grammar. *ESP* **2008**, *27*, 459–479. [CrossRef]

73. Biemiller, A. *Language and Reading Success*; Brookline: Newton Upper Falls, MA, USA, 1999.

74. Stahl, S.A. Beyond the instrumentalist hypothesis: Some relationships between word meanings and comprehension. In *The Psychology of Word Meanings*; Schwanenflugel, P.J., Ed.; Erlbaum: Hillsdale, NJ, USA, 1991; pp. 157–186.

75. Townsend, D.; Filippini, A.; Collins, P.; Giancarosa, G. Evidence for the importance of academic word knowledge for the academic achievement of diverse middle school students. *ESJ* **2012**, *112*, 497–518. [CrossRef]

76. Nunnally, J.C.; Bernstein, I.H. *Psychometric Theory*; McGraw Hill: New York, NY, USA, 1994.

77. Deno, S.L. Curriculum-based measurement: The emerging alternative. *Except. Child.* **1985**, *52*, 219–232. [CrossRef] [PubMed]

78. Deno, S.L.; Mirkin, P.K.; Chiang, B. Identifying valid measures of reading. *Except. Child.* **1982**, *49*, 36–45. [PubMed]

79. Fuchs, L.S.; Fuch, D.; Hosp, M.K.; Jenkins, J.R. Oral reading fluency as an indicator of reading competence: A theoretical, empirical, and historical analysis. *Sci. Stud. Read.* **2001**, *5*, 239–256. [CrossRef]

80. McGlinchey, M.T.; Hixon, M.D. Using curriculum-based measurement to predict performance on state assessments in reading. *SPR* **2004**, *33*, 193–203.

81. National Governors Association Center for Best Practices & Council of Chief State School Officers. *Common Core State Standards for English Language Arts and Literacy in History/Social Studies, Science, and Technical Subjects*; National Governors Association Center for Best Practices, Council of Chief State School Officers: Washington, DC, USA, 2010.

82. Graesser, A.C.; McNamara, D.; Louwerse, M.M.; Cai, Z. Coh-metrix analysis of text on cohesion and language. *Behav. Res. Method. Instr. Comput.* **2004**, *36*, 193–202. [CrossRef]

83. Zutell, J.; Rasinski, T.V. Training teaches to attend to their students' oral reading fluency. *TIP* **1991**, *30*, 211–217.

84. Loo, R. Motivational orientations toward work: An evaluation of the work preference inventory (Student form). *MECD* **2001**, *33*, 222–233.

85. Nunnally, J.C. *Psychometric Theory*, 1st ed.; McGraw-Hill: New York, NY, USA, 1967.

86. Streiner, D.L. Starting at the beginning: An introduction to coefficient alpha and internal consistency. *J. Pers. Assess.* **2003**, *80*, 99–103. [CrossRef] [PubMed]

87. Moser, G.P.; Sudweeks, R.R.; Morrison, T.G.; Wilcox, B. Reliability of ratings of children's expressive reading. *Read. Psychol.* **2014**, *35*, 58–79. [CrossRef]

88. Smith, G.S.; Paige, D.D. A study of reliability across multiple raters when using the NAEP and MDFS rubrics to measure oral reading fluency. *Read. Psychol.* **2018**, in press.

89. SRI: Technical Guide. Available online: https://www.hmhco.com/products/assessment-solutions/assets/pdfs/sri/SRI_TechGuide.pdf (accessed on 29 September 2018).

90. Hasbrouck, J.; Tindal, G. Oral reading fluency norms: A valuable assessment tool for reading teachers. *Reading Teacher* **2006**, *59*, 636–644. [CrossRef]

91. Baron, R.M.; Kenny, D.A. The moderator-mediator variable distinction in social psychological research: Conceptual, strategic, and statistical considerations. *J. Personal. Soc. Psychol.* **1986**, *51*, 1173–1182. [CrossRef]

92. Preacher, K.J.; Hayes, A.F. SPSS and SAS procedures for estimating indirect effects in simple mediation models. *Behav. Res. Method. Instrum. Comput.* **2004**, *36*, 717–731. [CrossRef]

93. Preacher, K.J.; Kelly, K. Effect size measures for mediation models: Quantitative strategies for communicating indirect effects. *Psychol. Method.* **2011**, *16*, 93–115. [CrossRef] [PubMed]

94. Preacher, K.J.; Curran, P.J.; Bauer, D.J. Computational tools for probing interaction effects in multiple linear regression, multilevel modeling, and latent curve analysis. *J. Educ. Behav. Stat.* **2006**, *31*, 437–448. [CrossRef]

95. Hiebert, E.H. The forgotten reading proficiency: Stamina in silent reading. In *Teaching Stamina and Silent Reading in the Digital-Global Age*; Hiebert, E.H., Ed.; TextProject: Santa Cruz, CA, USA, 2015; pp. 16–31.

MDPI

St. Alban-Anlage 66

4052 Basel

Switzerland

Tel. +41 61 683 77 34

Fax +41 61 302 89 18

www.mdpi.com

Education Sciences Editorial Office

E-mail: education@mdpi.com

www.mdpi.com/journal/education

www.ingramcontent.com/pod-product-compliance
Lightning Source LLC
Chambersburg PA
CBHW041140120626
46547CB00020B/3058